12/94

# THE COMPLETE BOOK OF
## ─HARDY─
# PERENNIALS

# THE COMPLETE BOOK OF
# HARDY
# PERENNIALS

## RICHARD BIRD

WARD LOCK

For Jane Sterndale-Bennett

# ACKNOWLEDGEMENTS

The publishers are grateful to the author for
granting permission to reproduce all the
colour photographs, with the exception of
the one on p.125, which was taken by
Bob Challinor.

First published in Great Britain in 1993
by Ward Lock Limited, Villiers House, 41/47 Strand,
London WC2N 5JE, England
A Cassell Imprint

Text filmset by Litho Link Limited, Welshpool,
Powys, Wales
Printed and bound in Hong Kong
by Dah Hua Printing Co. Ltd.

CIP data for this book is available upon application
from The British Library

ISBN 0 7063 7076 7

# Contents

# Preface

Hardy perennials have had a tremendous resurgence in popularity of late. This is partly due to gardeners becoming more aware of the plants either while visiting gardens or through television. This increased awareness of perennials and what can be done with them has been reflected in nurseries and garden centres where more varieties of plants are available than probably ever before.

What gardeners have begun to realize is that perennials are not a time-consuming luxury, but tough, trouble-free plants that help create a garden scene in a way that no other plant can. The time has gone when borders were made exclusively of herbaceous plants. Although some still exist, there is now a more enlightened attitude towards borders in which plants of any category – annuals, shrubs and even trees, as well as perennials – can be mixed together to give a better picture. These mixed borders have the advantage that they can span the seasons. Thus they are interesting during the winter as well as the summer, as long as the gardener has got the mix right.

There is a misconception that hardy perennials are plants that can only be used in sunny borders. Fortunately there are large numbers of plants that can be grown in differing amounts of shade. This allows gardeners not only to create borders under trees and shrubs but also on the shady side of buildings and against tall walls and fences.

Hardy perennials offer the gardener a wide range of plants. While most people are concerned with creating a decorative border, for which purpose they select their plants, others get hooked on the plants in their own right. These plantsmen amass large collections of plants, sometimes only paying lip service to their decorative relationships in the border. They often like to collect the rare and the curious, sometimes restricting themselves to one or more favourite genus. On the other hand some gardeners combine both these approaches. Fortunately hardy perennials seem to be almost limitless in their number, with new ones constantly being created in the form of cultivars and hybrids, as well as seed of plants new to cultivation being introduced from the wild. Perennial gardening is an exciting area, with much to explore.

In this book perennials have been examined from all points of view. Starting from the basics of garden layout, through the principles of design, including the use of colour, shape and texture, on to the techniques of gardening, including ground preparation, plant selection, planting, maintenance, pests and disease, and on to the plants themselves. The plant list comprises about half the book and discusses the individual plants in a discursive way, talking about their merits and demerits and how they should be grown.

It is hoped that both the beginner and the more experienced gardener will find a lot of useful and interesting information that will help him or her create a garden, not only of which they are proud but, more importantly, which they will enjoy. Gardens really are about pleasure and the presence of hardy perennials is one way of ensuring that this comes about.

**R.B.**

# CHAPTER 1

# *Background to Hardy Perennials*

Gardeners are fond of categorizing their plants, calling them annuals, alpines, water-plants, herbaceous plants, bulbous plants and so on. Unfortunately all these definitions are imprecise. The plants they call annuals, for example, are often perennial, although sown every year. Similarly many alpines come from regions that are distinctly un-alpine. The expression 'hardy perennial' looks straightforward at first glance but can equally mean different things to different people.

## What are hardy perennials?

Strictly speaking hardy perennials should include all plants that are both hardy and perennial. In theory this would include trees and shrubs, but in practice these are usually excluded; the term being restricted to non-woody plants. This is not entirely true as the expression also includes many sub-shrubs that are half way between the two. There are also a few true shrubs, such as *Perovskia*, that are generally included in hardy perennials as they are treated in the same way and cut back each year.

It may be thought that herbaceous plants are synonymous with hardy perennials, but the former die back each year below ground for a period of dormancy. While most hardy perennials follow this practice, many – hellebores for example – remain in leaf throughout the year.

At least the word 'perennial' means what it says: all perennials are perennial! However, there are also some 'annuals' that are in fact perennial. Many of the so-called annuals that are bought from seed merchants each year are short-lived perennials and if left in the ground at the end of the year will flower again the following season. Wallflowers (*Cheiranthus*) and sweet williams (*Dianthus barbatus*) are both examples of this. There are other perennials which are tender and so are re-sown every year, thus giving the impression that they are annual.

The life-span of a perennial varies considerably. Some, such as the pinks (*Dianthus*) and lupins, are relatively short while there are others, bergenias and peonies for instance, that seem to go on forever. A plant's longevity can depend on the soil and other conditions. Thus a pink will usually last longer on a well-drained soil than on a heavy wet one. Conversely astilbes will thrive and increase in moist soils, but will languish and soon fade away in a dry one.

The word 'hardy' is much more difficult to deal with. Essentially a hardy plant is one that will withstand a winter outside, but winters vary considerably from one area to another, just a few hundred miles apart. Not only do plants vary in hardiness from one part of the country to another, but they can also vary from one part of a garden to another. Most gardens have areas that are colder than others, sometimes having quite deep frost pockets. Generally plants that are on the tender side will thrive up against south walls which hold the heat and are out of the cold northerly winds.

A plant's hardiness is not wholly concerned with its ability to withstand frost. Winter dampness also seems to be involved and it is often found that a plant will survive a winter in a well-drained soil whereas it will succumb in a damper one. Just because a plant comes from a cold country, it does not follow that it is completely hardy. Many alpines come from thousands of metres up mountains where the cold is intense, but the plants are cosily tucked up under a blanket of snow. In lowland gardens they have no such protection and find difficulty surviving the cold winter winds. Another problem can be winters with a stop-start quality about them. A warm spell in the middle of winter will start a plant into growth, while the subsequent cold spell will check it, sometimes killing it outright.

The hardiness of plants is still not fully understood and often there are surprises when plants that are thought to be tender come through relatively cold winters. However all this should not worry the beginner. The majority of perennial plants that are commercially available are hardy and are able to stand surprisingly severe winters. Those that are marginally hardy can be protected in some way such as digging the plants up and overwintering them inside, as one does with chrysanthemums or dahlias, or by protecting the dormant plant with a mulch of bracken or leaves (see page 58).

When referring to hardy perennials gardeners and gardening writers usually restrict their definition to plants that will grow in a border. Alpine plants are strictly speaking hardy perennials but the practice of growing them is a specialized one and so they are usually excluded from the general category. However there are a large number of low-growing plants, including such things as violas, primulas and many low carpeting plants such as aubrieta, that will happily grow in a border, usually at the front and are included in the definition.

Bulbs are also thought of as a separate category, but by excluding them many good border plants would be left out of the book so they have been included here. It is hard to imagine a border without lilies for example. Hardy perennials need not be grown as flowering plants. Some, such as ferns, are purely foliage plants while others, hostas for example, although they flower are grown mainly for the effect of their leaves. Grasses are grown both for their foliage effects and for the decorative effect of their flower and seed heads.

So we have arrived at a working definition of hardy perennials as being non-woody perennial plants that are suitable for growing in a border or garden setting and which will survive an average winter.

## Origins

Although many hardy perennials have been bred in cultivation they all have their origins as wild plants. Initially the majority of flowering plants that were introduced into gardens were of a practical nature. They were usually herbs for cooking, for strewing on the floor to keep down lice and prevent flies, or for use for medicinal purposes. Many of these plants would have grown in the hedgerows, woods and meadows and would have been transplanted onto ground near cottages so that they would be close at hand when needed. Undoubtedly others were also introduced, especially into gardens of grander houses, purely for their decorative qualities.

Gradually the quality of the plants improved as better forms were selected, perhaps those with larger or more flowers, or those with brighter or different colours. Certainly curiosities, such as double flowers, were noted and introduced. At first pollination was a natural process and all improvements were brought about by nature unhelped by humans, except in that they gathered plants together which may have interbred.

As travel was extended, explorers brought back plants from overseas and more exotic plants entered our gardens. Some of these escaped and became naturalized and are now often considered native. As gardening became more organized nurseries began to specialize in plants, selecting the best forms and generally improving the availability of plants. They often funded expeditions to remoter parts of the world to collect plants to add to their catalogues and by the end of the nineteenth century there was an incredible range of perennial plants available for gardeners. By then the mechanism of hybridization was understood and many new varieties were being created. Most of these were new cultivars but some were considered unique enough to be designated new species and yet others new genera, usually where two genera were crossed to form a bi-generic hybrid (see page 82).

In more recent times it has been possible to create new plants by causing mutations by irradiation or other means. Genetic engineering now offers even greater possibilities of creating totally new plants. However, while this has been going on there has been an increasing awareness of the simple beauty of the original species and many gardeners have forsworn the bigger, brasher flowers of the hybridists and scientists and have returned to cultivating the 'true' plant, thus turning the story of garden plants in a full circle. There is a constant supply of new plants being introduced from the wild, usually in the form of seed, as collecting the plant itself is now, justly, frowned upon for conservational reasons. These introductions are not just from the local hedgerow, but from all over the world.

## The appeal of hardy perennials

Until the recent tremendous resurgence of interest in hardy perennials, they had been suffering a decline that goes back to the Second World War. There were two reasons for this. They were always considered to be labour intensive and, with the decline of paid gardeners, many garden owners switched to a predominance of trees and shrubs which were thought easier to maintain. Another change that came about was the decline of the traditional nursery in favour of garden centres. For many years these found it difficult to offer hardy perennials as container plants and so there was a sharp decline in the number of plants readily available.

Fortunately the position has now changed. People now realize that herbaceous plants are not necessarily difficult to maintain and many more species and varieties are again available from garden centres and from the increasing number of traditional nurseries. Not many gardeners have gone back to the Victorian and Edwardian concept of purely herbaceous borders; most now have mixed borders that include a few shrubs to give the border a permanent structure, especially during the winter.

The majority of perennials are easy to look after, require quite ordinary soil and are easy to increase. They may need occasional splitting or dividing, but the work on them is not so urgent or critical as it is with annuals or shrubs. From the visual point of view they provide a very large range of colour, textures and shapes with which to decorate the garden. Their range is sufficient to provide colour in the garden throughout the year. The number of different species available is enormous and this diversity means that you very rarely see two gardens of hardy perennials that are the same. Unfortunately there is much more uniformity in gardens that rely on annuals and shrubs.

The range is so large that it is possible to create themes of one sort or another. For example it is possible to have a one-coloured garden, perhaps restricting the flowers to white. It is also possible to restrict the planting to more individual themes, perhaps even personal ones, for example using only plants that include the name 'Ann' in their title. Another big advantage of growing hardy perennials is that you will rarely be without flowers for the house, as a large number of them make ideal cut flowers.

Most hardy perennials can be easily raised from seed and cuttings and so a large collection of plants can be grown for a small outlay. Many gardeners get a tremendous amount of excitement out of growing their own plants. This is occasionally intensified when, amongst the seedlings, is found an exceptionally good plant which may exhibit a new or better colour that any that have gone before. Creating plants in this way is one of the greatest joys in gardening with hardy perennials and it is open to anyone, not just the experts.

It would be naive to suggest that hardy perennials do not suffer from any problems, but on the whole they are trouble-free and require little in the way of chemical sprays or other treatments. Many have come down to us from earlier generations of gardeners and the very fact that so many have survived is indicative of their toughness and their proof against pests and diseases.

Hardy perennials are a good topic for conversation and most growers soon find that they get to meet others in their area and will soon spend many happy hours wandering around gardens discussing the merits of various plants. It is not only tales that are swapped, plants too get exchanged and soon, even the beginner will find that gardening with hardy perennials has an extremely friendly side to it. It is possible to formalize these friendships into a local society or to join one of the national associations such as The Hardy Plant Society (in the United Kingdom and the United States), which organizes many local events including plant sales, as well as producing informative literature in the form of journals and books.

# PART I

## PLANNING THE GARDEN

# CHAPTER 2

# *Basic Layout*

Hardy perennials are normally thought of as border plants and therefore it is usual to consider them in this rather limited situation rather than in the garden as a whole. However, the borders must be placed in context and so it is essential to look at the complete garden before we narrow our focus down to the borders and what they contain.

## Purpose and uses

Before thinking about anything else it is essential to consider the purpose of the garden and the uses to which it may be put. This will save a lot of time in the long run, particularly in the need to move things.

The overwhelming desire may be to grow hardy perennials, but if there are young children (or even older ones) in the family recognition must be given to the fact that they will want to play in the garden, not necessarily just on a swing or in a sand pit tucked away discreetly, but also on bicycles and with footballs or tennis racquets which will require a great deal more space. To a certain extent these activities can also be destructive as well as space-consuming, particularly if children and dogs go chasing after balls into the borders. Obviously the use of island beds in the middle of lawns will not be very successful under these circumstances.

Not all children take over the whole garden, but when considering the garden their interests must also be taken into account. If the garden is big enough it may be possible to set a lawn and perhaps a 'wild' area aside for them. At the other extreme, many modern gardens are far too small for this and decisions will have to be arrived at as to whether the garden is big enough to contain the various activities that could go on there.

Children are not the only ones to have special needs in the garden. One of the great revolutions over the last fifty years is that people have made more time to relax in their gardens and there is now a vast leisure industry providing all manner of chairs, tables, barbecues and so on for use in the open air. Most gardens now have at least one paved terrace or patio, often adjoining the house, which is used as an outside room. A lawn may also act similarly, although it is not so accommodating during or after wet weather as a hard surface.

To many, an essential part of any garden is the vegetable and fruit produce that can be obtained from it. Decisions on how much you want to produce will determine how much space (and time) it will require and how much is left over for other things. If fruit trees are involved then these may produce shade that is unwelcome in other areas of the garden. Depending on the scale of your gardening it may also be useful or desirable to have reserve beds for plants waiting to go out into the borders or beds for cutting flowers.

A final consideration is to what extent you will want to use parts of the garden as utility areas: places in which to keep dustbins, compost heaps, space for a bonfire, areas devoted to a greenhouse, cold frames, sheds and so on.

Having looked at all the possible demands that may be put on the garden it is important to weigh them up against each other to see what can be achieved and how much space is given over to each. Failure to consider them all at this stage can result in unsatisfactory compromises at a later stage; for example it could be necessary to put a greenhouse on part of a border, upsetting its shape and appearance. The smaller the space the more important it is to work out what you want to do with it before you start work on laying it out.

It may be possible to plan for changing circumstances so that in time, you achieve what you desire. For example, children do not stay children for ever and areas that are left for them can be placed in such a position that they can be incorporated into a more decorative scheme once they have grown up. Lawns, for instance, can be turned over to borders; toy sheds can be converted to tool sheds.

Another factor that must be considered when thinking about the garden as a whole is the amount of time it will take to maintain the garden of your dreams. The more there is under cultivation the more time it is going to take. Since it is presumed that the intention of the reader is to grow perennial plants then it must be assumed that they are prepared to spend time working towards this end. There is no doubt that creating and maintaining a living garden does take time; there are few short cuts if you want to do it properly. If you want a maintenance-free garden then this must be taken into account at this stage of the planning, but, unfortunately, you will also want a different type of garden to the one we are planning.

It is difficult if you are inexperienced to work out in advance how much time it will take to look after a particular garden. More can obviously be achieved if there are two of you keen enough to undertake it, or if one partner is at least willing to mow the lawns and trim the hedges. If you intended to have a vegetable garden as well as flower borders, remember that this will take up a surprising amount of time if carried out properly.

## Planning

Having looked at all the factors above you should have a clearer idea as to what garden you want and are able to achieve. The next stage is to see whether it will fit into the space that you have available. Often a compromise will have to be reached as the garden will be too small to accomplish everything you demand of it. As already suggested, perhaps one method of com-

promise will be to look ahead and see which areas can be temporarily used for children and which can be brought back into the garden at a later stage. It may be that a paved terrace will also serve the same function as a lawn (or *vice versa*) for some families.

Trying to fit all your requirements into the garden is always an exciting exercise but it does demand an ability on the part of the gardener to be able to visualize: you need to be capable of seeing in the mind's eye the complete garden in place of the wilderness or bare ground that is currently there.

While I do sketch out plans on paper, I am a great believer in standing and staring. I can spend hours strutting about a garden looking at it from all possible angles trying to visualize what it will be like when it is complete, if necessary sticking stakes or marking out areas with string to help give some idea of how the various areas will appear.

If I were a professional designer I would probably starve as I spend a great deal of time over this process. A few years ago, for example, I added another three quarters of an acre to the garden and I spent over six months looking at it. I imagined every possible permutation taking into account its shape, the lie of the land and, of course, (something that designers often forget about) the variation in soil quality across the area, the differences in moisture content, the direction of the prevailing winds and direction of the sun. These will all be looked at in more detail later, but my point at the moment is that time is not wasted by standing and staring, even if you do prefer to plan on paper.

It is a good idea also to outline things on paper, even if you have only a rudimentary ability with a pencil. (Remember that no one other than yourself need ever see your sketches, so as long as they mean something to you that is all that matters.) At the planning stage all that it means is drawing broad sweeps on the paper as to where everything is roughly going to go; the detailed shapes of things do not matter at this point. When roughing in the outlines think not only in terms of how the areas will relate to each other, but how they will affect the overall appearance of the garden. Draw in, for example, the sightlines from the main windows of the house and from planned sitting areas in the garden so that you can get some idea of what you will see from these various positions.

These drawings can be made either in the comfort of an armchair or preferably out in the garden itself. If you prefer to walk around and plan on the ground with sticks and string, it is still useful to jot down on paper what decisions you arrive at.

Amongst the basic things at this stage is to determine roughly where everything is to go. Most people prefer to have a terrace near the house so that it is possible to wander in and out. On the other hand, if this area is in shade for most of the day it might be preferable to have it in a more sunny position, but still handy to the house. Utility areas should be tucked away, as inevitably they are not the most decorative of features. However, if you are a greenhouse enthusiast and spend a great deal of time there, then it should be placed reasonably close to the house and near such facilities as water and electricity. Play areas for young children should also be close to the house. Dustbins, coal stores and other practical things should be reasonably close to the house, too, and connected by a solid path.

There is a tendency in modern gardens to relegate the vegetables to the bottom of the garden, but in cottage gardens they were often very close to the back door to save having to go too far to pick them. In either case vegetables must have a reasonably fertile soil and a sunny, open position. Herbs were also located near to the house and there is still a strong case for this position.

Since flower borders are the main consideration of this book, their positioning will be given a section to itself.

All these factors are for you to decide, but decided they must be, because once the general outline of the garden is settled upon it can be a great upheaval to re-do it. Look at the reasons for having a garden,

what you want to achieve with it and then, without going into detail, allocate general areas for each activity based on where it will be most usefully accomplished and where it will be most aesthetically sited.

## Positioning borders

The position of flower borders can depend on a number of factors. If a lot of time is spent in the house near a window then it makes sense to position flower borders so that they can be seen from there. On the other hand, one of the most frequently met tenets of garden design is that a garden should contain mystery and not all of it should be seen at a glance. This means that the position of all borders should not be too obvious, recognizing the fact that it is extremely pleasant to be able to stroll around a garden constantly coming across new delights, even in a small garden.

As well as aesthetic considerations, positioning of borders also relies on physical factors. The direction of the sun and wind are important, as well as the soil conditions.

### Soil

If the flower borders are your first priority in the garden, then they should be given the best soil. It is possible to alter the soil, as we will see in a later chapter, but the natural quality of the soil can easily vary from one part of the garden to another. An area of good loam that is free-draining and yet moisture retentive, for example, should not be passed over for a patch of clay simply because you want to put a terrace on the loam. If at all possible use the clay for the terrace, or, if you have the time and energy, move the soils around.

### Sun

Most hardy perennials are sun lovers. There are, of course, many that will grow in shade, but apart from the true woodlanders, the majority of these flower better and keep their shape best in a sunny position. This means that overhanging trees should be avoided for the main borders. Remember that if a border is in full sun but is on the south side of the garden, many of the plants will have flowers that will turn and look at the sun or will be most floriferous on the side pointing away from the garden, giving your neighbour the benefit of your planting. Another problem with a border towards the south of the garden is that the front of it is likely to be in shade so that any short plants might not get much benefit from the sun (Fig. 2.1). This is not to say that you should never put borders on the south side of a garden, but rather that you should consider carefully the plants you wish to put in it. Hostas, for example, will do better in a south rather than a north border as they will get some protection from the sun by their taller companions.

**Fig. 2.1** Tall plants in the borders on the south side of the garden may shade those plants in front of them.

### Wind

It is essential, when planning a garden, to take into consideration any prevailing winds, especially near the coast where they are likely to be a regular feature. It may be expedient to put in some hedges or other form of wind break. Avoid placing borders where they are in the direct path of winds that are funnelled between two buildings. Even in the mildest breeze the wind here can be accentuated and it will be a difficult area to grow plants successfully. Again, it might be possible to break the wind by placing tough shrubs in its path. Generally it is better to filter wind through a hedge or shrubs than to block its path with a solid wall or fence, as the latter will create turbulence – the effects of which can be worse than the original wind (Fig. 2.2). However it must be said that a garden without any air movement can also be deleterious, as damp stagnant air is good for promoting rots and mildews. If you have a border in a very sheltered spot you may have to be careful what you plant there – for example, michaelmas daisies should be avoided in these positions.

**Fig. 2.2** Wind will filter through hedge (*left*), reducing its force, making it a perfect windbreak. A wall or solid fence (*right*) will block the wind forcing it into swirling vortices that can create a lot of damage.

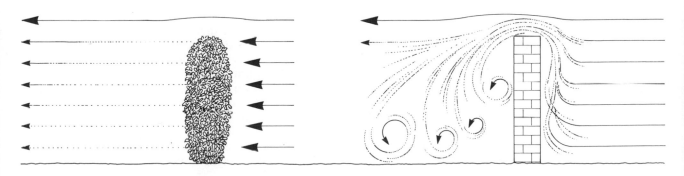

*Frost*

Another factor to take into consideration when placing borders is frost. It is surprising how different parts of the garden attract frost more than others. Some parts of my garden, for example, can be several degrees above others. Obviously walls with a southern aspect provide a much warmer climate than those with a northern one and any plans to grow the more tender plants must include borders in these favoured positions. Conversely, borders open to northerly winds will be much colder and will either need some form of protection or their planting restricted to really hardy plants. Southern slopes will be warmer than northern ones, but any garden that slopes is likely to have frost pockets at some point where the cold air collects and cannot drain away. If this is caused by a hedge, then a hole can be cut into it to allow this air to disperse, thus raising the temperature appreciably. Other ways of coping with frost will be dealt with in the chapter on maintenance.

*Damp*

In my experience, frost pockets often, but not always, tend also to be damp. Apart from bog lovers, most plants do not like wet positions, or at least places where both the moisture in the soil and in the air is stagnant. Avoid placing borders in a damp part of the garden; if, however, your overall plan requires that they are, then take steps to drain the area. This will be discussed in a later chapter.

## Detailed design

Having looked at the purpose and general layout it is time to consider the design in more detail. Since this book only deals with hardy perennials and is not a general design manual we will, from now on, only consider aspects which relate to this type of planting.

### Backgrounds

One of the important aspects to concern anyone who is considering the detailed planning of a garden is the structural items such as hedges or fences that provide the boundary to the garden, and barriers and screens within it. Besides acting as a physical barrier around and giving privacy to the garden, hedges and fences from our point of view have two important functions: they keep out the wind and they provide a background against which to see the borders.

Windbreaks, as we have already seen, are important to a perennial flower garden where the plants are not as strong as the more woody trees and shrubs. Staking can be unsightly as well as time consuming to execute, and the less there is to do the better.

The background to a border, I feel, is very important. It acts as the canvas on which the picture is painted. Without it plants tend to hover in empty space or, worse still, get mixed up with the plants and other impedimenta in the distance – distracting and confusing to the eye. Island beds (see page 20) are often not very successful, as one can see straight through them, there being nothing solid against which to anchor the plants.

### Hedges

Hedges should be preferably one colour. Tapestry hedges where, for example, green and copper beeches are alternated make too fussy a background and one against which it is difficult to plant satisfactorily. Yew (*Taxus baccata*) is one of the most pleasing and, in spite of its reputation, does not take that long to reach an acceptable thickness and height.

To the beginner, in particular, it often looks a waste of space to have a path between a hedge and the border but its necessity becomes immediately apparent as soon as the hedge requires cutting. Attempting to cut a hedge, or even worse still, trying to clear up the resulting clippings, is a nightmare if you have to step over and lean over clumps of flowering plants, especially the taller ones at the back of the border. Another reason for having a space between a hedge (or even a solid fence or wall) is that plants close to it will grow outwards to get maximum light and are thus likely to flop forward and need staking. So when planning your borders allow ample space (60 cm/ 2 ft is probably adequate) if you can spare it.

Most hedges, especially yew, are thirsty and hungry and will take a great deal from the soil of a border, so it is essential to feed the areas near the hedges. Incorporating organic material will not only enrich the soil but will help retain the moisture, making it available to both the hedge and the border plants. Remember that hedges will create a rain shadow and that the area in their lee will be drier than the rest of the border. Walls and fences do not rob the soil of nutrients and moisture but they can still cast a rain shadow.

### Fences and walls
Fences and walls make a good alternative to hedges. The latter are preferable, especially if they are of a mellow stone or brick, but they are expensive to construct if you are not lucky enough to have one already. Avoid pierced concrete blocks that are available in a variety of patterns. These are fussy and do little to enhance the garden within. Wooden fences can look a bit stark at first but will soon weather and improve, particularly once their line is broken by plants. They should be treated with preservative to prolong their life, but avoid creosote as many plants will die if they come into contact with it or with its fumes, which are given off for several years after treatment. There are several proprietary wood preservatives specially formulated for use in the garden, which will cause no distress to nearby plants.

One advantage that walls and fences have over hedges (apart from not having to cut them regularly!) is that they will support climbing plants of various sorts. It is possible to grow climbers through hedges but this makes them very difficult to keep trimmed and can cause die-back if the climbers have a dense foliage. One exception to this is that some people like to grow the flame-red *Tropaeolum speciosum* up through a yew hedge, which only needs cutting once a year.

### Trees and shrubs
Hedges and fences are essentially lines, straight or curved, but it is possible to create backgrounds with a mixture of trees and shrubs, arranged in an irregular pattern. This is particularly useful in dispelling any feeling of formality and will help disguise the rectangular nature of the garden. It also allows a feeling of continuity throughout the year as the background shrubs often give a feeling of structure and interest to the beds, even when there is little in flower. The use of individual shrubs can also help to give variety but since they can be chosen to blend in with the rest of the border they should not cause the same kind of distraction that a mixed or tapestry hedge will cause.

Any background hedges or trees and shrubs should be got into the ground as soon as possible as they will take a while to reach maturity and the borders will not look at their best until they have.

## Border shapes
Since this is a book about perennial plants it must be assumed that the reader wants to create a garden in which these can be grown. It concentrates, therefore, on traditional layouts rather than the more modern designs in which plants often only put in a token appearance.

The shapes of the borders are absolutely crucial to the appearance of the garden, but, unfortunately it is one of the most difficult things to get right. Essentially the front of a border is a line, but while most people can draw a straight line, many have difficulty in producing a satisfactory curved one. But before we look at shape it might be best to look at size.

### Size
A flower border can be as long as you like, the only limiting factor being the size of your garden. In reality, however, a long border disappearing into the distance can be rather boring and it is much more interesting to break it, giving the impression that it continues but hiding it so that you cannot actually see it until you turn a corner or go

17

**Fig. 2.3** The greater depth afforded by a corner of a narrow border can be used to accommodate taller plants.

round a large shrub or pass through an arch of some sort. It is amazing but you can have two similar gardens, one of which you can see everything at a glance, while the other requires the viewer to wander around from area to area before it can all be seen; although they can have exactly the same

planting, the latter will be far more exciting and interesting. This is why a lot of the most successful gardens, such as Sissinghurst Castle in Kent, have the whole garden broken down into smaller gardens, each containing its own borders.

The width of a border is also important to consider. Many people try to create herbaceous borders which are far too narrow. The rule of thumb is that the width of a border should be twice the height of the tallest plant you wish to grow in it. This means that if you wish to grow tall plants such as delphiniums or maclayeas you must have a border that is at least 3.7 m (12 ft) across. This kind of size can be difficult to create in a small garden: here, obviously, narrower beds can be created, but these should be planted with shorter plants. Height can then be created by growing climbers up the wall or fence behind the border and by planting taller plants in the corners, which can be made deeper (Fig. 2.3).

However, always try to make the widest borders you can. It is much easier to create a pleasing picture as you will be able to have clumps of plants one behind the other, not only creating a three-dimensional effect but also allowing you to have plants of varying flowering periods which will increase the length of interest of the border. In a narrow bed the planting tends to be more linear, and gaps begin to appear as the season progresses.

*Shape*

Do not rush into creating a garden: take time, as I have already suggested, to think about it. If possible go and look at as many other gardens as possible before you start your own layout. Look at the way the borders fit into the garden as a whole; notice how they follow the natural lie of the ground; see how they respond to fixed features; decide which curves are pleasing in shape and which tend to jar the senses; and note the effect of straight lines.

Straight edges to a border give an air of formality. It also tends to draw the eye down its length (Fig. 2.4). Borders with curved front edges form bays which tend to

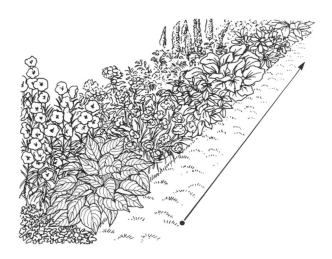

**Fig. 2.4** Straight edges to a border tend to draw the eye down its length.

hold the eye, and headlands which act as full stops, preventing the eye from moving on to the next part of the border before it has seen what lies in front of it (Fig. 2.5). Curves and hidden parts of the garden create more tension and excitement than a straight line.

The problem is that straight lines are easy to create but curves are very difficult.

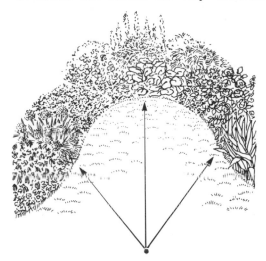

**Fig. 2.5** Curved and indented borders tend to interrupt the visual flow, preventing the whole border being seen at a glance.

have made. Either way it is useful to dig along the line of the pipe as this makes a more permanent line to work to once construction of the border begins.

Bold sinuous lines tend to look best. Avoid having too many in and outs, which look fussy and disturb the eye. If handled well, a deep loop into a bed can be used to focus attention onto a particular plant or object (Fig. 2.7).

**Fig. 2.6** Flexible hosepipes are ideal for planning curved outlines to borders. Once you are satisfied with the shape they can be used as a cutting guide.

**Fig. 2.7** In a large garden, deep bays of the lawn, or wide paths, are ideal for creating focal points, such as a piece of sculpture.

Within a given space (i.e. the shape of the garden) some curves will be right and others wrong; it is very difficult to lay down the rules. You can start by drawing shapes on paper and trying to visualize how they will fit into the garden. But perhaps a better way to solve the problem is to obtain a long length of hosepipe and stretch it out on the ground, pushing it into the shape that will suit the front of the border. Move this around until you are satisifed (Fig. 2.6). Leave it and come back another day and see if you still like the shape; if you do then you can start work on the border.

An alternative, if it is a lawn that you are cutting into, is to cut out a line of turf, about 5 cm (2 in) wide along the line of the pipe, and come back several times and see whether you can live with the shape you

Another way of looking at the shape of the borders is to look at the reverse shape it makes with the lawn or whatever backs on to it. After all, you only have to realize that the word border, means just that, it borders on something else. So do not make a series of borders without looking at what will be left (Fig. 2.8). In the case of a lawn, this should have its own definite shape that will be pleasing to the eye and not just be the bit in the middle after the borders have been created.

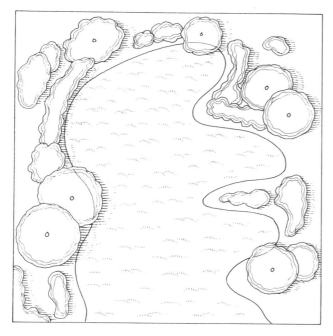

**Fig. 2.8** When creating the outline to borders, look back at the shape of the lawn that this will make. It may be too curvaceous to make sense.

If you cannot come up with a suitable shape (and I have one lawn that has been worrying me for years), you might dispense with it and turn over the whole area to beds with broad paths threading through them. The visual advantage of having lawns is that they give somewhere for the eye to rest: they are a peaceful contrast to the hurly burly of the borders. For this reason they can be an important part of the garden but

it is possible to dispense with them if the paths are wide enough to serve the same function.

Perhaps one should not be over conscious of the line of the border, as the planting is eventually likely to overlap onto the lawn or path. It is likely to only be in the initial planting stages and perhaps during the winter that the true outline will be seen. Bearing this in mind the gardener might like to confine his or her internal shapes to a circle, square or rectangle, leaving the plants to provide the interest in breaking this line. Certainly these shapes have a simplicity that takes a lot of beating. Circles will work well in any shape of garden, even triangular ones.

*Island beds*
Many of us looking at plants in a garden prefer to see them against a background of some sort, but it can be argued that in nature many plants are usually seen without this advantage. It is possible to create so-called island beds which can be viewed from all sides as they are placed in lawns or are at least surrounded by paths.

These are difficult beds to design well as, besides the problems of their initial shape, the planting has to be very well carried out as the plants must relate to each other in all directions at once. Bare patches left by plants once their season is over can be more apparent than in a conventional border.

One of the problems with island beds is choosing their shape. They can be geometric such as squares, rectangles, ovals or circles. The first two are generally far too formal for perennial planting. The latter pair are better as long as they are not too small and they do have the advantage of being simple. However, to many gardeners island beds look better if they are irregular in shape, but unfortunately irregular shapes are the most difficult to bring off successfully. Curves are obviously more successful than straight lines, but these should be sinuous and not too sudden in their changes of direction. The lie of the land might well dictate the shape and in the more successful beds this is often a significant factor.

The positioning of island beds is another problem. They can all too easily appear to float, unanchored in the middle of a lawn, a bit like an ice-floe that has wandered off from its parent ice-sheet. There is no doubt that the most successful island beds are those which are large enough not to show their independence. On the bigger ones it is possible to have a spine of shrubs or even trees which will give some heart to the planting. Without this many island beds seem to invite the eye to pass straight through or even above them, missing the plants altogether (Fig. 2.9).

One advantage of island beds is that it is likely to receive all-round light; the plants are not overshadowed by taller, denser trees and shrubs that make them push forward and flop over, necessitating staking. However if the island bed is big enough there are likely, as already mentioned, to be some shrubs, if not small trees, in the centre of it.

*Paths and other surfaces*

Borders and beds must front onto something. I suppose it is possible to fill the whole garden with plants but even here there must be some form of access and some viewpoint, otherwise the whole exercise is futile.

When considering paths, one of the first things to think about is that they should be wide enough for two people to walk side by side. One of the great pleasures of gardening is to be able to walk around the borders talking about their contents. This is partially denied if the people involved have to walk in single file!

Another reason for having wide paths is that unless strict formality is required, it is desirable that plants should flop over the edge of the border onto it. Some of my paths are far too narrow and it becomes quite a battle to get through them by the end of summer.

Grass paths can suffer from having plants permanently draped over them (Fig. 2.10) and, of course, are the very devil to mow with such obstacles along the edges. Consideration should therefore be carefully

**Fig. 2.9** Island beds need to be substantial to be of any aesthetic value. The eye will miss low or thin plantings, travelling to the plants or scenery beyond.

given as to the surface of the path. A solid one of gravel or paving slabs is more expensive, but obviates this problem and is much easier to maintain. Both grass and solid paths set off plants equally well. Solid

**Fig. 2.10** Plants hanging over the edge of grass paths and lawns will kill off the grass and leave ugly bare patches.

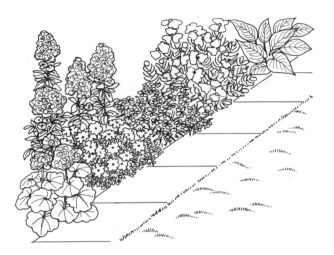

**Fig. 2.11** Paved areas to the edge of lawns ease the problems of mowing under flopping plants, as well as preventing the grass from being killed by lack of light.

paths have the advantage of being able to be used during or after wet weather without doing any damage to the path or shoes.

The shape of the paths will be dictated by the shape of the borders and should be considered at the same time and not left to chance. For me one of the most exciting paths is the one that curves away out of sight behind a bush or planting of some kind. This gives a hint of mystery and depth to the garden, even if the path stops dead up against a fence just round the corner.

Lawns are the other main surface that fronts onto borders. One of the big problems here is the same with grass paths: plants that flop over it. One solution to this is to lay one row of paving slabs round the edge of the lawn, slightly below the level of the grass (Fig. 2.11), thus providing the necessity of only mowing as far as the slabs and not right up to the troublesome edge of the border. Another solution is to ignore the problem and put up with a few brown patches on the lawn where plants have killed off the grass.

It is not a very good idea to have a raised decorative edge between the border and a lawn, such as bricks set on edge, as trimming round these when the lawn is cut can take hours. Edging between a border and solid surfaces such as gravel paths or paved terraces is a matter of taste.

The shape of the lawn has already been discussed but it must be reiterated that the lawn should not simply be an afterthought – the remains of the plot after the borders have been drawn up – otherwise it might not be visually attractive. If you are making a garden in an old field it is best to start any grass paths or lawns from scratch rather than simply rolling and cutting the existing grass, as often there will be creeping grasses which will constantly work their way into the borders. In some older parts of my garden there are some such field paths and it is a never-ending battle to keep these grasses from rapidly smothering the border. One day I will have to bite the bullet and re-sow.

# CHAPTER 3
# Designing with Plants

The usual recommended method of planning or designing flower borders is to outline the border to scale on squared paper and then to draw in on it the position of the plants you wish to use, carefully considering their colour, shape, texture, season, height and so on. This has a lot to recommend it, particularly if you have the type of visual mind or training that enables you to do it. But a lot of people only design one or two gardens in their life and often at a time when they are relative beginners to the subject. One difficulty is in making the visual jump from a few lines on a piece of paper to a border full of flowering plants. Another difficulty with this approach is that many people laying out gardens are beginners and have not got an intimate knowledge of all the plants they want to grow. It is impossible in the depth of winter, a time when such a plan is often being drawn up, to visualize the precise shade of a particular phlox or know exactly how high monardas will grow on your soil, especially if you have never grown them before. There are, of course, lists of plants in books, but their limitations are soon realized when precise information, relating to your conditions is required. A further problem with this type of approach presupposes that you have enough money to buy all the plants, usually several of each type, in one go. By all means attempt this type of planning if you can achieve it, but do not worry if you can't: it does not mean that you are a gardening failure.

## First steps

Although it goes against all principles recommended by designers, the majority of gardeners probably lay out their garden entirely by trial and error and really there is nothing wrong with this. Indeed it often introduces a note of sponaneity that is lacking in more formal designs. It is found by putting some basic plants in the ground and then adding others as they become available, perhaps moving plants around and adjusting the colours in the meantime. Gradually a border begins to appear with which the gardener is pleased. Gaps left for later planting can be temporarily filled with suitable annuals.

Even with this approach it is still a good idea to sit down with some sheets of paper along with catalogues and gardening books. First decide what kind of border you want. Perhaps it is a general one based on a few plants that you cannot live without; perhaps it is one based on a particular colour theme, yellow and white for example. It may be that the border is a shady one and, therefore, preference must obviously be given to shade-loving plants.

Once the theme has been established in your mind, make a list of all the plants you would like to grow and then by going through illustrations and descriptions of plants, make up another list of the plants you think might mix in with your original list. Draw out the shape of the border, preferably to scale, and then superimpose on it any dominant features such as shrubs and any plants that you want in a particular position (Fig. 3.1). You may, for example, want a phormium in a particularly eye-catching focal point. Now sketch in some of your other desired plants, matching in more from your second list so that the bed gradually fills up. Plants can be related to each other by colour, shape, height, time of flowering, and so on. It is likely that you will have to redraw the border several times before you get roughly what you want (Fig. 3.2).

**Fig 3.1** Draw out the shape of your border, marking on it the main features and the amount of space they will occupy.

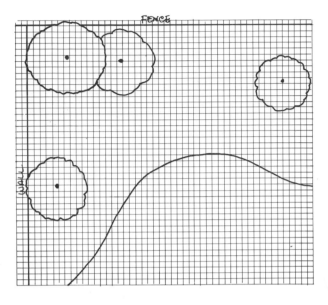

It may be that to purchase all the required plants is going to be way beyond your means, so the next thing is to consider whether some plants can be swapped either temporarily or permanently for others. For example if you want to include a clump of the pale cream *Kniphofia* 'Little Maid' it might be prudent to buy just one plant and bulk it up in a spare bed until there are enough to fill the space. In the meantime it might be possible, for example, to beg from a friend some pieces of their super-abundant *Sisyrinchium striatum*, which also has pale yellow flowers and the same upright habit, and which may well temporarily fill the gap while you await the kniphofia. We will look

**Fig. 3.2** Once you are satisfied with the bones of the border add the detailed planting, indicating the colours. You may need one plan per season.

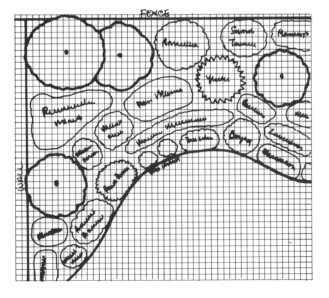

at the ways of acquiring plants in a later chapter (page 60).

Try making a plan on paper, then, but do not despair if you have difficulty in reducing your vision of the perfect border to a few pencil lines. Standing in front of an empty border with a wheelbarrow of plants might be much easier. Do not rush the planting. Lay them out on the ground and stand back and try and visualize the result, move a few around and stand back again. Sometimes in an older garden it becomes necessary to dig out a bed and replant it. This gives the gardener an opportunity to bring together existing plants from all over the garden into a new design, perhaps eventually replanting the whole garden, redesigning it as you go. I am always shuffling plants around like this. Gardens should never be static and a lot of enjoyment can be had by grouping plants into new combinations.

One difficulty where beginners become unstuck is in visualizing how much space a mature plant will take up – in other words, in knowing how close to place plants to each other. As a rule of thumb, allow the equivalent of half the height of the plant between each plant. This is an over-simplification, but will suffice if the gardener has no other information. Many books and catalogues include information on the spread of a plant as well as its height, while some state how many plants are required to the square metre. The latter is not a very useful piece of information as one rarely wants to plant exactly a square metre and converting the number for an irregular piece of border is not always easy.

Even after years of experience I still, out of habit, plant too closely but it has long ceased to bother me as it means that the border looks mature sooner and if things become over-crowded I dig them out and start them off again so that the borders always look full and fresh.

## Mixing plants

We are, of course, primarily concerned with hardy perennials in this book but few gardeners would so artificially limit themselves to such plants. Nearly every garden is bound to contain some shrubs and trees, as well as a few annuals of one sort or another. In late Victorian and Edwardian times there was a vogue for pure herbaceous borders, in which everything dies back to the ground each year, but this has almost disappeared as a style of gardening. This is partly because of the amount of time needed to tend them (no one can any longer afford large numbers of gardeners) and partly because herbaceous plants have a limited season, roughly from late spring until autumn, so that for the rest of the time the borders are devoid of interest. Pure herbaceous borders can really only work in a large garden where there are other parts to be visited when they are not at their best.

Herbaceous and other hardy perennials are therefore usually mixed in with other plants which give a framework of continuing interest to the border. The most obvious of these are the shrubs, which even when out of flower retain their leaves and shape. Shrubs also provide a certain amount of physical protection, from cold or drying winds for example, often creating micro-climates in which more tender plants may survive a winter.

Choose shrubs that blend well with hardy perennials, complimenting them both when they are in flower and in leaf. Avoid those that are boring when they are out of flower. However delightful you might think a flowering lilac (*Syringa*) is – and I definitely do – it is a terribly stiff and boring plant when it is out of flower, and will add little to the border other than in spring. Avoid conifers in a border as these tend to be too unchanging and stark, rarely matching the colourful exuberance or romanticism of perennials. Roses on the other hand, especially the long season shrub roses, blend in very well, as do shrubs such as *Lavatera olbia* which seem to flower non-stop.

There are some types of hardy perennials that need to be associated with trees and shrubs. These are the shade-loving plants, many of which flower in the spring. A later chapter will be devoted to them (see page 90).

**Fig. 3.3** It is easier to arrange an odd number of plants into a pleasing group than an even number.

the same type together rather than a single plant. In fact, if possible, always plant an odd number as the asymmetry of their grouping is more effective than the symmetry of an even number of plants. For example it is usually difficult to make four plants look right, whereas a group of five always seems to fall into place (Fig. 3.3). It is not always necessary to buy several plants; as we will see later, one plant can be purchased and bulked up, or sometimes can be divided immediately into a number of pieces. Ignore seedmerchant's packets which contain mixed colours, as unknown colours, and mixed at that, are difficult to use in a border and are likely to result in a spotty, restless picture. If you want to grow lupins from seed, for example, select a packet that will produce one colour.

Annuals will be dealt with in a little more detail later in this chapter (see page 33), but suffice it to say here that they are particularly useful for filling gaps in spring and later in the season, and as a temporary cover for new plantings.

When planning the border try to think in terms of broad sweeps. Drifts of colour merging one into another are much more restful to the eye than spots dotted here and there. Always try to plant several plants of

Occasionally the use of just a single plant can make an exciting change. A large plant, a spiky yucca for example, or one of a striking or contrasting colour, can be used as a focal point to draw one's eye into the border (Fig. 3.4). Try not to use groups of the same perennial plants in several different places in a border. If you want to repeat a colour try and find a different plant that will give the same effect. Seeing the same plants over and over again in a garden becomes very boring to anyone looking at it; variation will hold the interest. Sometimes it is useful to repeat shrubby or architectural

**Fig 3.4** A single bold plant will act as a focal point in the border.

plants to effect some sort of rhythm, or if you are creating a symmetrical pattern, but in informal settings repetition of perennials should generally be avoided.

As well as trying to blend colours and shapes when laying out a border, it is always a good idea to try to plan it so that as long a season as possible is achieved. Early-flowering plants should be planted next to later ones so that they can take over the interest from each other, or even as just suggested, covering the spot where the earlier one grew. An obvious example of this is with bulbs. Tulips and narcissus can be grown between clumps of emerging plants which will eventually cover the dying foliage of the bulbs.

The whole art of associating plants with one another is a very difficult one for the beginner, and indeed even the experienced grower is bound to make mistakes. It is essential not to be disheartened with any failures, as they happen to all gardeners, and to remember that you will probably learn more from mistakes than successes. You should always be prepared to move plants about. It is all very well preparing a plan on paper but only when the plants are flowering in all their colourful three-dimensional glory will you really see what you have planned. Be critical and prepared to move things; most perennials, with the main exception of tap-rooted plants, move quite readily. Constantly pick small bunches of flowers and hold them up against other plants to see whether the colours go together and then move them in the autumn if you think they will make an improved combination.

When considering how to relate one plant to another, a whole range of factors must be taken into account. Colour of the flowers and foliage, shape and texture of the foliage, and of the plant as a whole, are probably most important and these will be looked at in detail later in this chapter.

Do not consider one factor alone. If you choose plants just for the colour of their flowers, then the border will be rather spotty and boring for a large part of the time. Choose plants that have a range of qualities; for example those that provide interest through their foliage or shape, even when they are not in flower, will help to keep the border alive and full of interest.

Next is the height of the plant. As a rule of thumb the taller plants should go at the back of the border (or centre if it is an island bed) and the shortest at the front. This makes obvious sense as everything can then be seen, but it does make the border look a bit like a choir standing to attention in a concert hall (Fig. 3.5). Vary it a bit by pulling some of the taller plants towards the middle or even the front so that they break the symmetry of the border and form interesting barriers to deflect and stop the eye (Fig. 3.6). There are some tall plants, such as *Verbena bonariensis*, the mulleins (*Verbascum*) and some of the taller onions (*Allium*), which can be planted at the front of the border with great effect. They are not

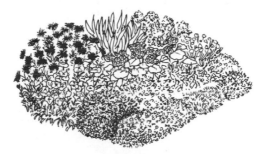

**Fig. 3.5** Do not make the border too regimented in the way plants are arranged according to height.

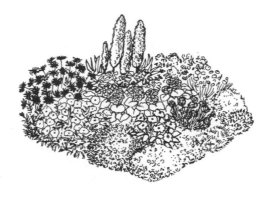

**Fig. 3.6** Bring some of the taller plants towards the front to break the symmetry.

'solid' plants but ones that can be seen through or between so they do not obscure the border but break it up, preventing it from becoming too bland or regimented.

Some plants are more untidy than others, especially when they are dying back. The oriental poppies (*Papaver orientale*) look dreadful once they have finished flowering. This type of plant should be planted in the middle of the border and should have later flowering plants behind and in front that will envelop it, hiding its decaying stems, or the space from where the stems have been cut down.

Not all gardens, of course, have been consciously arranged in this way. Some gardeners have an innate visual sense and plant their borders without any thought of design. The classic examples of this are the old cottage gardens where plants were left to self-sow amongst themselves and new plants were introduced only where there were gaps. The whole was a wonderful tapestry of colours, completely free from any overall plan. Somehow we are a bit too self-conscious now for this kind of gardening to work: we all know a little about what we are trying to achieve and so we try to orchestrate it a bit, but it never seems to work in the same way as it did for our forefathers; it seems to come out contrived. The nearest we can get to it now is in meadow or wild flower gardens (see page 102).

## Colour – flowers and foliage

To most people colour is the most important aspect of a garden. When they talk about it they generally refer to the colour of flowers but, of course, it must be remembered that foliage also has a colour, even if it is only green, and this is very important. Remove all the leaves and you would have a very dull garden in spite of the flowers. To many other gardeners the colour of the flowers is relatively insignificant; to them the basis of interest is the foliage, with only the occasional flower to create an accent.

Foliage forms the background colour to the flowers and to the border as a whole. It seems amazing to me that nature nearly always, but not invariably, matches the colour of the flowers with the colour of the leaves of a plant. For example citrus yellow flowers often have bright green leaves, frequently shiny, that set the flowers off well; while the yellows of a more reddy persuasion are backed by bronzy or reddish-green leaves. Compare, for example, the leaves and buds of the greenish-yellow-flowered *Oenothera biennis* with those of the reddish-yellow-flowered *O. stricta*. It is rare that flowers and leaves are not sympathetic towards each other.

Some people find that a garden devoted to foliage is a very restful place but I am afraid I get bored very quickly when there is a total absence of flowers. And it is really their colour that announces a plant's presence.

In overall terms, drifts of colour merging one with another are more successful than small patches dotted here and there. With the latter the eye jumps from one patch of dominant colour to the next, never finding, it seems, anywhere to rest. The neighbours with which colours merge must be chosen with care as they have great influence on each other.

It may seem surprising but the colour of a flower can appear to be different depending on the colour of the flowers next to it – a red amongst purples, for example, will look quite different to the same red amongst yellows. It can also vary in different lights – a pale blue on a hot summer's afternoon will appear totally different to the same colour in the dwindling light of evening. This is well worth remembering if you spend most of the day away from the garden and only ever see it during the evenings.

Some colours are more sympathetic to certain other colours, meaning they are in harmony with them. On the other hand there are colours that appear to be opposites and clash with each other – that is they are contrasting (these colours are known confusingly as complementary colours). Artists and colour theorists have been aware of this phenomenon for centuries.

Probably the first thing to do is to go out and look at the colours of flowers (go to the florist's shop if it is winter). One of the first things you will notice is that flower colours are very rarely pure, they are usually flushed, striped, or spotted with another colour, often giving the overall appearance of a completely different colour. Another aspect of the varying colour is the texture of the flower. A velvety surface will give a deeper, richer appearance, whereas the same colour on a shiny petal will appear bright and gay.

Another thing you will observe is the variation in one colour. For example yellow can veer towards green, giving quite a cool impression, whereas other yellows have a hint of red in them moving them in the direction of the oranges. These yellows are much warmer in appearance. This is very important to note as the two different yellows will often not go together very well. It is the same with most colours. For example reds can vary between the fiery reds with a touch of orange and the purply reds which have been influenced by blue. Place plants of these two colours together and the result can be hideous.

One of the important divisions of colour is that of cool and warm. The former tends to be based on blue and includes all the colours that have a hint of blue in them, including the harsher whites and the pinks that are touched with blue. On the other side, the warmer colours are a result of the influence of yellow and so we have the creams, the salmony pinks, the oranges and the fiery reds of the sunset colours. The choice of the terms 'cool' and 'warm' are not arbitrary, as the respective colours have a distinct effect on our moods. A bed of cool colours can be peaceful and restful whereas the hotter colours are more stimulating and exciting.

As already hinted above, warm and cool colours should not be mixed together as the result will be uncomfortable to the eye. If you wish to create a border that includes plants with flowers from each group, then grade the flowers so that the colours merge, possibly using greens or greys as a connector between colours that do not naturally blend.

Sometimes mixing contrasting colours can be exciting as long as this is not over-done. A clump of blue flowers in a predominately yellow border acts as a focal point – it naturally draws the eye. Apart from the drama in this there is also the practical point that it draws the eye away from somewhere else, which may, for example be a part of the border where the flowering is already over, leaving a temporary gap. One curious fact about strong and pale, misty colours is that paler colours seem to move away from the eye whereas the brighter stronger ones approach it. Thus if pale blues or lavenders are planted at the end of a border, an optical illusion is created in that they seem further away than they really are. This is useful in making short borders or small gardens seem larger. Conversely the really hot colours planted at a distance will seem closer than they really are. This phenomenon is often noticed on colour photographs where a red poppy, for example, seems to leap out of the picture.

These, then, are some of the points about colour that must be taken into consideration when planning a border. They will, doubtless, seem terribly complicated to the beginner but one should not be put off by this. While it helps enormously to understand how colours work it is possible to use them intuitively. Most plants can easily be moved around the garden, and trial and error – finding what is satisfying for you – is an approach through which you will learn a lot. Pick flowers and walk around the garden, putting them next to other plants to see how they go together, and go to other people's gardens and see how they mix their colours, making notes of what plants go with what plants.

I have only touched on colour theory here as it is quite complicated, particularly for the non-artist, and other books are available which tackle the subject in more depth.

## Shape and texture

Many gardeners only consider colour when they select their plants, but there are also other important factors to take into consideration. One of these is the shape of the plant. Put crudely you can get round plants, flat spreading ones, tall thin ones, ones that

**Fig. 3.7** If a border is made up of plants that are all the same shape, low hummocks, for example, it will look very boring.

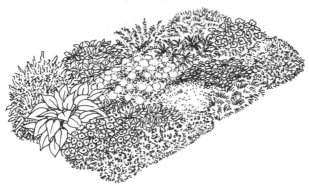

**Fig. 3.8** Once this is broken by the introduction of other shapes, upright plants, for example, it immediately becomes more interesting.

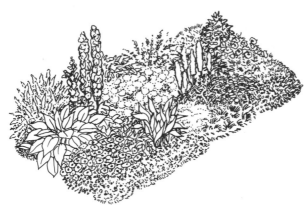

**Fig. 3.9** The best borders are an integration of shapes and textures as well as colour. This may be difficult to achieve in one go, but move plants around until you are happy with the result.

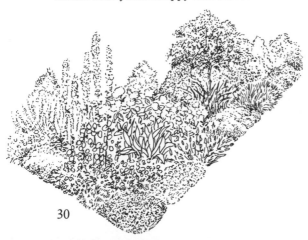

fan out and so on. It is not only the shape of the plant but the shape of the leaves that makes an impression on the eye. Again there can be round leaves, thin ones, feathery ones, long strap-like ones and so forth.

The use of these shapes can radically determine the appearance of a border. Often the shape of a plant is in place and retained long before and after a plant has flowered and therefore can extend the role of the plant. A border with low hummocks can look extremely dull and uniform (Fig. 3.7), but broken with rounded and occasional taller shapes it immediately becomes more interesting (Fig. 3.8). The use of trees and shrubs in a border makes it easier to achieve a border that is of interest throughout the year, but a lot can be done with perennial plants as they exhibit a tremendous variety of shapes and textures (Fig. 3.9).

Flat masses of plants do not excite the eye, they tend to be tranquil and lead on to other things. It is essential to have areas of this kind of plant to prevent the border becoming too restless. The rounded shapes, such as that of peonies, and the open upright shape that the majority of perennial plants form, create the main shapes of the border, their variety being in height and in texture. Tall upright shapes are far more dramatic and are one of the most eye-catching forms in the garden. They are very useful for creating focal points, frequently looking better if planted singly – a single large mullein (*Verbascum*) can for example, look more dramatic rising out of a border than a clump of them, although the latter also can have its place. The fan-like shape of such plants as *Phormium* or even ferns can also draw the eye and make a good contrast to more rounded and open forms.

It is the juxtaposition of these various shapes that creates the overall appearance of the border. Those borders that have contrast without being too restless are the most successful. Pleasing contrast can be achieved by relating, for example, the fan-shaped filigree leaves of a fern with the full rounded leaves of some of the hostas, or the upright growth of lamb's ears (*Stachys byzantina*) next to the round hummocks of a geranium. When looking at a garden try not to look at the plants individually but look at the structural groups created by shrubs and trees and try to deduce why one border or part of it is successful whereas others are not.

Texture is a bit more elusive. This can be created by the overall effect of the foliage of a plant, for example a carpet of ivy (*Hedera helix*) on the ground, or by the surface of individual leaves, such as the furry texture of the leaves of *Stachys byzantina*. Shiny leaves, on the other hand, give quite a different impression as they reflect the light and can be useful to lighten dark corners even if the leaves themselves are quite dark. Holly (*Ilex aquifolia*) is a good example of this, or in the perennial field some of the hostas. Some plants have an airiness about them that makes them float, gypsophila for example, while others have a solidity about them that no breeze would dare move. *Crambe cordifolia* is another ebullient, frothy plant that if planted next to the gyposphila would look all wrong, but when anchored with more sturdy friends looks fantastic.

Size can also cause drama, for example the huge leaves of *Gunnera manicata* always excite comment (Fig. 3.10). Similarly the tall linear form of the grass *Arundo donax*, or the giant candelabras of the Scotch thistle *Onopordum acanthium*.

## Scent

Although it is possible to create a perfectly acceptable garden without thinking about perfumed plants, there is no doubt that they do add another dimension which most of us would not like to be without.

Not all scents, of course, are attractive. Some people like the smell of the curry plant, *Helichrysum angustifolium*, but others hate it; either way its scent is far too overpowering for it to be planted near the house. There are some that are downright foetid, such as *Lysichiton americanum*. At the other extreme there are scents which are so sweet that many people find them sickly.

However the majority of perfumed garden plants are appreciated and it is well worth including them in your short list of plants for the borders. It is ideal to have them spread around the garden so that you are always within nose distance of at least one. But there are certain places that are more obvious for such plants than others. Anywhere near a bench or terrace where people sit is a perfect location. Another classic place is beneath or around the windows of a house (Fig. 3.11).

Many of the scented flowers are of a light colour, and are pollinated by moths and other insects that fly at dusk and at night, so it is at this time that their scent reaches its peak. There are some that change smells at this time of night. *Cestrum parqui*, for

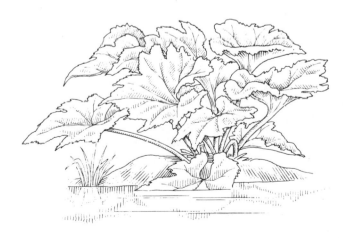

**Fig. 3.10** Large-leaved plants, such as this *Gunnera manicata*, will always add a sense of excitement to a border.

31

devoted to different times of the year, but in smaller gardens borders have to serve as long a period as possible. Careful thought must therefore be given to the plantings, if possible mixing plants from various periods of the year so that there is a continuous stream of bloom with as few gaps as possible.

One way to achieve this is by underplanting deciduous shrubs and trees with shade-loving woodland plants that naturally appear and flower in early spring (Fig. 3.12). Another method of underplanting is to arrange for bulbous plants, such as narcissus, to grow through or next to later-flowering plants.

Some plants can be made to serve more than one season and are worth their place. Pulmonarias flower in spring but some retain their attractive, silver-splashed leaves right through to autumn. Others, such as some of the euphorbias, also flower in the spring but take on fiery tints in the autumn.

Many of the winter-flowering plants are unexciting for the rest of the year and should be planted in such a position that they are covered by more interesting things as they fade. This is particularly so of such plants as hellebores, which can be in light shade towards the back of a border and still easily be seen in the winter when there is little else around.

## Ground cover

Many gardeners like to fill their borders so full of plants that no bare earth is showing, thus giving weeds little chance of germinating and growing. However, there are some plants that are better than others at creating this type of cover and which are used extensively in protecting areas away from formal borders, such as under shrubs and trees, or odd pieces of ground that are not frequently visited.

Any area that is covered in this manner must be absolutely free from weeds before you start, otherwise the idea will not work. Once the ground cover has been planted, keep an eye out for weeds until the plants have merged to form a complete blanket over the earth.

**Fig. 3.11** Place scented plants near a terrace or under windows where their fragrance can be appreciated.

example, has a strong savoury smell of Oxo during the day but as afternoon lengthens into evening it is transmogrified into a sweet, almost sickly, smell.

Scents can be very elusive and I have often followed one around a garden trying unsuccessfully to locate it. A surprising number of winter-flowering plants are scented, including snowdrops (*Galanthus*), a good reason for planting them near paths.

## Seasonal plantings

The true herbaceous borders have a limited season over the summer and early autumn. In days when gardens were large it was possible to have different parts of the garden

**Fig. 3.12** Flowers that appear in early spring can be planted under deciduous shrubs and trees, where their remains will be screened by foliage later in the season.

Unfortunately ground cover can look rather boring. Because of its purpose there is a tendency to use it in large swathes. Another problem is that it has to stay in leaf all year to be effective and can therefore begin to look a bit tired and tatty, especially if it is in an odd bit of ground that catches fallen leaves in autumn and bits of paper and other rubbish during the year.

In a small garden large areas of the same plant can unbalance the appearance and it is better to concentrate on filling the borders with attractive plants and to be prepared to take out the odd weed. There is nothing wrong with weeding if you do it regularly and approach it with the right frame of mind. It provides an ideal opportunity to examine the border and its plants in detail.

## Use of annuals

Annuals and biennials can be very useful for filling gaps in the border or for adding colour. There are some, such as foxgloves, *Digitalis purpurea*, that one would never like to be without and, indeed, need never be without as they copiously self-sow. There are quite a number of these perennial annuals, as it were, which come up every year without any help on the part of the gardener. *Limnanthes douglasi, Nigella, Collomia grandiflora, Omphalodes linifolia, Myosotis* are all among those that regularly occur in my garden, the only attention I give

them being to remove any I do not want.

On the other hand there are also quite a number of annuals that must be sown every year by the gardener, either in trays or direct into the soil. This obviously takes up time and many gardeners either do not bother or buy the plants from nurseries.

It is a shame not to use some annuals as they can contribute a lot to the garden. Unfortunately many gardeners mix the colours and dot the plants all over the place, which makes a restless unattractive picture. Avoid buying packets of seed that have mixed colours. Choose one colour that blends in with your plants for the border and plant it in drifts in the same way as you would with the perennials. Some of the more highly bred self-sowers will not come true to the original plants of the first sowing. For example whatever the colour of the first *Eschscholzia* you grow they are likely eventually to produce seedlings that are orange.

Annuals can be used as fillers for temporary gaps in new plantings. They can also be used to fill gaps at certain times of year, following on from spring-flowering plants for example, or used with short-term flowers such as the classic tulips and forget-me-nots (*Myosotis*) combination. Another popular use is of course in tubs and other containers, which can be used as an integrated part of the garden scene.

# PART II
## TECHNIQUES

# CHAPTER 4

# *Border Preparation*

Giving advice on gardening matters is fraught with difficulties, one of which is that every garden is different from any other. One of the most basic differences is in the soil. Even in the same area, indeed, even within the same garden, the soil is likely to vary considerably, provoking a different response from plants. The main difference is between alkaline and acid soils. I was brought up in a heavy clay area that tended towards acid and I can still remember my sheer amazement at the difference of the flora when I first walked across the chalk downs less than twenty miles away.

From the point of view of gardening with perennials, the variation in alkalinity/acidity does not make as much difference as it does in growing, for example, shrubs amongst which are a lot of ericaceous plants that are lime-haters. There are a few plants that are not compatible; dianthus, for instance, prefer a soil that is alkaline although they will grow in neutral soils, and, if they are well-drained, in very slightly acid conditions. Many of the woodland plants are happier in a leafy soil which tends towards the acid side of neutral.

Gardeners like most other people seem to be rarely satisfied with what they have got and those living on chalk yearn to grow rhododendrons and those on acid soils would love to grow dianthus. On the whole, however, it should not worry perennial gardeners too much.

Perhaps more of a problem is caused by living on light or heavy soils, as the lack of moisture in the first and the excess in the latter, can be restrictive unless action is taken to alter things. Light soils are the sandy ones through which water passes rapidly. The heavier ones are the clays which hold the water, especially during winter, but once they have dried out can create a very harsh environment for plants to live in.

The ideal soil is a good loam which contains plenty of organic material to feed the plants and to retain moisture, but at the same time is porous enough to allow excess moisture to drain away. Given time and effort the two extremes can be turned into something more like an ideal soil. Earlier I referred to being brought up on a heavy soil. It was the worst possible sticky yellow clay when we first moved in and yet now, forty years later, it can be easily forked over in mid-winter (it did not take that long to get it to that state).

## Soil improvement

### Drainage

If the garden is a wet one then the first thing to consider is drainage. Very few plants, other than bog and pond plants, can survive wet conditions, which somewhat restricts the scope of the gardener.

There are two ways to improve a wet soil. The first is to install a drainage system and the other is to improve the drainage of the soil itself by incorporating a drainage material such as grit or gravel.

If the water lies around in the whole or part of the garden then it must be removed. This can be done by digging drainage channels below the level of the topsoil and filling them with an aggregate such as pea-beach or with drainage pipes (Fig. 4.1). The difficulty, of course, is getting rid of the water that the system collects. In a large garden it may be possible to lead it away to a ditch round the perimeter but if this is not possible, and it is certainly unlikely in small town gardens, then a soakaway must be

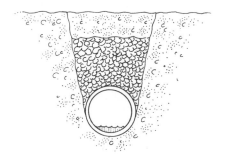

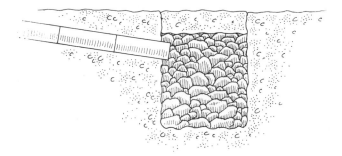

**Fig. 4.1** In areas that are permanently wet, land drains will have to be installed to make the soil suitable for borders.

**Fig. 4.2** If there is no ditch to take land drains, construct a soakaway at the lowest point of the garden, to remove the excess water.

constructed. This is a large hole in the ground at least a cubic metre (35 cu ft) in volume which is filled with old bricks or stone. The water is channelled into this. (Fig. 4.2). Another possibility if the lie of the land will allow it, is to take advantage of the excess water by creating a pond into which it will flow.

Comparatively few gardens need go to the extreme of constructing full-scale drainage systems, the majority being able to improve drainage simply by improving the soil. It may be that the soil itself is heavy clay, which holds water which would otherwise drain away. This can be improved by digging grit or gravel into it. Heavy soils of this type should also have organic material added: as this breaks down it will also improve the drainage.

If you dig deep holes for planting trees or shrubs, be careful that they do not act as sumps and fill up with water from the surrounding ground. If there is the likelihood of this, dig a drainage channel leading away from the hole and fill it with small stones.

### Enrichment

Enrichment can take two forms: firstly to improve the moisture retentiveness of the soil and secondly to make it more fertile.

Any fibrous organic material can be used to improve moisture retention. In the past peat has been a popular medium. This popularity has over-stretched production

and is now thought to present environmental problems. Interestingly, it is not the best material to use anyway, as it seems to disappear very quickly into the soil, leaving very few benefits behind. It is much better to use well-rotted farmyard manure or garden compost, which has some nutritional value as well as the ability to retain moisture. On light soils a good layer of compost placed at the bottom of the spit as it is dug, plus some mixed in with the soil seems to be the best combination (top dressing will also help).

Well-rotted organic material will also help to feed the soil and should be added to any type of ground. When preparing the borders, plenty should be dug into them. Once they have been planted it is a good idea to top dress them once a year, usually in early spring. Where there are plants with shallow roots it is best to leave the dressing on the top, letting the worms work it into the soil. In other areas it can be lightly forked in. Some materials, such as farmyard manure and home-made compost, are more likely to contain weed seed than others and these should not be used for top dressing.

*Farmyard manure*
This is once again becoming relatively easy to obtain, depending on where you live. Horses are on the increase, particularly around the edges of towns, and the problem of disposing of their waste is becoming acute and many stables are willing to let you have

as much manure as you can take and often free at that. A day in the country takes on a different meaning if you are accompanied by half a dozen bags of horse manure in the boot. It should, however, be well rotted before you put it on the borders and by this time it should be completely odourless. If it is still smelly stack it, possibly adding some to the compost heap, until it has rotted down and is quite friable (crumbly). Farmyard manure can contain seed left from hay that has been fed to the animals. This form of organic matter can come from any animal – horses, cows, sheep, chicken, or goats – as long as it is well rotted.

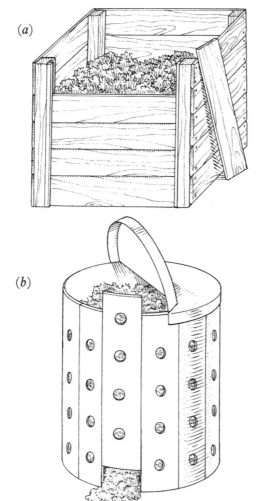

(a)

(b)

**Fig. 4.3** Home-made compost bins (a) are efficient and can be made from scrap materials. There is a wide range of commercially available bins, some with easy access for extracting the mature compost (b).

### Home-made compost

The cheapest form of organic material is that created by the gardener from garden and kitchen waste. There are always plenty of weeds, dead and dying parts of plants, grass cuttings, old leaves and so on that can be composted. Most vegetable waste from the kitchen can also be added.

To make seed-free compost you have to be selective with the weeds you compost. Nothing that is going to seed should be added, otherwise you will be spreading them over the whole garden. Some authorities claim that if the temperature of the heap is hot enough it will kill the seed but in practice this never seems to work. However I still believe in composting even weeds in seed. These can be put on a separate heap which is eventually used not on the top of borders but dug down deep when plants that are not going to be moved, such as shrubs, are planted. Here any seed is well out of harm's way and yet the rest of the rotted plant material is of great benefit.

Be careful with perennial weeds that have a creeping rootstock such as couch grass (*Agropyron repens*), which can infest a compost heap and odd fragments can get back into the borders where they will reek havoc. Either dispose of them in some other way, such as on a bonfire, or kill them off by drying in the sun until they are dead before adding them to the heap. I tend to create mountainous compost heaps which I do not use for a couple of years and have found that if couch is put at the bottom of the heap it exhausts itself before it reaches the surface and dies, but don't do this if you have smaller heaps or a shorter cycle.

Compost can be made in special containers which are available from ironmongers and garden centres or in home-made enclosures (Fig. 4.3). They are most efficient if they have a lid on the top to keep out excess moisture and to retain the heat. In fact, I am never in a hurry to produce compost as I always have plenty to spare so I use the traditional country method of just piling everything up in an orderly heap, turning once so that the outside goes into the middle and vice versa. Every spring I start a new heap and use the previous year's to grow marrows on. The following year I break it up and use it.

The compost rots down easier if the ingredients are well mixed. If there is, for example, too thick a layer of grass cuttings it tends to slow down the process. It is possible to buy activators which speed things up, but a little horse manure added at intervals will have the same effect. It is also usually advised that occasionally a layer of soil is added to the heap. I find that there is usually sufficient soil on many of the weeds. If borders have regular additions of manure or compost they will soon begin to build up in height so that the loss of some soil on the weeds helps to redress the balance.

In recent years many gardeners have invested in shredders with which they cut up the coarser material such as hedge clippings and old cabbage stalks which would not normally rot down. This not only uses up material that hitherto could not be used but also provides a useful mulch (see page 54). Like compost it should be stacked and composted for several months before it is used. It is not only useful as a mulch but also as a soil conditioner. The general recommendation seems to be that you should buy the most powerful shredder that you can afford, as some of the cheaper ones are underpowered.

Every autumn we are sent a free load of nutrients for the soil in the form of leaves. It is a terrible waste to burn these. Make a container out of four posts and some chicken wire (Fig. 4.4) and let them decompose into leafmould, an excellent soil additive. Leafmould can be a little disheartening in that what starts off as a full bin of leaves dwindles to only a fraction by the time it has broken down. Obtain as many leaves as you can, but do not go and raid your local woods as the continuing existence of the trees depends on the nutrients they gain from the fallen leaves.

### Mushroom compost

There are also quite a number of other forms of organic material that can be acquired as by-products of farming and industrial processes. Spent mushroom compost, for example, is an excellent material and can usually be obtained quite cheaply, especially if purchased in bulk. This tends to contain a little chalk so that it is especially of value for those living on acid soils. It is generally quite inert and can be safely used as a top dressing.

### Chipped bark

Crushed or chipped bark is another waste product that is being used a great deal nowadays. In an uncomposted state it is best used as a mulch but if it is left in a heap for a

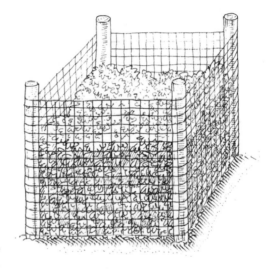

**Fig. 4.4** A simple enclosure made from stakes and wire-netting can be used for composting leaves.

year it will start to break down and can be used mixed in with the soil. It should be stacked for a while in any case to let any resins evaporate off as these could damage plants. You can add uncomposted bark to the soil but it needs nitrogen as it breaks down and therefore the soil is likely to become depleted rather than enriched.

The cheapest way of buying bark is by the lorry load, but if it is purchased by the sack you can find variations on the theme, with chemical fertilizers added to it to boost its decomposition and to feed the soil.

### Hops

Spent hops from breweries can be a useful addition to the soil, as can a variety of other waste products such as cocoa-bean shells (although the latter can form a gooey mass in wet weather which looks as though it could harbour a number of moulds).

I have spent a lot of space writing about the various organic materials that can be added to the soil. If you wish to have the best of borders you must take serious note of them. In areas of low rainfall the addition of this kind of material helps to retain moisture in the soil, in spite of the high temperatures above it.

### Other additives

Three other additives should just be mentioned. Bonfire ash is a useful addition in that particles of soil that were on the roots of pernicious weeds that have been burned, get lightly fired and turn almost into pottery. These particles will not return to soil but will act like small stones and help improve the drainage. They are particularly useful on clay soils.

Soot is another useful ingredient as long as it is used in moderation (too much will make the soil tacky). This helps to darken the soil, which will keep warmer during the winter and warm up faster in the spring. If you do add soot to the soil, weather it in a heap for six months before use.

Finally, there is ground chalk or lime. The acidity of some soils can be counterbalanced by the addition of lime which will adjust the pH (the scale used to measure the acidity/alkalinity of the soil) towards neutral. Instructions as to quantities are usually found on the packaging, or in the soil-testing kits which you will need to use to determine the pH of your soil. Do not add soot and lime to the soil at the same time.

## Soil preparation

Before you can plant a border the soil must be thoroughly prepared. This cannot be over-emphasized. If the border is properly prepared it will save a great deal of work in the future and it will last much longer until it has to be dug out and replanted.

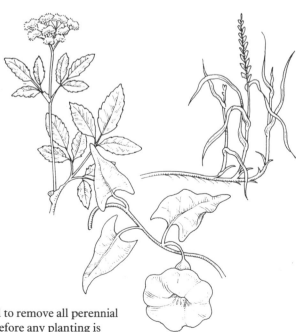

**Fig. 4.5** It is essential to remove all perennial weeds from a border before any planting is attempted.

## Removing weeds

The first and most important thing is to remove all perennial weeds (Fig. 4.5). How you do this is up to you. For many people chemical weedkillers are the answer and if used correctly they are certainly an effective answer to the problem.

However, there are an increasing number of people who are less than happy to use chemicals in the garden. The main method for them is to dig the bed thoroughly, searching each spade or forkful of soil to make certain that there are no pieces of root lurking there to re-shoot. This is very time consuming but you certainly get to know your soil and you can check for pests, such as wireworm, at the same time. If possible dig the bed six months or so before planting and remove any weed that shoots from any piece of root left in the soil. They will usually come out very easily if the soil is still loose.

If you have a good loam soil such a method is not at all arduous or difficult, but on clay soils it is not as simple as I have made it sound as bits of root remain undetected, embedded in the sticky clay. Here an alternative is to cover the soil with black polythene or an old carpet or something similar, to starve out any weeds which will be deprived of light with which to photosynthesize. Unfortunately this takes a long time to be effective and the garden can look rather unsightly in the meantime. It may be that chemicals will have to be used on this type of soil. If you are reluctant to use any chemicals, it is worth remembering that this is a one-off usage if the garden is properly maintained thereafter.

Although all the perennial weeds may have been removed there will still be plenty of annual weed seed left in the soil, but this does not matter so much as it can be easily dealt with (Fig. 4.6). If possible leave the prepared soil for a month or so before planting so that any annual seedlings that appear can be easily hoed off. After planting there will still be plenty to remove, but they will be much easier to remove than perennial weeds and after a couple of seasons the number will decline if they have not been allowed to seed themselves.

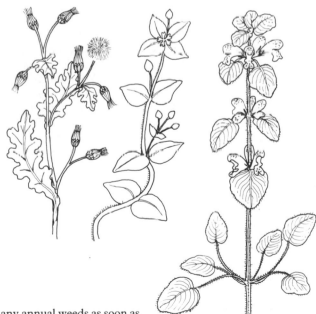

**Fig. 4.6** Remove any annual weeds as soon as they occur so that they do not seed.

**Fig. 4.7** Perennial borders are likely to be undisturbed for years so prepare them thoroughly by double digging.

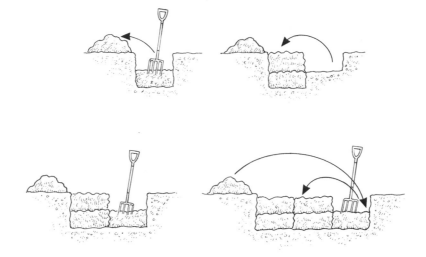

Once the weeds have been dealt with the soil should be dug over. Organic material as described in the previous section of this chapter should be incorporated, preferably at the bottom of the spit. If possible it is useful if the soil can be double dug or at least have the bottom spit broken up and organic material mixed in with it. The technique of double digging involves digging a trench and then digging over the soil on this lower level, turning the next top spit onto this and then digging the newly uncovered bottom spit and so on until the end of the plot, which is filled with the soil taken out of the original trench (Fig. 4.7). The soil from the two spits should not be allowed to mix. During the recent severe droughts in parts of the UK, double digging has certainly paid off. Newly set-out plants have sent their roots down into the manure, which has provided them with sufficient nutrients and moisture to keep them going through the long hot summers, whereas on older beds, where the manure had been broken down and used up, the plants have flagged miserably.

Once the border has been dug, break it down into a reasonably fine tilth, raking it back slightly from the edges if it neighbours onto grass, so that it is possible to trim after mowing.

If possible leave the border a while before planting so that any weeds that might germinate can be removed, as can any scraps of perennials that may have been left in the soil which will have shown their presence by sprouting. The ideal time for digging the border is in the autumn and for planting is in the following spring. This gives plenty of time for removing any weeds and also allows the frost to work on the soil and the birds to remove any pests from the loosened earth.

It is now ready for planting.

# CHAPTER 5
# *Planting*

There is a very large range of plants to choose from. Over 58,000 are available from commercial growers in Britain alone. No-one could ever hope to grow such a huge quantity of plants and so, obviously some selection is necessary.

## Selecting plants

In the first place a list of desired plants should be drawn up, as discussed in the chapter on design (see page 23). There are very many illustrated books on gardening which may help you make up your mind as to what you want, and nothing could be more pleasant in the winter than thumbing through some, perhaps sitting beside a fire. Most libraries have a good selection for you to go through.

A much better way is to visit gardens and to see the growing plants. Many that are open to the public have all, or at least most, of their plants labelled. If not, ask. Here you will get a better idea of how plants grow, how big they get and with what they associate. Garden visiting is a very valuable way of getting to know your plants.

A third, but least satisfactory method is to see the plants growing in pots at the moment of purchase. You are likely to get a false impression of a young plant in a pot. The size of the plant, and the size and even colour of the flower are likely to differ once they are planted out and fully grown. The descriptions on the labels often leave much to be desired. Many of the specialist nurseries have gardens attached in which the plants can be seen growing and their knowledgeable staff are usually willing to give advice.

When selecting a plant from a batch on offer look at it critically. Choose one that has no obvious disease, leaves should be fresh, whole and undistorted. The plant should not be pot-bound, that is to say the roots should not be wound round and round the inside of the pot (Fig. 5.1). These plants have been in the pot too long and may be starved. The roots have got into the habit of growing round in circles and it is sometimes difficult to persuade the plant to grow normally. The plant, once planted out, will never do well and if you dig it up after a year you may still find the roots in a tight ball.

**Fig. 5.1** Never buy plants that are pot-bound, where their roots form a tight congested ring around the edges of the pot.

If you are too shy to take the pot off to look, you can normally tell by looking through the drainage holes on the bottom. Pot-bound plants have roots sticking out of the bottom. If the plant is in a plastic container you can often tell if it is pot-bound by running your fingers over the outside of the pot. The compacted roots are likely to have distorted the pot and the fingers will detect the irregularities in the plastic.

Not all pot-bound plants are necessarily a bad buy. I recently bought a *Tricyrtis formosana* which was so badly rootbound that the outside of the pot was really bumpy and totally distorted; I had to cut the plastic to get the plant out. By carefully unwinding the stolons I managed to pot up 43 plants out of the original one. All survived, making this a very good bargain. However, selecting plants that are pot-bound is something that comes with experience and beginners should avoid any such plants.

Don't necessarily go for the plants that are in flower; choose one that has a good even growth. If you are after a particular clone or colour form, and suspect that the nursery may have got their labels mixed up or have not labelled them correctly, then it is a good idea to choose one in flower to be certain that you have got the right plant.

The biggest plant in a pot does not always get away quicker than its smaller colleagues. A medium-sized, even a small one sometimes, will establish itself quicker than a big plant. This is because there is often a better balance between roots and top-growth.

**Fig. 5.2** Writing a limited cheque saves everybody a lot of time. Write the maximum amount that your bill can come to across the cheque and the nurseryman will fill in the precise amount.

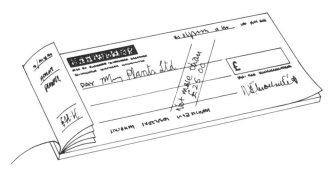

## Acquiring plants

There are a number of places from which you can buy plants. The most obvious these days is the ubiquitous garden centre. There is no doubt that you have to be careful when buying plants here. In spite of their protestations to the contrary, plants are often wrongly labelled and are frequently in very poor condition. They tend to be left in pots too long and can become very pot-bound. If at the beginning of the season the compost on the top of the pot looks fresh, it may be that it is a plant left over from the previous season that has had the top weed-infested layer of compost replaced. Push your finger in and if it meets an old layer of compost or tight roots, do not buy the plant. The selection of perennial plants from garden centres is also severely limited. In the main they go for plants that are easy to propagate, are in flower when they are sold and stand well in pots.

Old-fashioned nurseries are a much better bet. Here you are likely to find a much bigger range of plants, most of which will have been raised on the premises. The staff, because they are involved with plants all the time are usually very knowledgeable and are willing to give advice. It is in their interests to keep their plants in healthy condition and so they will throw away those that have become pot-bound or sickly looking. Because of the lack of overheads, the plants are more than likely to be cheaper than at a garden centre. Most nurseries try to change their stock annually or at least to introduce new plants to their range, so they are worth visiting at least once a year.

Many nurseries run a mail-order service which can be a useful way of acquiring plants that are not available in the immediate neighbourhood. All that offer this service provide a catalogue (for which you usually have to pay these days, as they are expensive to produce). These are often a wealth of information as besides giving the name and price, they usually include a description and cultural tips.

Nurseries only have a limited stock of plants, so when ordering by post be prepared that not all your requests may be fulfilled. Be certain to give ample second choices or, if you do not want any substitutes for missing plants, send an open cheque limited to a certain amount so that the nurseryman can fill in the exact amount. To do this leave the amount blank but write across the cheque 'maximum limit × pounds' (Fig. 5.2). This will save the nurseryman from having to make refunds or raise a credit note for you.

Plants are normally only sent out by post in spring and autumn. If you are likely to be away on holiday when the plants might arrive, ask the nuseryman not to send them during that period or arrange for a neighbour to open the parcel – a packet of young plants that have been sitting on a hot doorstep for a fortnight is not a very pretty sight. You are unlikely to receive an acknowledgement of your order automatically; if you want one, enclose a stamped addressed envelope.

When the plants arrive, unpack them immediately and stand them in a cool shady place until they have recovered. If they are not in pots, pot them up. Water if necessary but be careful not to overwater. Do not plant out until they have fully recovered and are showing signs of growth.

Another source of plants is from plant sales of various kinds. Some of the best are run by gardening societies. These often have an interesting range of plants, but it is essential to get to any sale at its start as the best plants go quite quickly. Some plants have obviously been dug from the garden and put into pots. There is nothing wrong with this, but check the plants carefully, removing the soil if necessary, to make certain that there are no pieces of weed root or pests, such as vine weevil, tucked away amidst the roots.

A final source of plants is not one that requires purchase. This is from friends. One of the joys of gardening is the generosity of all gardeners. It frequently happens that when walking around a garden you have only to give the slightest hint that you like a certain plant and out will come a fork and before you know what is happening you have a piece in a polythene bag. At first this can be embarrassing, and one has to learn to either hold your tongue or to refuse politely. However the way to cope with the embarrassment is, in the first place, not to be too greedy and, in the second, to become as generous yourself; if you give you will not be so reluctant to receive. Plants become associated with the person who gave it to the gardener and they will often refer to so-and-so's plant, especially if they have not got a name for it. This association of plants and friends makes gardening a very personal thing and gives many people great pleasure.

Many herbaceous plants increase with reasonable rapidity so it is no hardship to give pieces away. One aspect of giving plants away is that it does a great deal for conservation. The more people that have a particular plant, the less likelihood there is of it dying out. Giving plants away is a kind of insurance, because if you lose yours through some disease or mishap, you can always turn to your friends for a replacement. One thing that is worth doing is to label any plants as you are given them because, unless you know your plants well, you are bound to get them mixed up or forget what they are.

One cheap way of acquiring plants, of course, is to produce your own. Most perennial plants can be quite easily grown from seed, cuttings or divisions. As will be seen in a later chapter on propagation (see page 60), there are plenty of sources for seed in particular and this gives the opportunity for the gardener to build up a collection of unusual plants that may not be available from any other source. The keen gardener may also want to create his own unique plants by hybridizing, which is not as difficult as it may seem to the uninitiated.

Producing your own plants enables you to grow several of one species or cultivar, whereas you might only be able to afford one if you were buying. This means that it is possible to make larger-scale plantings. If you have space it is always worth while having a nursery bed where young plants can be brought on, ready to be planted out when they are required.

In many cases they may well be plants you have raised yourself but in others they may be a single plant that you have purchased, but have split up. When buying or otherwise acquiring a plant, look at it before planting to see whether it can be split up into several plants. It is amazing how many can be, particularly spreading plants that are sold in larger pots. I remember many years ago, in more impecunious days, buying a pot of *Phuopsis stylosa* which I immediately broke into seven pieces, of which I sold six to friends and planted one (which is still growing in the garden). Likewise it is possible to take cuttings immediately you buy a plant, so that later in the year you have several to plant out. Buy, for example, a penstemon in spring, cut off all the shoots and root them in a propagator, and by late summer you will have at least half a dozen more plants to set out.

## Planting out

Having acquired your plants it is time to plant them out. Plants in pots or other containers can be planted out at any time of year as long as the roots are not disturbed and provided it is not too cold, too hot or too windy, all of which can kill the plant. Those that are bare-rooted, that is dug up

**Fig. 5.3** If the soil is likely to be compacted, when it is wet for example, use a board from which to work.

direct from the earth, are best planted in either spring or autumn when the soil is warm and moist enough to promote regrowth. Some plants have a seasonal preference; *Paeonia*, for example, are best planted in autumn, while grasses should be planted out in spring. In colder areas it is probably best to leave most planting until the soil has warmed up in spring.

The ideal weather for planting is cool and overcast, preferably with an imminent period of drizzle or light rain. Thoroughly water the plants in their pots or in the ground if they are to be dug up, the day before they are to be planted. This will give the plant time to take up some moisture and by the time the plant is taken from its pot the compost will still be moist enough not to fall apart, but not too wet to handle. If the weather is dry soak the ground the day before planting. This will allow it to be moist, yet not muddy when planting starts. If the border is wet and likely to be compacted, work from a board or plank of wood (Fig 5.3).

The ultimate size of the plants, and therefore the distance at which they should be planted apart, is often difficult for the beginner to foresee. Many books include the spread of a plant which will give some help but as a rough rule of thumb, plants should have about half their final height between them and the next plant. Position all the plants on the area to be planted or otherwise mark their positions so that once the plants are out of their pots they can be put into the ground immediately, preventing the rootballs from drying out while you figure out where to put them. Work methodically across the plot so that plants already in the ground are not trodden upon.

Plants can be removed from pots by smartly tapping the rim of the inverted container on the edge of a wheelbarrow or handle of a spade, while holding one hand across the pot with fingers spread out on either side of the plant (Fig. 5.4). The rootball should then easily slide out of the pot.

Plants acquired in black polythene bags should have the bags slit from top to bottom with a knife and then the root-ball eased out

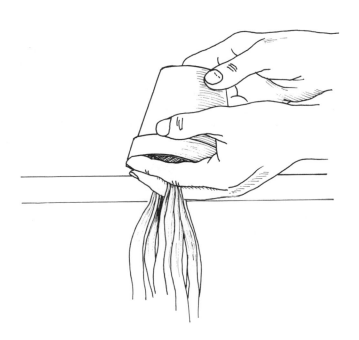

without breaking it. It is difficult to get the plant out by simply inverting and pulling it, as the compost usually falls apart. When cutting the polythene, avoid pushing the knife in too far as it might also cut any roots that are running round the inside of the bag.

### How to plant

Dig a hole, with a trowel for smaller plants and a spade for larger ones, that is wider than the root-ball of the plant. Put in the plant so that the stem is at the same depth that it was in the pot or in the ground (Fig. 5.5). If the plant is root-bound, with the roots spiralling round the ball of compost, tease them out gently. Some authorities advocate that roots should not be touched, but they are no good tied up in a tight knot which will prevent them from growing away. If the roots have been teased out, or if the plant is bare-rooted, spread the roots out evenly in their most natural position, and gently cover with soil. Firm in with the knuckles of your hands and water.

In really dry weather it is advisable to puddle in the plants. Place the plant in the hole as before, fill it with water and then refill with soil.

If the ground is not a newly prepared border, the area around where the plant is to be positioned should be dug over and some organic material or slow-release fertilizer, such as bonemeal, incorporated. Sometimes, even with newly prepared ground it is necessary to make localized additions to the soil. For example those that resent drying out, such as monarda might have an extra amount of organic material added to

**Fig. 5.5** Most plants need to be planted to the same depth as they were in the pot or nursery bed.

47

the soil. On the other hand plants such as *Iris unguicularis* prefer a spartan, well-drained soil and so it would be worth adding exta grit in the immediate area.

Once the plants are in the ground they should be labelled (see below) and the soil raked over to give an even finish between the plants. Make certain that any compacted areas, such as footprints, have been opened up, otherwise these might form pools of water. If you are intending to mulch the border then this should be done at this stage. It is possible to plant through a mulch, but inevitably it gets mixed up with the soil and needs replenishing. If the planting was done during the autumn keep an eye on the plants during cold spells as the frost can force the newly-planted root-balls out of the ground as it freezes.

### Labelling

To label or not to label is a dilemma that faces many gardeners. Some like to know what every plant is and where it is located and therefore label everything; others dislike the sight of 'tombstones' sticking up all over the garden and never label. It is a matter of choice.

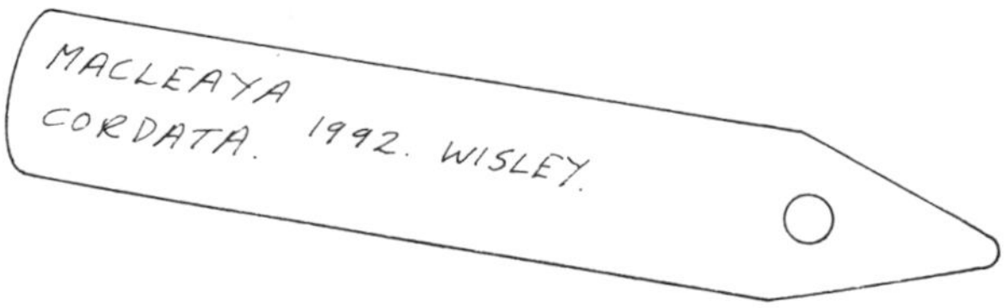

**Fig. 5.6** If there is space on the label include the date of planting and where you acquired the plant.

The advantage of labelling is twofold. In the first place it is a record of the plant: its name, the date of planting and possibly where it was purchased or where it came from (Fig. 5.6). This can be quite important if you have a bad memory for names, because you can easily check a label. In the second place the label marks the position of the plant, which can be very important when it is dormant. Some plants are very late into growth, *Cosmos atrosanguineus* for example, and they can easily be dug up or overplanted by mistake if there is no label to indicate their presence.

The ideal label is difficult to find. Cheap aluminium labels are a thing of the past and although they can still be purchased, they are now expensive. These are ideal in that they can be written on with pencil, with the inscription lasting for years. I still have a stock of these and always attach them to a long piece of galvanized wire which, when inserted in the ground, stops blackbirds and cats from scattering them everywhere (Fig. 5.7).

**Fig. 5.7** Attaching labels to pieces of galvanized wire holds them firmly in the ground.

An alternative is to use white plastic labels which can be stuck in the ground or, again, tied to wire stems. Although waterproof-pens can be purchased, pencil still seems to be the longest lasting. The problem with the plastic labels is that they quickly become brittle and break. One way round this – and the objection that they are unsightly – is to bury them so that just the tip is showing. This prevents the light getting at them and thus prolongs their life considerably.

Another alternative is to use plastic labels that have a black coating, through which you scratch the name. These have the advantage that they do not stand out like tombstones and, being coated, last longer. However, they are only coated on one side so the amount of information you can put on the label is restricted. You also have always to take the scriber with you, and I find it easier to carry a pencil.

Another possibility is to use an embossed tape which is either stuck onto a plastic label or a strip of wood. These always, at least to my eyes, look tatty. Another objection is that the large letters take up a lot of space, thus making the labels large (and hence obtrusive) or rather short of information.

It is a good habit always to put the label in the same position with regard to the plant. I always put mine at the top right of a plant (between one and two o'clock) so that even if the label has become buried in mulch I know roughly where to find it (Fig. 5.8).

A completely different approach is to keep records on cards or in a book. One method is to keep an alphabetical list of plants in which information regarding site, date of planting, where purchased and any other information is kept. This can be updated to record when the plant is divided or other such details. Another method, and one that I adopt, is to have a book in which I

have a rough outline of each border, or part of a border per page if it is a large one. On this I record in the form of numbers, each different plant or clump or plants. Below the drawing I list the numbers and what plants they represent and any information I want to note (Fig. 5.9). Several pages are left after every drawing so there is plenty of room for the current plants and any future ones. This enables me to find out what any given plant is in a border without having to tramp over it to dig up the label; and it provides a back-up system in case the label is lost or weather-worn.

**Fig. 5.8** Always put the label in the same place relative to a plant. Here they are on the right-hand upper corner of the plant.

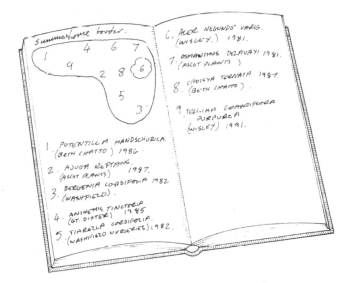

**Fig. 5.9** One way of 'logging' the plants in a garden is to make plans of the borders in a notebook, indicating the position of the plants with numbers.

# CHAPTER 6

# *Maintenance*

To keep the border in good heart and looking at its best it is essential to have a routine of maintenance. Indeed the old adage of 'little and often' is a good one in this context. Regular inspection of each border, removing weeds as they occur, is much less onerous than a once-a-year blitz.

## Supporting plants

Not all of our border plants will stand up without some form of support, especially those in gardens situated in windy locations. Some gardeners hate staking and refuse either to do it or not to have any plants in their gardens that require it. The first solution often results in a mess and the second denies the presence of many good plants.

There are some gardeners who meet the situation half way and plant sufficiently closely for the floppier plants to be held up by stronger neighbours. Others go so far as to cut the plants down to the ground after they have made 15 cm (6 in) or so of growth so that they have to start again, reaching flowering stage before they have reached their full height. I do this with *Sanguisorba officinalis*, not so much to prevent it blowing over as its wiry stems are quite stiff, but because I don't want it to grow too tall in the situation where I have it.

The majority of growers, however, bow to the inevitability of at least some staking. There is no doubt that any support should be provided before the plant has reached maturity rather than leaving it until it has started to flop and then tying it up with a piece of string like a stook of corn. We all have to prop up some plant from time to time, but it never looks very satisfactory. The art of staking is to do it early and in a way that is not conspicuous.

One form of evasive action that can be taken in advance is to plant a shelter belt in windy areas; this will make a great deal of difference. Another thing is to avoid planting susceptible plants where they can catch the turbulence billowing over a wall or funnelling between two buildings.

The best form of support is a matter of opinion but I prefer the use of pea sticks wherever possible. The best type are hazel (*Corylus avellana*) branches which tend to be flat and fan-shaped, but there are many other forms of trees and shrubs that can be used. The best time to cut them is during the winter before the leaves have started

**Fig. 6.1** Create a supporting cat's-cradle of woven pea-sticks above the emerging plant so that it will grow through sticks, hiding them from view.

50

forming. If you are really organized you can grade them into bundles of various sizes so that you do not waste time sorting through them when you are staking. Cut the ends cleanly at an angle so that they go easily into the ground.

Press some of the sticks into the ground around the plant to be supported, during the spring before they have grown less than half of their ultimate height. Bend the tops of the sticks over to form a horizontal framework above the plant, tying the twigs if necessary to keep them firm (Fig. 6.1).

The level of this network should be at the height that you want to support the plant. In most cases it may be about two-thirds of the way up. This platform is always best if it is down amongst the foliage and so it will be lower in plants with flowering stems that overtop the leaves by a long way. By putting the sticks in at this stage the plant will not only grow through the top mesh but will also grow through the sides so that the sticks will not be seen. There is just a short period when the plant is growing when the support will be in view.

There are also mechanical devices that will achieve the same results but these are expensive and not so flexible as pea sticks, which will cope with any size of clump. However, once purchased, they will last a long time. Some consist of a simple hoop supported horizontally on strong wires pushed into the ground (Fig. 6.2). Others also have a hoop but this is filled with a mesh, giving more support to the stems in the centre of the clump. A third example consists of inverted L-shaped pieces of thick wire, which link into each other so that a varying-sized circle can be constructed, with cross members if desired (Fig. 6.3). These all come in different sizes and heights, and for gardeners who do not have access to pea sticks, they are probably the answer. They are particularly effective for lower-growing plants that need support, such as double peonies. Emergencies always seem to occur at some point, and this method comes into its own when coping with plants after they have flopped over.

One home-made device for large clumps

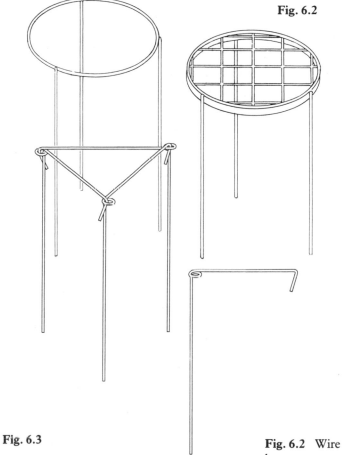

Fig. 6.2

Fig. 6.3

can be constructed from a piece of sheep or pig netting held horizontally between some posts (Fig. 6.4). Another is to put posts in the ground and weave a cat's cradle of string between them (Fig. 6.5).

Generally speaking it is best to let any supported plants have a certain amount of movement as this not only gives them a more natural look but it also prevents them snapping off in strong winds. All the above examples allow the stems to pass into a general enclosure which allows them to move.

Occasionally it becomes necessary to stake each stem individually. This is either

**Fig. 6.2** Wire hoops on stems can be used to support plants. The better versions have a few cross wires to give additional support.

**Fig. 6.3** Some wire supports are in the shape of inverted 'L's, which can be linked to create various configurations.

51

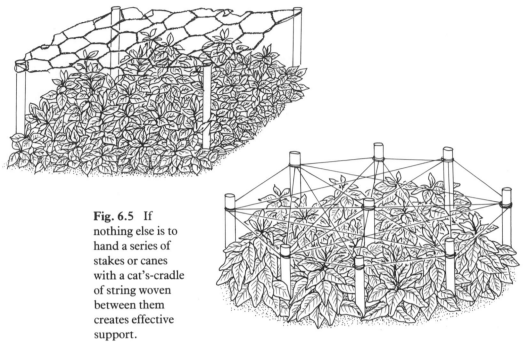

**Fig. 6.4** For large colonies of plants a sheet of wire-netting, slung horizontally between posts makes an ideal method of support.

**Fig. 6.5** If nothing else is to hand a series of stakes or canes with a cat's-cradle of string woven between them creates effective support.

because a horizontal support of some kind would be seen and look out of place, or because the plant consists of just a few very tall stems, such as a hollyhock or delphinium. In these cases each stem can be supported by an individual cane to which it is tied with a piece of soft gardening string, taking in new ties as the stem extends. If done well the canes are not too obvious, especially as the taller plants are usually towards the back of the border.

Keep notes of everything that needs staking so that nothing is missed and has to be 'hoiked up' by its bootstraps in an ungainly fashion after it has collapsed.

## Watering

The amount of watering required will be greatly diminished if the ground has been well prepared, with plenty of humus dug deep into it. I have found that plants thus treated have done even better than those that were mulched. Mulching will be treated in a later section, but it should just be mentioned here that a layer of chipped bark or the like will help prevent moisture evaporating from the surface of the soil so

that plants have a plentiful supply. Organic material in the soil acts, in effect, like a subterranean mulch and not only prevents moisture disappearing into the drier upper layer, but also holds quite a bit of it within its fibrous texture.

There is an old saying that states once you have started watering you must continue. This has been pooh-poohed over the years, but in recent times it has been proved right. If you water you are unlikely to soak the ground to any depth and, instead of putting down deep roots, the plants put out surface roots where they find the current moisture. Having done this, if you now stop watering the plant has no immediate access to the deeper-seated moisture and as a result may well die. Another factor is that plants develop a powerful suction action when in a drought situation, and watering reduces this power. I can only repeat that it is best to try and encourage deep-rooting by the addition of organic material to the lower levels of the soil.

Having said all that, there is of course often the need to water. Probably the greatest need is when the plants are establishing themselves. If only one or two plants need attention, or if the use of hose-pipes is prohibited, a watering-can can be resorted to. It is no good just sprinkling the surface with the water; it must penetrate well down. Until you are certain what you are doing, always check how far the water has gone down. The roots of a plant are not immediately below the plant but also spread out sideways, so soak the area round the plant as well. This often means that each plant will take the contents of a watering-can – it can become a tiring business.

If you are lucky you can use a sprinkler system and, next to rain itself, this is probably the best thing. But again it should be emphasized that the ground must be thoroughly soaked. The amount of water delivered can be checked by placing a jam-jar somewhere within the orbit of the sprinkler (Fig. 6.6): for efficient use it must show that at least 2.5 cm (1 in) has been received by the soil. Making a sweeping generalization, many places in Britain receive about 2.5 cm (1 in) every ten days or so, thus in hot dry weather it is important that the plants should receive this if they have no back-up reserves in the soil. So having delivered your 2.5 cm (1 in) you should repeat it in about a week's time and so on until natural rainfall takes over.

One problem with regular use of a sprinkler, or indeed a high rainfall for that matter, is that it does leach out many of the nutrients from the soil, so the ground will need extra feeding to replace them.

## Feeding

To keep borders of perennial plants growing vigorously, they must have an adequate supply of nutrients. If you cut back all the dying vegetation each autumn and cart it off to the compost heap or bonfire, you are removing much of the material that would otherwise be recycled. The ground will soon become impoverished if it is not replaced in some way.

The ideal feed is some form of organic material as this not only provides the nutrients, but also improves the nature of the soil, especially in its moisture-holding

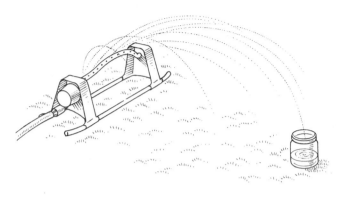

**Fig. 6.6** Check the efficiency of your sprinkler by catching water in a jar. This will tell you roughly how much water has been delivered to each area.

capacity. Not all organic material is high in food: peat, for example, is quite barren and adds little to the soil. Farmyard manure, on the other hand, is probably the richest, especially in nitrogen, which will help promote growth of stems and foliage.

Garden compost is in between the two and for general purposes is one of the best materials to use. It is one of the basic tenets of gardening that you recycle as much garden waste as possible in this way. However garden compost can suffer from its weed seed content. This is not so much of a problem if it is being dug deep into the ground but if it is being used as a top dressing, then a forest of weed seedlings can soon appear. One way of coping with this is to have two compost heaps, one solely for material that is free of weed seed, while the other is for any dubious material. The latter can be used solely for deep work, while the former can be safely used as a top dressing. Farmyard manure can also suffer from weed seed, especially if it contains odd bits of hay, but if the litter used was wood shavings or some other modern material, then it will be much freer from contamination.

Many of the other materials, such as mushroom compost (see page 39), are also good for feeding the soil. They should all be added to the top of the soil and then chipped into the surface using a border fork. The worms will probably help and soon take it all below ground.

Not everybody has recourse to supplies of farmyard manure, and many gardeners may have to rely on fertilizers. There is nothing intrinsically wrong in this except that they do not have the soil-improving qualities that the more fibrous materials have. One advantage of using fertilizers is that they are at least easy to apply: it is simply a matter of scattering the granules over the surface. Try and avoid getting it onto any emerging plants as the chemicals can scorch the leaves. Unfortunately, if there is no rain the fertilizer just sits there and does little good. Apply any fertilizer before applying a mulch.

A general, balanced fertilizer is the one to use in spring. This contains equal proportions of nitrogen (N), phosphate (P) and potash (K). This is often labelled a 7:7:7 fertilizer as it contains 7 per cent of each of the mentioned chemicals. In the United States the most commonly available fertilizers have slightly different proportions: 5:10:10, which contain less nitrogen.

There are all kinds of specialist fertilizers for different purposes. Some, such as liquid tomato feeds, are high in potash (5:5:9) and good for bud and flower formation. These can be applied in late spring, once the main plant growth has been established, to encourage flowering.

The compounds mentioned above are all inorganic, (i.e. they are chemically derived), but it is also possible to buy organic fertilizers of which blood, fish and bone, and bonemeal are the two most common. Their composition varies, but the former is stronger in potash than other ingredients, which makes it a suitable fertilizer for perennials. The advantage of organic fertilizers, apart from being 'natural', is that they are generally slow release, which means that the food they supply is available over a long period of time. This is especially true of bonemeal.

Chemical fertilizers should be applied at the rates given on the packets. There is little point in exceeding the dosage as the plants will not absorb them any faster and they will only be leached away and wasted. Granular ones can be applied by hand in spring. Quicker-acting fertilizers are applied in the form of liquid that can be sprayed onto the foliage of the plant or directed at the soil above the roots. When applying fertilizers, especially organic ones, wear gloves.

## Mulching

It is a good idea to mulch all borders. This involves covering the soil with a layer of organic material of some kind. You can use traditional leafmould, or a more modern alternative such as chipped bark or spent mushroom compost. The idea behind this is really twofold. In the first place it keeps moisture in, preventing it from being evaporated from the surface of the soil, especially by drying winds and in sunny conditions. In the second, it helps to suppress weeds.

The ground should be moist before a mulch is applied as some mulches tend to make the water run off the surface and therefore not get through to the soil where it is needed. It should also be weed free before the mulch goes down. There is no point in covering up perennial weeds as these will only grow through the cover. What it does inhibit is the germination of weed seed, thus preventing a new crop from appearing. Any weed seed that is blown in and lands on top is likely to germinate, but at least it is easy to pull out of the soft mulch.

It should be applied over winter or in spring before growth begins. When putting it on, apply at least a 10 cm (4 in) layer. This will compress down as it weathers and anything less will be far too thin to be of much use. Most mulches have not been broken down and will continue to rot as they lie on the ground. This process uses up quite a lot of nitrogen, which it obtains from the soil, so it is a good idea to apply a general fertilizer to the soil before putting down the mulch.

One of the simplest and most readily available of mulches is grass clippings from lawns. Do not apply them too thickly, though – 5 cm (2 in) is ample – as they will heat up as they rot, scorching and possibly killing plants that pass through them. If you find that borders look unsightly covered with grass cuttings, throw them along the back, out of sight, and allow the birds and worms to work them both gradually forwards and imperceptibly into the border soil. If it becomes compressed and too matted break it up with a fork and work it into the top layer of soil before adding a new layer.

One often sees the high-tech solution of a plastic mulch. The idea here is to cover the ground with black polythene, in which planting holes are cut and then the whole disguised with bark or similar cover. It very rarely works in a border, partly because perennial plants tend to spread and the hole will soon be too small, and secondly that, try as one might, the polythene always seems to show through, making the border appear terribly tatty. A final minus for it is that unless special porous material is used, water has difficulty finding its way through the membrane, creating pools in the depressions.

With new borders, do not apply the mulch until the planting has been completed. With existing borders, carefully scrape back the mulch before digging a planting hole so that the mulch and the soil do not get mixed up, and then replace the former after planting. If possible try to prevent the soil appearing above the mulch (moles have a nasty habit of mixing the two) as this often brings weed seed to the surface.

## Weeding

This is the one thing that most people hate about gardening, but it can really be rather a pleasant occupation. By the very nature of the operation one must be down amongst the plants and one sees so much and learns a great deal while one is in such a position. The real problem is that many gardeners do not prepare the ground sufficiently in the first place and leave it too late before taking action in the second, so that weeding becomes a chore and an uphill battle.

If the ground is thoroughly prepared before anything else is done, then half the battle is won; the only weeds that should

appear are seedlings. The second half is won if these seedlings are removed before they become substantial weeds. It is little use allowing them to grow to full size and then scrape around on the surface doing a cosmetic job or just removing the top-growth; they will be back again before you have got to the end of the border. As I said at the beginning of this chapter, 'little and often' are the watch words. If all the borders are tickled over several times a year, removing any seedlings that appear and keeping the surface loose so that it is easy to get those out that do survive, weeding becomes an easy and even enjoyable occupation. One final point: do not leave it too late before you start – many gardeners think of weeding as a summer task. If possible, have all the garden neat and tidy by the spring, this will get things off to a very good start.

Throughout the year I try to spend at least one hour in the garden every day doing various jobs, some pleasurable some boring (I hate cutting hedges). In that hour it is possible to work through a surprisingly large border removing any weeds, dead-heading, cutting off dead stems and generally looking at and admiring the plants. If you let things go, an hour's work will hardly get you anywhere.

If a border does become infested with weed don't try scraping them off the surface, dig the whole border out and start again. It might seem a chore, but it will save a lot of time in the long run and will produce a much more satisfactory bed.

Try to avoid using weedkillers on a planted border, partly because it should not be necessary and partly because accidents can so easily happen – sometimes unseen ones caused by drift of spray or translocation through the roots. The last thing you want is for treasured plants suddenly to keel over to lie along with the shrivelling weeds. If necessary use a weedkiller when first cleaning the ground, but if this is done properly, it should not be required again.

The best way of removing weeds from a border is either to work through it with a border fork, loosening the soil, or by going down on your hands and knees and digging it with a trowel or hand fork. Removing weeds individually like this will give you the opportunity to distinguish between weeds and self-sown plant seedlings that may be left where they are or potted up for future use (or, of course, relegated to the compost heap if they are not required). Some people like to use hoes, but this can be a dangerous tool to use in a crowded border. It is fine between straight rows in a vegetable garden, but amongst flowering plants there always seem to be some unfortunate casualties. It is possible to use one in the first year or so after planting, while there is still room to manoeuvre safely and while there is likely to be a large amount of annual seedlings still appearing.

As well as thorough border preparation, there are other ways of pre-empting the weed problem. One is to apply a mulch which will go a long way to suppressing weed seed that is already in the ground. The other is to create a densely planted border that will allow little light to get to the ground, thus denying weeds one of their basic needs.

## Deadheading

Some gardeners regularly practise deadheading while others totally ignore it. It has a twofold purpose, firstly to tidy the plants up and secondly to promote a second or continuing flush of flowers.

Deadheading to tidy up the plants is obvious and needs little explanation; dying flower-heads simply look tatty. Once they have been removed the plant will go on possibly serving as a foliage plant. For example *Pulmonaria* flowers in early spring but its leaves, especially those with silver markings, carry on making an attractive contribution to the border until the autumn.

The promotion of further flowering however is equally, if not more important. Once a flower starts to fade, a lot of the plant's energy is being channelled into seed production. If the developing seed is cut off along with the dead flower, all this energy is available for producing more flowers, which the plant feels are needed once its prime means of reproduction has been thwarted by

removal of the first flush of seed.

Another reason for not letting the plants seed is to prevent them self sowing. For some this is no nuisance at all, but others can produce masses of seedlings and, in a case like the deep tap-rooted *Meconopsis cambrica* (the Welsh poppy), the plant can become a pest. The seedlings may also produce plants that are not true to their parents and thus introduce inferior or different-coloured plants into the border. It is best to remove the incipient seed pods while there are still the fading flowers to remind you of the problems that could lie ahead.

Of course, not all seed production is bad and it is quite likely that the gardener will want to collect at least some from various plants. In this case the appropriate number of seed heads must be left on the plant. Unfortunately in some cases, *Hesperis matrionalis* for example, the seed takes a long time to set and ripen so the plant must be left in its decrepit state for some considerable period.

Another reason for leaving seedheads on the plants is that they can be decorative. Most gardeners would not remove the old heads of the stink iris, *Iris foetidissima*, whose seed pods split open to provide a lasting display of red berries. Similarly the silky seeds of *Pulsatilla vulgaris* are well worth leaving for their decorative display. Many grasses would also fall into this category.

The amount of the stem that is removed depends on the plant. In some cases, *Alchemilla mollis* for example, the plant should be cut to the ground (Fig. 6.7) so that it produces a new flush of foliage as well; in others it is just a question of removing the dead or fading flower, cutting back to the previous bud on the stem (Fig. 6.8). Many of the daisies are produced on long flowering stems and these should be traced back into the foliage and cut off, leaving the rest of the plant intact (Fig. 6.9). Some plants, such as *Hemerocallis*, obligingly drop their own flowers and so no action is needed except to cut off the flowering stem when the last bud has opened and faded.

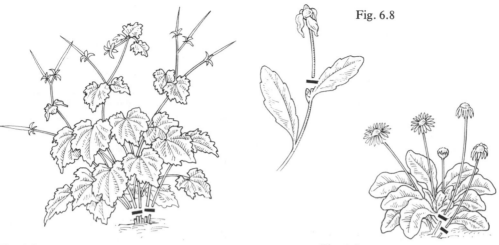

Fig. 6.8

Fig. 6.7

Fig. 6.9

**Fig. 6.7** If cut to the ground after flowering, many plants will shoot again, creating a fresh mound of foliage.

**Fig. 6.8** Some plants simply require deadheading, which involves removing the old flower stem from just above the nearest leaf or bud.

**Fig. 6.9** Where the flower appears on its own stem, this should be completely removed at the base.

## Winter maintenance

The busiest time in the border is between the time when the last plants die down for the winter and the time of the emergence of the new growth in spring. The precise timing as to when the work involved should be tackled is not critical, as long as it is completed by the time the vulnerable new shoots begin to appear. The reason is that however careful one is there will always be some that are damaged as the gardener moves around the border.

The basic tasks are to cut out all the dead material, remove any weeds, loosen up the soil to allow birds to get at any insect pests and to allow the winter rains to penetrate. You can also apply any feed or mulch that is required.

Whether to remove the dead material in autumn or in late winter is a matter of debate and both have their advocates. Removal in late autumn means that the borders are neat and tidy and there is less to do at the end of winter, when there always seems to be masses of jobs to do including sowing seed, pricking out young plants, planting and so on. If the dead stems are left on, it is argued, they give a certain amount of protection to the crowns of the plant from the frost. They also provide the birds and small mammals with a certain amount of food from the remaining seed heads and from insects that are hiding amongst them.

Finally, the dead stems can themselves be quite attractive, especially when rimed with frost, and provide something to look at in what otherwise would be a barren border. A disadvantage of the later timing is that if the weather is bad towards the end of winter, and it often can be, work may be delayed until the plants are well into growth. This makes it not only a terrible rush to get things done, but also difficult to accomplish without damaging the new shoots. Another problem is that dead vegetation lying around provides ideal living quarters for slugs.

Well, you make your own choice. I prefer to start in the autumn and work methodically through the borders as weather allows until I have finished them, usually well before the new growth commences. Gardening in winter can be a very pleasant occupation, especially on the many soft, still days that we seem to get.

So much for the timing. The actual work to be done has been mainly dealt with under the various topics, such as weeding and mulching. Cutting off the dead stems is just a further extension of deadheading and in the majority of cases involves cutting the plant right back to the ground and composting the resulting waste. There are a few plants with sap which can cause irritation and rashes to people with sensitive skins. *Euphorbia*, *Heracleum mantegazzianum* and

*Ruta* are three that immediately come to mind. These should only be touched by gloved hands.

Winter work also involves splitting up those plants that look overcrowded, or restricting those that are beginning to march into somebody else's territory. It is also easier to be more ruthless when the plants are out of flower, so it is the time of year to get rid of plants that are not earning their keep or that have fallen out of favour.

The question of winter hardiness is a vexed one. If it were a simple question of a certain plant dropping dead at a particular temperature – for the sake of argument if *Euphorbia rigida* always died at $-6°C$ – then life would be very simple as one would know where one stands. Alas, however, it is far more complicated than that.

One problem is that although a plant may be 'as tough as old boots' and can stand very low temperatures, what it cannot stand is a period of warm weather in the middle of winter. This gives it the false impression that spring has arrived; it is then coaxed into growth, only to be severely checked by a sudden cold spell. This has only got to happen a couple of times during the winter for the plant to give up.

One way that cold can kill is to freeze the ground to a considerable distance for quite a long time. This will obviously lock up all the water so that the plant will not be able to take up the small amount of moisture it requires to keep alive, and can therefore die of drought in midwinter. Fortunately the majority of us do not have to put up with penetrating frost of this kind. Mulching the ground around the plants is one solution.

One very serious problem is dampness. Although one thinks of a winter as being typically cold, there are in fact a surprising number of quite warm days. Down in the centre of a plant, out of the wind and perhaps tucked up by a mulch of dead leaves and other vegetation the temperatures can easily reach the point where rots can set in. Wounds are often opened up by slugs and there being no air circulating, the warm damp conditions are perfect for the plant to rot away. I suspect most gardeners lose more plants to this cause than any other, and the remedy is difficult to supply. Certainly keeping the slug population down is a great help.

Some plants benefit from a warm mulch because they are relatively tender and the lack of circulating air must be risked. Plants that are totally hardy, I suspect, are best left as open as possible so that the air can get in. To a certain extent this will also help keep the temperature down, which will prevent them breaking into premature growth. For some tender plants temporary protection seems to work well. When frosts threaten I cover them with tomato trays filled with several sheets of newspaper, but I leave them off during the daytime and when the temperature is unlikely to drop below zero. This method works even for tender bedding plants such as some of the verbenas, which have taken temperatures of $-10°C$ (14°F) or more covered in this way. It is labour intensive in that you have to be around to do it every day if necessary, before darkness and the temperature fall.

Cold winds can cause a lot of damage, particularly to plants that have prematurely come into growth. It may be possible to give protection against this hazard without actually covering the plants, screening them for example.

Snow, curiously enough, is not a problem as it puts a relatively warm blanket over the plants which keeps them at slightly above zero. It can also protect the plants from cold winds that are often associated with snow. However, it can be a nuisance if the plants are far enough in growth to bow down under its weight or even worse, break under the strain.

Certainly in cold areas it would be sensible to give protection to plants either from constant hard frosts or from continuous winds, but in warmer districts it can be a mixed blessing. Certain plants that are borderline, such as *Cosmos atrosanguineus*, can be lifted and stored like dahlias in dry peat in a frost-free shed or cellar. An alternative is to cover them with a mulch of straw, leaves, bracken or even the dead stems and leaves of the plant itself, as is the practice with *Gunnera manicata* (Fig. 6.10). It is sensible to put down some slug bait first and perhaps renew it a couple of times throughout the winter.

## Renovating borders

As well as the routine work on borders, from time to time it becomes necessary to carry out a bit of more serious renovation. It may be that a perennial weed such as couch grass or ground elder has penetrated the defences. In this case there is little choice but to dig out the infected part of the border and remove every piece, taking time to shake all the soil off the plants so that you are certain to remove every part of the weeds, whose underground shoots have a nasty habit of pushing right through the heart of a plant (Fig. 6.11).

Another need for renovation is that many perennial plants require splitting up every four or five years (or perhaps less) as they spread outwards with age, leaving dead, unsightly centres. They also become congested and lose their vigour. They must therefore be lifted and broken up and replanted. The best parts of the plants to use are the young growth round the outside of the old plant. Often when dividing a plant for replanting, only a small fraction of the original may be required and the rest can either be given away or put on the compost heap. Lifting plants also provides a chance for digging up any clumps of bulbs that have been planted between them as

these are also likely to need splitting up and replanting. Move carefully through the border, as it is very easy to accidentally damage them with a fork when there is little to see above ground, with the exception possibly of a label, to indicate where they are.

When plants are dug out for dividing, it is an ideal opportunity to dig a fresh load of organic material into the soil. This is particularly the case if several plants are lifted at the same time, clearing quite a space.

Not all plants appreciate being disturbed; peonies, dictamnus and Japanese anemones, for example, prefer to be left where they are, otherwise they will take two years or so to settle down again. Most tap-rooted plants, such as the eryngiums, are also very difficult to transplant and should be left in place.

The timing of renovation is not critical, but it is not a good idea to do it during the summer as this is not the best time for dividing plants. Autumn, particularly in warmer areas is a good time, but spring is just as good and may be better in colder areas.

**Fig. 6.11** When ridding a bed of perennial weeds remember to remove those pieces that go through the roots of the plants.

# CHAPTER 7

# *Propagation*

Many gardeners regard propagation as a mystical art and the word 'green-fingered' is conjured up to describe somebody that has the ability to accomplish it. In fact there is very little mystery about it, it just requires commonsense and a certain amount of patience. The more you do and the more experienced you become, the easier it will be, but there is no reason why any gardener should not attempt it.

There are several reasons for producing your own plants. In the first place it is cheap and therefore may be the only way you can obtain sufficient plants for your needs. Then you may already have the plant and wish to have more. It is possible that you may wish to produce plants to give away or sell from plants you have in the garden. Some gardeners, realizing that they have a rare plant, wish to reproduce it so that if it dies they have back-up plants. There are many plants which are impossible to obtain commercially but are available from seed. A good way of building up a collection of interesting plants is to avail oneself of the large amount of seed available from gardening societies' seed exchanges. Perhaps one of the most important reasons is that it is very satisfying to produce your own plants.

There are three principal methods of propagation: by sowing seed, by dividing the plants and by taking cuttings. The second two are known as vegetative means of propagation, as they take a part of a plant and recreate a new one from it. Since they are grown directly from the original, all resulting plants are identical to each other and to their parent. This method of increase, then, is very important when you want to be assured of reproducing the same plant in all respects, colour, shape, habit and so on.

On the other hand, plants grown from seed can often vary considerably. Sometimes the plants are so similar to their parents that to all intents and purposes they are the same, but in many cases the variation is quite noticeable, especially if the parents differed from each other. But even if the parent plants were the same, there is no guarantee that the offspring will resemble them. Seedlings from cultivars, in particular, are likely to vary and any plants obtained in this way should not be given their parent's name. Thus seed produced from offspring of *Helenium* 'Moerheim Beauty' should not be given this name. They should simply be referred to as seedlings or given their own names if they are distinct enough.

Some plants can be reproduced equally well by any of the above methods, but often there is one form that is more appropriate for a given plant than another.

## Growing from seed

One of the advantages of growing plants from seed is that you can acquire a large number of plants for very little outlay. However it is not always a quick method, in spite of the fact that some plants will germinate and flower in one season. Some plants, particularly bulbous ones, can take several years to reach that state. There is also the problem of variability of the offspring but in the majority of cases this is not significant enough to cause worry and, of course, there is always the excitement of raising some new and interesting form.

### Sources of seed

The most obvious source of seed is from seed merchants, either bought from shops or through the post, but there are several other important sources. One of the most important is the seed exchanges attached to many of the gardening societies. Britain's Royal Horticultural Society runs such a scheme as does the Hardy Plant Society, which of course specializes in perennial plants. These exchanges offer members the choice of a certain number of packets which they can select from the several thousand different varieties on offer. There are also specialist societies, such as the Cyclamen Society, which also offer lists restricted to their particular subjects. It is a very good way of obtaining a range of unusual plants that cannot be purchased through the normal commercial channels. You have to be a member of the societies to be able to avail yourself of their offers.

One very exciting source of seed is that offered by seed collectors who have been on expeditions to various parts of the world. Quite a lot of the seed is of plants that are not in cultivation and there is the thrill of raising what are potentially unique plants.

There are two methods of acquiring seed from this source. It is possible to take out a share in the expedition, currently about £50 or $100, for which you get a predetermined number of packets. This could be as many as 100 different ones, which stands up as remarkable value when compared with seed of common plants offered by commercial concerns. The other method is to buy them by the packet from a list produced after the expedition has returned. Finding out about these collecting trips is not easy but they are usually advertized in either the RHS journal *The Garden* or in the Alpine Garden Society's *Bulletin*.

Another method is to collect seed from your own garden of the plants that you want to increase. This is not a difficult task (see page 73) and many gardeners undertake it each year both to use themselves and to send into the seed exchanges. Similarly it is often possible to get seed from gardening friends who have plants that you want to grow.

## Seed compost
Most seed requires very little from its compost. The seed itself contains its food-stock, which will carry it through until it has established roots and its first leaves. All it requires is moisture and physical support – something in which it can grip to hold itself upright.

Seed composts are, therefore, usually simple mixtures that contain no added fertilizers. Both soil-based and soil-less seed composts can be easily purchased from garden centres or stores and are generally adequate for most purposes. If you wish to make your own then equal portions by volume of loam (preferably sterilized), horticultural grit, and peat or sieved leafmould, should be mixed together. The loam provides a certain amount of nutrients to keep the seedling going once its own stores are depleted, and provides an anchor for the emerging roots; the grit ensures that there is not an excess of moisture left in the soil, something that seedlings abhor; and the peat or leafmould holds sufficient moisture to keep the seedlings supplied with water. The compost should be just moist.

Not all plants are happy to adjust from a soil-less compost to soil of the garden so I always prefer to use a soil-based compost, but this is a matter of individual preference. If you prefer to work with a soil-less compost and get results from it, then carry on using it.

## Sowing seed
When to sow is always a vexed question. There are some seeds that definitely need to be sown as soon as possible after they ripen. Most of the buttercup family, the Ranunculaceae for example, require it. If you sow hellebores straight from the pod you will get almost 100 per cent germination. If you delay until the following spring, germination will be very slow and erratic. Similarly *Pulsatilla* have earned a reputation of being difficult, but they will come up like mustard and cress if sown fresh. There is no point in sowing all seed as soon as it comes off the plant, otherwise you have got the problem of getting all the seedlings through a winter and not all will take kindly to it.

With most seed there is little choice as you do not get it from seed merchants or seed exchanges until the winter or early spring. If you have the seed early, but are in doubt what to do with it, sow half of the packet in the autumn and the other half in the spring. That way you should always win and, at the same time, gain valuable experience as to which seeds want which treatment.

Most gardeners start their propagation with annuals and thus get used to sowing large quantities of seed in trays or half-trays. When considering perennials a gardener will soon realize that he or she does not require anywhere near the quantity of plants that a tray will hold. More than enough seedlings can be germinated in a 9 cm (3½ in) or even a 7.5 cm (3 in) pot.

Fill the pot with compost and tap on the bench to settle the compost, compressing *lightly* if necessary to level off the surface. Sow the seed thinly and evenly across the pot. If the seed is known to have a poor germination rate, then it can be sown a little thicker. Large seed such as that of lilies should be spaced out evenly across the pot. If there is not enough room in one pot for this larger seed, use two pots rather than a bigger one, as it is easier to cope with pots if they are all of the same size.

Once the seed has been evenly spread, cover it with a 0.75 to 1.25 cm (¼ to ½ in) layer of grit (Fig. 7.1). The best grit is that supplied by pet shops or agricultural merchants as chick grit. There are several reasons why seed should be covered by what appears to be a harsh medium. It makes watering more even, as it is less likely to run off the surface onto one side of the pot. It holds the seed in place and so this does not end up washed to the lowest point of the surface, often at one edge. Importantly, it provides a dry collar around the new seedlings. This is the point where damping off occurs. It acts as a mulch and helps to keep the compost moist, warmer in winter and cooler in summer. Since perennials are not necessarily quick germinators the pots may be standing around for quite some while, sometimes several years. In this time they are likely to attract moss, liverwort and weeds. The grit helps to deter this and when

**Fig. 7.1** Top dressing pots of seed with a layer of grit has many advantages and is to be recommended.

they occur it can make it much easier to remove them without also losing the surface of the compost and the seeds with it.

An important duty to carry out at this stage is to label the pot. All pots of seed look the same and all gardeners have experienced delaying the labelling only to find that they have forgotten what is in which pot. It is a good idea to write the date of sowing as well as the name of the plant. I find it is also useful to write down the number of seed in the pot if it is less than six. The reason for this is that if two seeds are sown and two seedlings come up, I know it is not worth waiting for more to appear. Similarly if six seeds are sown and two come up, I can either decide to wait a little longer or carefully remove those two, leaving the rest of the seed undisturbed. I also normally include the source of the seed in case something remarkable happens and I want to refer back to it.

Once the seed has been sown, covered and labelled, the pot should be watered. This can be done in one of two ways. Some growers prefer to stand the pot in a shallow tray of water which reaches about half-way up its side (Fig 7.2). Once the surface of the grit changes colour it has imbibed sufficient water. The alternative method that others prefer is to water from the top with a fine-rosed watering-can.

Most seeds of perennial plants do not require heat for them to germinate. The sown pots should be placed in a shady position, out of wind and sun and kept watered until germination occurs or until it is decided to throw the pot away. Some seed has an in-built dormancy that prevents it germinating until favourable conditions prevail. Sometimes this may take a long time to break down. For example, some seed requires a period of chilling before germinating. This indicates to the seed that it has passed through a winter and now that warm weather has arrived it is time to burst forth. If it does not get the chilling, it imagines that it is still autumn and therefore lies dormant.

The chilling required is not very deep and most seed sown in autumn or early winter and left outside, will experience sufficient frosts to break any dormancy. If sown too late to be chilled, the seed will remain dormant until the following spring, after it has gone through the next winter. The chilling of late-sown seed can be artificially carried out by placing the pot, wrapped in a polythene bag, in a refrigerator for six weeks or so.

**Fig. 7.2** Stand the seed pot in a bowl of water until the surface of the grit darkens, showing that the compost is thoroughly soaked.

There are other types of dormancy. Some seed has a very tough coat and will only germinate after the rains have come and softened it. Sweetpeas (*Lathyrus odoratus*) are a typical example of this. Their dormancy can be broken either by soaking in water (simulating the rains) or by breaking the coat, by filing or chipping to allow moisture in.

If you have patience there is no need to worry about dormancy until you have more experience of seed sowing; simply place the seed pot in the open and allow nature to do the work. Never throw away old seed pots before at least three years are up. I have had some that have produced nothing, and then suddenly in their fourth year all in the same week, a forest of seedlings has appeared.

Although there is no need to worry about excess cold, excess moisture can be a bit of a problem. If the compost was made up correctly it should be free-draining and there should be no problems. However, the compost is likely to compact, especially if it is stood for several years in the open. It is a good thing, therefore, to be able to cover the pots in time of high rainfall. The ideal position for seed pots is in an open coldframe which can be shut during wet weather and covered with a shade frame during hot, sunny periods.

**Aftercare**
If the seed germinates during a warm spell in winter and more cold weather is imminent, move the pot into a greenhouse or closed coldframe to give the young seedlings some protection from the frosts. Seed that was freshly sown in the late summer or early autumn may germinate before winter. This should also be placed in its pot in a similarly protected position. There is no point in potting the seedlings up in either case until the spring when growth will again resume.

When the first true leaves appear (i.e. the second pair, not the first two, which are seed leaves) (Fig. 7.3) they are ready to be potted up. The best compost for this is a John Innes No. 3. Again, I prefer to use a soil-based compost for plants that will be planted out into ordinary soil, but many

**Fig. 7.3** Once the first true leaves appear the seedlings are ready to be potted up.

Pot the seedlings into 9 cm (3½ in) pots. Hold the seedling by a leaf between finger and thumb over the centre of the pot, steadying the hand by resting the little finger on the rim of the pot. Gently pour compost around the roots until the pot is full to the brim (Fig. 7.4). Tap it on the bench to settle the compost, pressing it down *lightly* if there is a need to level the surface. Label the pot, before you forget what the plant is. If the plant is likely to remain in the pot for more than a couple of months, I like to top dress the compost with a 1.25 cm (½ in) layer of grit. This affords the same benefits to the plant as were mentioned on page 62.

Stand the pot in a tray of water until the surface of the compost or grit is moist, and then stand aside to drain. The pots of newly planted seedling should be placed in a closed coldframe and covered with a shade frame (consisting of a framework of wood with netting stretched over it (Fig. 7.5)) if the hot sun is likely to shine on the plants. Once the plants have become established, open the frame for progressively longer periods each day to harden them off. Once this has been achieved they can be stood in an open frame or elsewhere in the open.

others always use a soil-less one. It seems that the choice of compost depends more on the preference of the gardener than the plant. Having said that, I do find that roots of plants that have been grown on in a soil-less compost seem to be reluctant to leave their peaty base and venture out into the soil. I also find it easier to control the water content in a soil-based compost but, again, this is a matter of personal preference.

**Fig. 7.5** After potting up, seedlings should be placed in a closed frame. Cover this with netting during sunny weather.

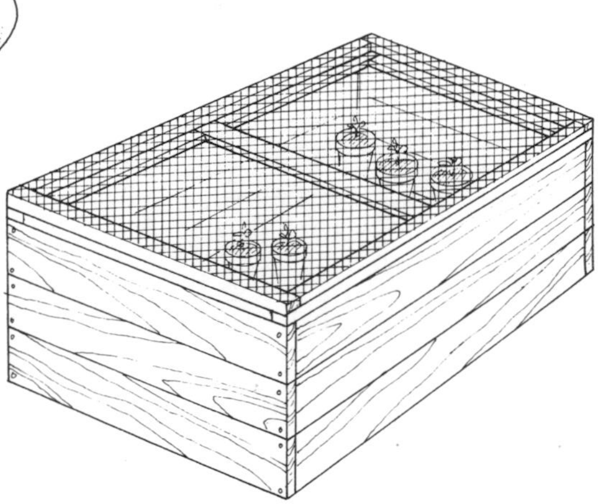

**Fig. 7.4** Hold the seedling by one of its seed-leaves in the centre of the pot and gently pour compost around it.

The green of the foliage acts as a good foil to this
white, cream and gold border.

A colourful stream-side border that includes
native plants as well as garden ones.

*Lysichiton americanus* and *Primula denticulata* in a sunny border in spring before the foliage closes in to create light shade.

*Below:* The vivid colours of a hot border at the height of summer. Colour themes like this need very careful handling.

A colourful border showing the careful use of different-height plants and the value of a background.

*Opposite:* Dramatic as these spiky shapes are, they can get boring if they are not relieved by some other shapes and textures.

Although all these leaves are green, their different shades of colour, texture and shapes make a very satisfying picture.

*Above:* Similarity in flower colour can also be dramatically contrasted by variation in shape as seen with this *Kniphofia* and *Solidaster*.

Colours that merge well together can become rather boring. Injecting a contrasting colour livens the scene considerably.

71

A similar effect can be had by using foliage. Here the variegated hosta sets off the soft misty colours of the *Allium pulchellum* and the sedum.

Having reached sufficient size, they can be planted out into the open ground in their flowering position. This is usually done in the autumn, but for fast-growing plants it can be earlier. Certain tap-rooted plants, and plants that do not like to be disturbed, should be planted out as soon as possible. If they are to remain in pots for any length of time use the deeper 'long tom' pots, which will allow better provision for their long roots.

### Self-sowing seed

It is surprising how many plants self sow in the garden. While weeding is the time to spot them and it can become a good discipline to identify any seedling – perennial or weed – that one comes across. Not all are worth keeping. Those that are sown from cultivars, such as michaelmas daisies (*Aster novi-belgii*), are in particular likely to be worthless, but many of the species are well worth keeping for planting elsewhere or to give away.

If you want plants to self sow, remember not to cut them down before they have seeded. Reduce the number of seedlings around the parent plant to an acceptable number. If too many are left they will crowd each other out and will be rather poor plants.

As with conventionally sown seed any seedlings with tap roots should be moved to their final flowering position as soon as possible.

### Sowing in open ground

Many perennial plants can be sown directly into the open ground. It is generally best not to sow them where they are to flower but to use a special nursery bed. Prepare the ground, removing all weeds and breaking it down into a fine tilth. Draw out shallow drills and thinly sow the seed. Cover with a thin layer of soil and lightly water in. Label the row. When the plants are big enough to handle, either thin out the row or transplant the seedlings to a reserve bed or spare part of the vegetable garden. Move the plants to their final position in the borders in the autumn. Do not delay moving plants with

tap roots, such as lupins, beyond this date otherwise they will have difficulty in settling down.

### Collecting seed

All gardens produce a wealth of seed each year. It is always good policy to collect some of it as, even if you do not want it, somebody else might. It can even be sent to society seed exchanges or taken to the local horticultural club, where it can be given away or used in a raffle. In cases of rarer plants or those that are not long lived, the gardener may require to keep it for his own use.

Seed collecting is not just an autumn occupation. Some of the early spring-flowering plants, such as the wood anemone (*Anemone nemorosa*) and hellebores, will be producing seed long before midsummer. The time taken between flowering and seed producing varies considerably. The anemone mentioned above takes only a few weeks, whereas *Cyclamen hederifolium* takes nearly a year – sometimes flowers and seedpods can be seen on the same plants.

To tell when the seed is ripe is a matter of experience, which will come after a short while collecting. Some seed changes colour (hellebores change from green to black, for example), and in many cases the seed capsules change colour from green to brown. The seed will often come away or out of the capsule as soon as it is ripe. For example the seed of the wood anemone, although still green when it is ripe, will easily fall away when rubbed gently with the fingers. Similarly the fluffy seed of *Pulsatilla vulgaris* and many of the Compositae family, will rub off as soon as they are ripe and ready for collection.

Many plants indicate that the seed is ripe by splitting their capsules. Most of the lily family open their capsules from the top and the seed wait in their open chalices (Fig. 7.6) to be collected (unless there is a strong wind). Poppies have a similar habit. Unfortunately there are those like hellebores which insist on opening from the bottom of the seed pod, shedding the seed onto the ground. As soon as these feel ripe (and

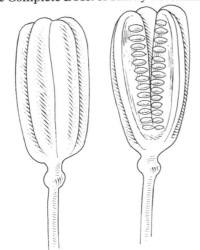

**Fig. 7.6** The upright capsules of lilies and other members of their family obligingly hold their seed until it is collected.

experience will soon tell you when) and before they split, the capsule should be opened and seed abstracted. Alternatively the seed head can be picked as it is about to ripen and put into a paper bag, where it will finish ripening and open itself.

This last method is a very useful one for those plants with explosive seed mechanisms, such as the peas (*Lathyrus*) and the hardy geraniums. The plant has developed the technique to spread the seed far away from the parent plant but this is not much use to the seed collector who must capture it before it disappears.

Put the seed or the seed-head into a paper bag, having written the name of the plant on the outside (it is surprising how seed from different plants can resemble each other, and being confronted with 20 bags of assorted but unlabelled seed is a nightmare). Once indoors remove all the obvious pieces of seed capsule, stems, leaves and other detritus. Leave the seed to dry in a cool airy place out of the sun. The bags can be left open to aid drying but those that contain seed held in explosive mechanisms should be kept shut until they shed their load; otherwise they will be scattered all over the place through the open top. When the seed is dry to the touch remove the rest of the chaff and detritus. This can be done in a variety of ways. Gently blowing over it will remove much of the lighter material to the far corners of the kitchen. A series of sieves can be employed. The larger ones will allow dust and seeds to pass through, retaining the larger pieces, while finer-meshed ones will hold the seeds back letting the dust fall

through. Of course, larger seed can be picked out with the fingers of a pair of tweezers.

Once cleaned the seed can be placed into sealed paper envelopes or bags until it is required. Store in a cool airy place away from sunlight and mice. At each stage a label should be kept with the seed so that no confusion may arise. This may seem obvious but years of experience of receiving wrongly labelled packets from the seed exchanges indicate that many people ignore this simple advice.

## Cuttings

This vegetative means of propagation requires that a part of the parent plant is taken and kept in such a manner that it develops roots and thus becomes a new plant.

The majority of perennial plants can be grown from cuttings, which often surprises many gardeners as they imagine that this is mainly the province of woody plants such as shrubs and trees. The cuttings can be the tips of shoots, the lateral or side shoots, intermediate parts of the stems or basal shoots. Cuttings can also be taken from roots but this will be treated separately.

### Compost and equipment

Cutting compost is a simple affair: 50% (by volume) peat, 50% sharp sand. The peat may be substituted with coir, fine leafmould or perlite. If you have none of these materials to hand, then an ordinary potting compost will do. Professional growers need to get 100% strike for economic reasons; the amateur grower does not have to be so efficient. A 9 cm (3½ in) pot will take a dozen cuttings or more but the average gardener is only likely to want a maximum of, say, six of any one plant so he can afford to have only a 50% success rate. I am not advocating sloppy propagation procedures but simply pointing out that it is not essential to have the ideal conditions which are available to the professional. In this case potting compost will make a perfectly good substitute for a cutting compost, as long as it is free draining.

The equipment can vary from the simple and inexpensive to the complicated and the expensive. For the home grower with small demands then the simplest will suffice, but as he or she begins to propagate more tricky subjects then investment in propagators and mist units might be worthwhile.

The simplest propagator is just a cover to keep the cuttings in a moist, buoyant atmosphere. Most books advocate the use of a polythene bag slipped over the pot and held closed with an elastic band (Fig. 7.7). Although simple, it has several disadvantages: the bag often touches the cutting, in spite of having wire hoops, and rot sets in; and condensation on the inside of the bag

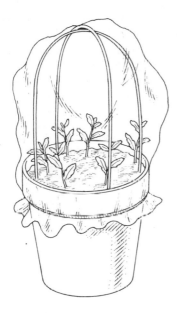

**Fig. 7.7** A simple propagator can be improvized by placing a polythene bag over the pot of cuttings. Use wires to keep the bag from touching the plants.

means you cannot see the contents and it is not very convenient to get inside. An equally simple but better method is to cut the top off a plastic sweet jar (often available free from sweet shops) and invert it over the pot (Fig. 7.8). Being rigid it holds itself away from the cuttings and can be easily removed. Condensation can be dispelled by

**Fig. 7.8** Another simple method is to invert a clear plastic sweet-jar, that has had its neck removed, over the pot.

a flick of the wrist as the jar is taken off. If the pot of cuttings is stood on a bed of moist sand this will help to keep the compost and the air moist. It will also provide an airtight seal if the neck of the inverted jar is pushed into it.

In effect the jar forms a small version of the commercial propagators, of which there are a number on the market. The simplest is a seed tray with a clear plastic lid (Fig. 7.9).

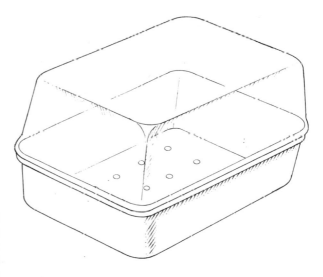

**Fig. 7.9** A basic propagator is just a seed tray covered with a clear plastic lid.

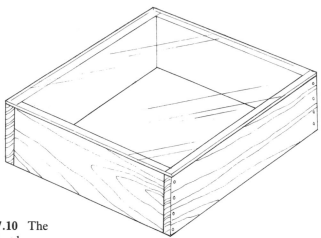

**Fig. 7.10** The simplest home-made propagator consists of four strips of wood nailed together, covered with a sheet of glass.

**Fig. 7.11** Further sophistications can be added such as sloping two of the sides, framing and hinging the glass lid and providing heating wires.

This basic model can be refined by enclosing the glass in a frame to make a proper lid, and cutting the wood in such a way that the lid is sloping (to allow any condensation to run off). Further heating coils can be installed in a bed of sand under the propagator, and additional ones can be arranged around the wood sides, above the level of the sand, to keep the air temperature up (Fig. 7.11). Thermostats can be attached to both. Kits for this kind of heating are widely available.

The propagators can include or be stood on a bed of sand. Cuttings can be planted directly into this or into pots which are stood on the bed. The advantage of the latter is that they can be removed to another propagator to be hardened off, without affecting the rest of the contents. If the cuttings are placed directly into the bed, the whole frame must be hardened off at the same time and is thus better if it is filled with only one type of plant at once.

When in use, any propagator should be in as light a position as possible without being stood in direct sunlight. If it is necessary to put it in the sun, then cover it with shade netting or whitewash the glass. Watch the temperature as you could end up cooking the cuttings, especially if the propagator is on the bench in a greenhouse or conservatory.

More sophisticated versions have an aluminium frame with plastic or glass panels. These also come with heating wires and a thermostat built into them.

It is possible to make simple home-made propagators. The simplest comprises four pieces of wood nailed together to make a square box about 15 cm (6 in) deep, with a pane of glass laid over the top (Fig. 7.10). The proportions of the box can be any convenient size, perhaps reflecting that of a spare piece of glass. The inside of the wood is painted white to keep the interior as light as possible. I have used such a propagator for many years.

### Taking cuttings

Cuttings can be taken at any time of the year when the plant is in growth, as long as the material is firm enough and not too floppy, or not too old and woody. Experience will soon show the new propagator which material will take and which will not.

Basal cuttings are taken in the spring soon after the plant comes into growth. The shoots are removed from the base of the plant when they are about 5 cm (2 in) long (Fig. 7.12). There are many plants that can be increased in this way including most of the Compositae (daisy) family – such as asters and chrysanthemums – and delphiniums and perovskias for example. Some plants can have basal cuttings taken later in the year, when they should be sheared over

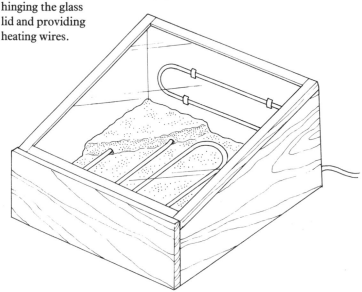

about 10 days before they are needed, to promote new basal growth (Fig. 7.13). Good examples of this are some of the violas such as *Viola cornuta*.

Other cuttings are taken later in the season from the tips or other parts of the stem. In most cases the tip is the best, but there are some plants that root very easily from virtually any part of the stem. Examples of these are the diascias and penstemons. It is useful to take stem cuttings late in the season from plants that are slightly tender, so that they can be overwintered under glass, potted up in the spring and used as replacement plants if necessary.

Give a good watering to the plant from which the cuttings are to be taken, the day before you start work. All cutting material should be placed into a polythene bag as soon as it is removed from the plant. They should be taken as soon as possible indoors, keeping them in the shade if possible. Do not remove from the bag until you are ready to use them.

### Striking cuttings

Fill a 9 cm (3½ in) pot with damp compost and tap on the bench to settle it. Remove the cuttings from their bag one at a time. Cut through the stem with a sharp knife or scalpel just beneath a node, leaving about 5–7.5 cm (2–3 in) of shoot. Remove the lower leaves from the cutting, being careful neither to tear the shoot or leave a ragged stump (use a sharp scalpel). Dip just the tip into a rooting compound and place into the compost towards the side of the pot. Do not push the cutting into the compost otherwise it will lose its powder and the sharp sand will possibly open up wounds that will become infected with rots. Make a hole with something like a pencil, pot in the cutting and then firm the compost round it (Fig. 7.14). Be careful not to leave an air gap around the area where you want the roots to develop. The use of a rooting compound is not always essential as many plants (e.g. penstemons) will root happily without it, but it also contains a fungicide which is useful in protecting the wounds from infection.

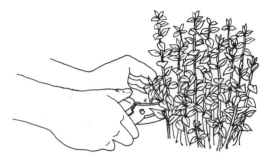

**Fig. 7.12** Basal cuttings are the young shoots that are found at the base of the plant.

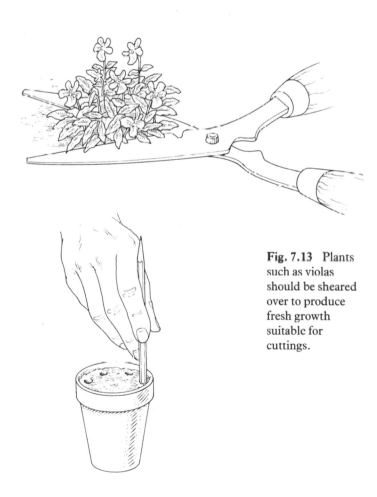

**Fig. 7.13** Plants such as violas should be sheared over to produce fresh growth suitable for cuttings.

**Fig. 7.14** Make a hole in the compost and place the cutting in it, firming it in gently so that there is no pocket of air around the stem.

Continue with the other cuttings around the edge of the pot until it is full (Fig. 7.15) and then water from the base by standing it in a tray of water. Place into the propagator. If a plastic bag is used, make certain that the polythene does not touch the cuttings.

**Fig. 7.15** Continue putting cuttings around the edge of the pot until it is full and then water from below.

Leave in the propagator until the cuttings have taken. In the meantime keep an eye out for any dying and decaying leaves or stems, which should be removed at once to prevent the whole lot going. Make certain that the compost remains damp, but not wringing wet. Experience will tell you when the cuttings have rooted. The cuttings begin to put on new growth with buds and shoots appearing in the axils (where the leaf or leafstalk meets the stem). One method, if you have enough plants to spare, is to try easing one out of the compost to see if it has roots. Once they have rooted, harden them off by gradually returning them to room temperature and humidity by opening the vents or propping open the lid of the propagator.

When they have been hardened off, knock the cuttings out of the pot and pot them up individually into 9 cm (3½ in) pots, using a John Innes No. 3 soil-based compost (or whatever compost you prefer, bearing in mind the remarks made on page 61). After watering, place the newly potted-up plants

into a closed coldframe (with shade netting if required) until they have settled down, and then harden them off.

If cuttings are taken with some roots already formed on them, then chances of success are great. These are basal cuttings

**Fig. 7.16** 'Irishman's cuttings' are those which are taken from near the base of the plant that already have a few roots attached to them.

that are usually found around the edge of the plant, especially of asters and other Compositae. They are removed as close to the parent plant as possible, and either treated as a cutting or potted up and put into a frame straight away if they have a number of good roots. They are generally known as 'Irishman's cuttings' (Fig. 7.16).

To the uninitiated, taking cuttings seems a complicated and fiddly procedure but it is surprising how quickly most gardeners become adept at it.

## Division

The other basic method of increasing perennial plants is by division. This is not only a method of propagation but an important means of keeping many plants alive and vigorous, because unless they are regularly lifted and divided they will languish and die out. Border plants that look congested or are dying out in the middle need to be treated.

Not all plants can be divided. The easiest are those that have a spreading rootstock, either forming clumps such as *Helenium*, or those that run underground making large colonies, such as lily-of-the-valley (*Convallaria majalis*). Other plants that make small clumps can be divided, especially if the stems put down roots where they touch the soil, such as pinks (*Dianthus*) and violas. Plants with tap roots, sea hollies (*Eryngium*) for example, are very difficult if not impossible to divide.

The two usual times for dividing plants are in the autumn or the spring. It can be undertaken at other times if the divisions are put into pots rather than back into the ground, or are kept well-watered. The basic technique is very simple: the plant is lifted from the ground and then divided up into separate portions and replanted. The outside of the clump normally is the youngest material and this is the part that is reused; the centre is often old and woody and should be thrown away. This is no hardship as most perennials that have been in the ground for a few years will provide far more material than is needed simply to replant the border, and will also furnish the gardener with a few spares to give away.

Water the plant to be lifted on the day before operations begin. Loosen the plant all round with a fork and then lift it. There are some plants that will fall apart in your hands (try *Sisyrinchium striatum*, which is one of the easiest of plants to divide) and others that are real beasts. Fortunately the majority fall in between and once the various techniques have been learnt should cause little problem. If the clump is too large to lift, split into smaller sections by using two back-to-back forks pushed into the clumps and then levered apart (Fig. 7.17). This is a crude method of division and should only be used for breaking larger clumps down, or for real thugs that can take this kind of treatment.

Once you have manageable portions, hold a piece in both hands and search for a natural dividing point with your fingers. Shake the plant so the earth falls off, at the same time gently easing your hands apart. With luck the plant should now come apart. Sometimes the various sections need to be

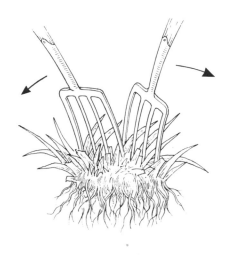

**Fig. 7.17** Large clumps of plants can be divided by using two forks, back to back, to prise them apart.

snapped or cut apart, but on other occasions they just part. If the plant is being obstinate, carry out the whole operation in a bucket of water and once the soil has washed off the plant should part quite readily.

The plant should come apart in natural pieces with a growing point and roots (Fig. 7.18). Keep dividing until it will divide no further. Some plants are much tougher to deal with and require a lot of patience to divide them down into individual portions.

**Fig. 7.18** Smaller clumps should be divided by hand, so that it falls apart into natural divisions.

The roots of hostas, for example, can become very entangled and can take an age to deal with. Here most gardeners, unless it is a rare plant or they want to get the maximum out of it, take a short cut and simply cut the solid root-mass into convenient chunks with a spade, ensuring that each piece has several growing points and roots. This is not a practice to be generally recommended as it is a waste of good plant material; it also leaves plenty of scope for disease to get into the plant, but it has been used as a quick method for generations so it would be silly to deny its efficacy.

Once the plant has been divided, replace the divisions into the soil as soon as possible, before the roots dry out. If it is a bit of a wrestle and takes a long time to divide up one plant, cover the pieces with a damp sack or put them in a bucket of water. Plant them as you would any new plant, firm in and water. Smaller pieces can be potted up individually into 9 cm (3½ in) or larger pots. A John Innes No. 3 potting compost should be used and the plants put into a cold frame.

Sometimes, if you simply want one plant to give away to a friend, it is possible to split off a portion from the side of your plant without taking it from the soil. I would be reluctant to try this with some of the more delicate or tricky plants, but those which are more vigorous, such as the michaelmas daisies (*Aster novi-belgii*), will come to no harm if a fork is inserted and a piece levered off.

## Layering

This is another vegetative method of reproduction which, in general, is more applicable to trees and shrubs. However, it is still a useful method to have in the tool kit. Self-layers of many plants that root when they touch the soil can be useful when you want the odd plant and this can often be encouraged. For example, if I see a straggly stem appearing from a viola I often just cover it with a little soil. In a few weeks there will be a new plant that I can dig up and use elsewhere in the garden, or give away to somebody looking around the garden if they happen to admire the parent.

There is a more formal way of layering a plant and it is mainly used with some pinks and carnations. The stems are bent over and held in place just below the surface of the soil using a wooden peg, wire pin (like a hairpin) or a stone (Fig. 7.19). It is often

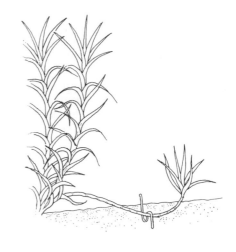

**Fig. 7.19** Layer a plant by pegging down a shoot and covering it with soil. When it has rooted it can be severed from the parent and dug up.

advantageous to split the stem where it is held under the soil (Fig. 7.20). If the soil is not particularly good it is possible to dig a little out and replace it with a potting compost. Alternatively a hole can be excavated and a pot of compost placed in the ground so that the layer roots directly into the pot, making it easy to transport and transplant once it has been severed from its parent.

The length of time taken for a layer to put down roots varies considerably, and in the case of woody subjects it can take several years. Once roots have been put down and the layer is obviously growing on its own it can be severed from the parent plant and dug up when required.

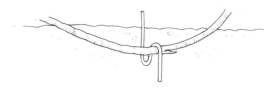

**Fig. 7.20** A wound, in the form of a cut in the stem, will often help to form roots on the layer.

On the whole the majority of plants that can be layered can be more conveniently propagated in other ways, but it is a useful method when you want to produce just the odd plant and can be initiated whenever appropriate material is spotted.

## Root cuttings

Root cuttings is a technique known about by all gardeners whether they propagate or not. If you break off the top of a dandelion or leave part of its root in the soil, a new plant will develop from it. Similarly a small piece of couch grass, ground elder or bindweed will produce the same result. They are all growing from what we would call, in a more controlled situation, root cuttings.

This technique can be used for a whole range of fleshy rooted plants: eryngiums, acanthus and oriental poppies (*Papaver orientale*) being three of them. It is a useful method as this type of plant is often impossible to divide and cuttings might not be easy to strike, making root cutting the easiest way of vegetative reproduction. It is also useful for some plants, such as phlox, that suffer from eelworm or other diseases in their above-ground parts, which makes it pointless to increase them using normal methods as the disease will only be passed on. As the roots are disease free, they are a good method of producing identical but clean plants.

The plant is dug up in the early winter and some of the fatter roots removed. The plant can then be replaced if so required. Another alternative is to dig down beside the plant and remove a few roots without disturbing the rest of it. These roots are cut into 5 cm (2 in) sections with a cut straight across at the end nearest the crown, and a diagonal cut at the root-tip end (Fig. 7.21). This does nothing to improve the performance of the cutting but it does show which way up to plant it.

Fill a 9 cm (3½ in) pot with cutting compost (see page 74) or ordinary potting compost. Make a hole with a pencil and place the cutting in with the horizontal cut at the top, just beneath the surface. Several cuttings can be put into the same pot. Put

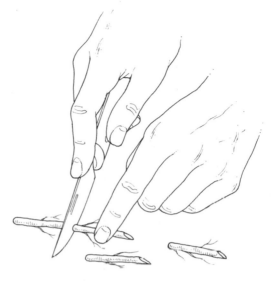

**Fig. 7.21** Cut straight across the top of root cuttings and diagonally across the base to indicate which way up to plant.

the pot in a coldframe over winter and keep the compost moist. By spring there should be signs of growth and as soon as leaves start appearing, pot up individually and treat as rooted cuttings. Some plants seem to prefer that the cuttings are laid on their side, in which case it is more convenient to use a tray or a wide diameter half-pot.

A similar technique involves taking rhizome cuttings. This method is particularly useful for plants with thick fleshy rhizomes, such as bergenias. Cut a section of rhizome about 2.5 cm (1 in) in length, ensuring that it contains a dormant bud, usually hidden behind a leaf scale (Fig. 7.22). Plant the piece in a pot of potting compost with the soil covering the roots, but leaving the bulk of the rhizome above ground. Place in a coldframe and keep moist until growth starts and the new bud develops.

**Fig. 7.22** Rhizome cuttings can be made from sections of the rhizome, each containing a dormant bud.

## Creating new plants

It is well within the powers of amateur gardeners to create new forms of plants either by hybridization or by keeping an eye out for sports.

### Hybridization

The vast majority of new cultivars and hybrids in cultivation have come about by deliberate or accidental hybridization. To take the second first, accidental crosses are happening all the time as bees transfer pollen from one plant to another. Not all plants are compatible but a few are and the resulting pollination results in seed that produces a new plant. The vast majority of these are useless from the gardener's point of view, but just occasionally there is a new form that is a winner. If new plants are referred to as a 'chance seedling' then this is how they were created, although it might possibly refer to the result of a gardener also doing random pollination.

With deliberate hybridization the gardener sets out with the purpose of creating a new plant and systematically pollinates flowers, keeping records of what he does. The purpose of hybridization is not necessarily to produce better flowers. It may be to produce plants that are shorter and therefore will not need staking; or to breed a hardier plant that will stand a greater degree of frost; or even to grow one that is more disease resistant. A good flowering plant can be ruined by having a poor constitution and it is to everybody's benefit if the breeder can improve it.

Generally speaking compatibility between plants is restricted to members of the same genus, so one species of *Dianthus* is likely to cross with another. In fact *Dianthus* cross very easily and this promiscuity means that if two different species are near each other, it cannot be assumed that any seed on either will be true to that plant. Not all genera cross with such willingness and in some, *Corydalis* for example, hybrids are rare.

There are a few genera that will cross with each other producing bigeneric hybrids. They are usually denoted by '×'. An example would be × *Heucherella*, which is a cross between *Heuchera* and *Tiarella*.

Cultivars are just a selection of good forms that occur within a species. If seed of *Sidalcea malviflora* is sown, the chances are that the resulting plants will have flowers of different shades of pink. If one of these is deemed to be significantly different, it can be given a cultivar name. It is possible to cross different colour forms of the same species deliberately in an attempt to create new cultivars.

The gardener can create new plants either in a random fashion or in a more systematic one. The simplest is to put two plants next to each other, hoping the bees do the work, and then collect any seed when it is ripe and sow it. More deliberate and controlled hybridization can be achieved by hand pollination.

For most practical purposes the two plants that are to be crossed should be in flower at the same time but it is possible to keep pollen for up to a fortnight. If it is carefully dried it can be stored in a freezer and used at any time up to about a year, making it possible to cross two plants that normally flower at different times.

The sexual organs of a flower are made up of the anthers that carry the pollen (the anther plus its stem is known as the stamen) and the stigma (the stigma plus its stem is known as the style), which receives the pollen and transmits it down to the ovary where fertilization takes place and the seed develops (Fig. 7.23).

**Fig. 7.23** The stamens include the anthers that produce the pollen and the style carries the stigma which collects the pollen.

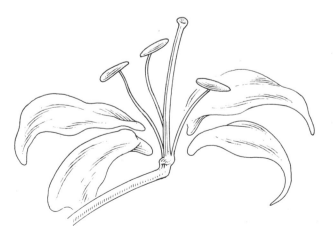

The process of hybridization is very simple. Pollen is transferred from the anthers to the stigma. It will soon become obvious when the pollen is ripe simply by looking at it. The stigma is receptive when it becomes sticky. In plants that are not self fertile the pollen and the stigma are not ready at the same time, thus ensuring that pollen from a flower cannot fertilize itself. Pollen can be transferred either by lifting several grains on a soft artist's brush and transferring them to a stigma in a flower on another plant, or by removing the whole anther with a pair of tweezers to the second flower and rubbing it up against the receptive stigma.

To make certain that bees do not interfere and either carry out a cross first or just after your back is turned, it is best to emasculate the flower just prior to the stigma becoming receptive. This means removing the petals, which are liable to entice bees (Fig. 7.24). This is best done as the flower is opening. Another way is to encase the flower in a muslin bag.

Mark the flower heads that you have crossed, either with labels or with different-coloured pieces of wool. Keep a record of what you have crossed. If the cross has been successful the seed pod will swell and the seeds can subsequently be harvested and sown in the normal way.

It is essential to be ruthless and throw any substandard plants onto the compost heap. Do not assume that just because you bred them they are all worth keeping. If you give them away instead of dumping them, inferior quality plants can get into circulation.

**Fig. 7.24** Remove all the petals from the flower so that bees or other pollinators are not attracted to it.

## Sports

Not all new forms of plants are grown from seed resulting from hybridization. Occasionally a plant will throw up a stem that will have different foliage or a different-coloured flower, caused by some form of genetic mutation. If you are lucky it will be possible to remove this stem and use it as cutting material to produce a new plant, which should bear all the characteristics of the mutation. This plant can then be increased vegetatively to produce more and so on.

Many of the variegated plants arise in this way. Not all sports are stable; many will revert quite quickly to the original, while others will just occasionally produce a stem similar to the original plant. It is important to cut out any such reversions before they swamp the rest of the plant. Some plants are more stable than others. *Dianthus* 'Doris', for example, has produced a number of sports that have been commercially successful.

# CHAPTER 8

# Pests and Diseases

It would be naive to say that hardy perennials do not suffer from pests and diseases but they do not seem to be as much trouble as many other plants, roses for example. One of the reasons for this is that mixed borders seem less prone to serious outbreaks of disease than monocultures. Another reason is that many of the border plants have survived from previous centuries and the only way that they have been able to survive is that they have been tough. In other words, the majority of plants that have come down to us have done so because of their own trouble-free nature.

Generally pests are more of a nuisance than diseases, but both can be partially combated with a certain amount of good housekeeping, especially by removing dead and dying foliage that provides protection or succour for both pests and diseases. Producing good, vigorous, healthy plants that have a balanced diet and adequate supply of moisture, will help a great deal. Both of these can be satisfied by the addition of organic material to the soil. It needs hardly

to be said that you should never buy or otherwise introduce plants to the garden that are sickly or are covered with pests.

## Pests

### Slugs and Snails

One of the biggest problems that most gardeners seem to confront is that of slugs and snails (Fig. 8.1). The work of these voracious eaters can result in disfigurement at best and death at worst. A few mouthfuls of hosta leaves will soon leave the clump in an unsightly mess that will not be rectified that season. Similarly a year's growth will be lost when a slug fells a trillium by eating through the stem.

The simplest way of killing slugs and snails is by using chemical bait. This can be in the form of pellets which attract and then kill the pests, or a solution which is watered onto the ground. This is useful against those that live beneath the soil. There are brands that are not dangerous to other forms of wildlife. If you use the more toxic kind, cover them with a pot or tile so that they are inaccessible to anything other than slugs.

The other way to remove them is by hand. One way is to leave pieces of tile or even upturned grapefruit skins on the ground as a shelter for the slugs and to visit daily and remove them. An alternative is to go round at night with a torch and collect up as many as you can see. You will be startled by the numbers if you try the latter method. A walk across a lawn at night will reveal thousands. Several night patrols will reduce the population to manageable proportions.

What to do with them once you have captured them is a problem. For those that dislike killing them, a trip to some waste ground is the answer; but for others they can be dropped into a jar or water containing a little washing-up liquid. The quickest method of all is with the heel of a boot but this is not to everyone's taste!

Some gardeners prefer prevention and it is often suggested that a layer of sharp gravel or ashes will deter slugs from getting to a plant. However a trip out at night with a torch will soon prove that slugs are made of sterner stuff than gardeners often give them credit for. It is also suggested that hedgehogs are useful in reducing their numbers. This is so, but they will make little inroads into the average garden's slug population.

## Mice and moles

Moving up the scale a bit, mice and voles can be a bit of a nuisance, although never on a large scale unless they exist in plague proportions. Mice can be a terrible nuisance by digging up bulbs, and voles' main vice is gnawing through the stems of plants. They are something to live with unless serious damage is caused, in which case traps (either ones that kill or capture alive) should be set. Cats will also generally keep populations down to an acceptable level.

Cats will also capture the occasional mole. Moles are pests on two levels. One is that their runs through the soil will often leave plants with roots dangling in air, which is particularly disturbing during times of drought. The other is the production of unsightly molehills, which can swamp smaller plants. Most traditional methods such as using smoke-bombs or planting caper spurge are little more than wishful thinking. The only sure methods are poison or trapping, the latter possibly being a live trap so that they can be released elsewhere. Unfortunately once a mole has been removed another always seem to take its place, so the best philosophy is to live with it.

## Cats

Cats themselves can be a nuisance, mainly in using freshly turned soil as a litter tray. There are cat peppers that are supposed to deter them but they never seem to work and, besides, they need replacing so frequently. The solution is just to enjoy the cats and ignore their shortcomings.

## Dogs

Dogs not only foul the garden but also can be a bit boisterous, often charging through borders. Both these problems can be overcome: by training if the dog belongs to you, or by good fences if it does not.

## Rabbits

Fences are important in the fight against rabbits. Anyone who has had these long-eared pests in the garden will know the havoc they can wreak in a night of munching. The only real defence is to erect a fence of small mesh wire-netting, burying at least 15 cm (6 in) below the ground to prevent the rabbits burrowing under it. Traps should be used if one or two manage to get in. These can be of the sort that catches them alive so that they can be released further away, if you are averse to rabbit pie.

## Deer

In terms of size, the biggest pests usually found in gardens are deer, which seem to be on the increase. Again fences are the only real answer, but in this case they have to be tall ones, 2–3 m (7–10 ft) in height will be needed to deter the deer from jumping it. These can be ugly, but give a wonderful opportunity for growing climbers. A tall hedge is another possibility but this solution is not so immediate.

## Insects

Returning to the other end of the scale, we have the insect pests. These can manifest themselves as grubs, caterpillars or adults. The main nuisance they cause is by chewing the roots, stems, leaves or shoots of a plant, weakening or killing it. They can also act as a vector for bringing disease to a plant.

**Fig. 8.2**
Caterpillar.

Some pests are specific to individual species. Thus the caterpillars of the mullein moth (Fig. 8.2) will live on the leaves of verbascum often reducing them to tatters. The aphid specific to lupins cover the young growth with a sticky mass of grey bodies.

The commonest of such pests is the *aphid* or *greenfly* (Fig. 8.3). The adults eat tender shoots in particular and will soon distort it. Some of the worst affected perennial plants are artemisia (by blackfly) and lupins (by lupin aphid). Fortunately control is rarely needed in a mixed border as there are usually sufficient flowering plants to attract both hoverfly and ladybirds, which are voracious predators of aphids. If the outbreak is severe then a chemical spray may be used, but choose one specifically targeted at

**Fig. 8.3** Aphid.

aphids and not a general one as this may kill beneficial insects as well. An alternative is either to squash the offending insects with the fingers or to remove the affected stems entirely. Populations of aphids should not be allowed to build up as they can introduce viral diseases and, while natural predators are likely to control most outbreaks, they must be given a helping hand if the problem becomes acute.

Probably one of the worst problem insects in the garden is the *vine weevil* (Fig. 8.4). This is a nuisance on two fronts. The adults make holes in leaves of many plants. This in

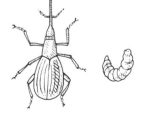

**Fig. 8.4** Vine weevil; adult and grub.

itself is a nuisance but not threatening. However it is the grubs that produce the threat. They chew their way through the roots of plants, leaving the tops to wilt with no chance of rescue. The first sign of trouble is when the plants keel over.

Vine weevils are very difficult to eradicate There is only one chemical that can be

guaranteed to kill them but that has now been banned. There are some that claim to kill them, amongst a host of other things, but they really have no effect – indeed one nurseryman claims to have seen vine weevils eating chemicals with great relish! There is hope that sprays that will prevent the adults breeding may be effective.

Biological control has been developed but this is only for glasshouse crops. The adults are well camouflaged and very difficult to find. If disturbed they immediately drop to the ground and lie doggo on the soil. One way to catch them is to place a sheet of newspaper under a plant that you suspect they are feeding on and then shake the foliage. This is fine if you grow rhododendrons, but it is not a very practical proposition in a bed of epimediums.

The grubs are the real scourge. They like any plant that has fine roots, in particular hardy geraniums, primulas, epimediums, tiarellas and many others. If a plant suddenly dies, dig it up and examine the soil around its roots. The weevil grubs will be seen as small cream horse-shoes. They can be prolific. I have found 50–60 in one forkful of earth. Unfortunately they tend to breed all year round, so that even if you carefully riddle the soil and remove all the grubs, there are probably adults around to produce more.

Prevention is the best mode of attack. Vine weevils cannot fly, only walk, so they are usually introduced into a garden on plants that are brought in. Examine all such plants and wash off the soil. This applies to plants in pots as well as bare-rooted ones.

*Cockchafers* (Fig. 8.5) and other chafers are a similar pest below ground. These are much bigger than vine weevils but have the same habit of chewing through the roots, killing the plants. In theory they are only found in newly cultivated ground but in practice they can be found in any soil. Dig over the border regularly and remove them by hand. A persistent chemical such as HCH can be added to the soil but this is impractical over the whole garden. Concentrate on protecting valuable plants, adding it to the soil at the time of planting.

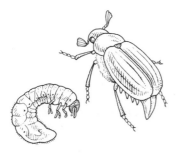

**Fig. 8.5**  Cockchafer, grub and adult.

*Wireworms* (Fig. 8.6) are yet another pest of the same ilk, although they are not so much of a nuisance in the flower borders as in the vegetable patch. They can be dealt with, if it is thought necessary, in the same way as chafers.

**Fig. 8.6**  Wireworm or click beetle.

*Caterpillars* of both moths and butterflies can be a nuisance, but apart from the mullein moth which reduces verbascum leaves to tatters, they are generally not too bad in the flower garden; it is in the vegetable patch where they become a nuisance. If there is an infestation, removal by hand is the most effective method of control. Chemicals can be used but they are also likely to kill off beneficial insects as well.

*Red spider mite* can be a problem in hot dry summers but they are really a pest of glass houses and beyond the scope of this book.

*Eelworms or nematodes* can be a pest for some species, in particular border phlox. The plants show symptoms of an infestation by becoming stunted and distorted. The best way of coping with this is to burn the plants, but before you do so take root cuttings to start a new batch of plants. The nematodes exist in the plant's stems but not the roots and so clean stock can easily be propagated. Do not, however, replant them in the same piece of ground.

Most of the other pests cause floral despoliation rather than killing the plant.

*Earwigs* (Fig. 8.7) tend to eat pieces out of petals and are especially cursed by growers of chrysanthemums and dahlias. The traditional method of dealing with them is to put an inverted flowerpot full of straw on the top of a cane thus providing the earwigs with accommodation. Examine these regularly and remove any pests that are found.

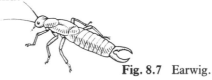

**Fig. 8.7**  Earwig.

*Thrips* can also be a nuisance by eating buds of flowers, often leaving white flecks on what would otherwise be perfect blooms. They can be treated with chemical sprays but most gardeners can live with such blemishes.

**Beneficial insects**

Not all insects are pests. There are some, such as bees, flies and moths, which are useful in the pollination of flowers; and there are others, such as hoverflies (Fig. 8.8) and ladybirds (Fig. 8.9), that are predators on some of the worst insect pests such as aphids. It is important, then, that the gardener does not reach for the spray gun as soon as he or she sees an insect on a plant. Most of us are familiar with ladybirds and even hoverflies, but how many know their larvae? These grubs are important not only because of what they turn into, but also because they have voracious appetites for greenfly.

**Fig. 8.8**  Hoverfly.

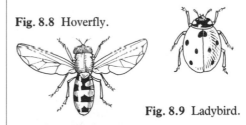

**Fig. 8.9** Ladybird.

It is not often that chemical sprays are really necessary in the flower garden, but if they are choose one that is specifically prepared for the pest concerned and only spray that part of the plant that is infected, not the whole plant which may well also be harbouring beneficial insects.

*Leaf miners* can make a mess of a plant's leaves by digging tunnels through them. If worried by a serious infestation, spray.

## Diseases

Fortunately there are not a great many diseases that affect the flower borders. The worst is probably the powdery mildews that can be seen on many plants, especially michaelmas daisies and monardas. These show clearly as a white powdery deposit on leaves and stems of the affected plant. Contrarily, these can be seen at their worst in hot dry conditons and in damp, muggy conditions. Plants can be sprayed with benomyl at fortnightly intervals to reduce the risk but there are two better ways of prevention. The first one is to choose varieties that are less susceptible to mould. The second is to plant those plants that are likely to succumb in an open position where the air will circulate around them. Make certain, too, that they have plenty of moisture at the roots by adding organic material to the soil and by mulching. Anything suffering from mildew should be burnt when it is cut down at the end of the season, to reduce the number of spores.

Leaf spot or blotch is relatively common on many plants such as hellebores and irises. As the name suggests, diseased blotches form on the leaves. The affected leaves should be removed and burned and the rest of the plant sprayed with Bordeaux mixture.

All the above are fungal diseases and there are a number of others that may cause problems with individual genera. Peonies, for example, suffer from peony wilt.

There are also viral diseases that are often brought in by aphids. The plants look sickly and often have yellow markings on their leaves. There is not much you can do about this except to check all incoming plants to make certain that you are not introducing the disease, and to burn all infected material.

## Other problems

Plants can also suffer from various other problems, of which nutritional ones are probably the worst, with plants looking sickly and generally out of sorts. These can usually be avoided by good cultivation. Avoid giving the border too much nitrogen as this only promotes excessive foliage growth at the expense of flowers and the overblown, lush growth can more easily become victim to pests and diseases.

Over-watering, or ground that is boggy, can produce plants with yellowing leaves and eventually a rotting death. Make certain that all flower borders are free-draining.

Mechanical damage often occurs with perennial plants in a windy position, if they are not staked. It is always wise to make certain that all susceptible plants are well supported (see page 50).

Plants often grow out of character if they have too much or too little light. Always take into account the plant's preferred habitat. Some plants that normally prefer shady conditions will grow in a sunnier position if they have a moisture-retentive soil. Many of those that usually grow in the open will grow in light shade but their flowering is impaired.

If you use herbicides anywhere in the garden, be careful of accidental drift. Plants may seem ill because they have received wind-blown spray intended for weeds. Some plants are allergic to certain pest or disease-control sprays. Read the packet or bottle carefully before you use them.

There is an old adage in gardening that if a plant is looking unhappy, move it. It is surprising how often this works; in some cases the plant need only be moved a short distance. If a plant stands still and does not seem to develop after it has been planted, or if it looks unhappy but is not obviously diseased or being eaten by pests, try digging it up and moving it. This is obviously best done in autumn or winter with most plants but if it is well-watered both before and after the move, it can be done at any time as long as the weather is neither scorching hot nor very windy.

Having dwelt on this subject at some length, it should be stressed that with well-grown plants and a check on all in-coming material, there should be few problems for the gardener to worry about.

# PART III
## SPECIAL AREAS

# CHAPTER 9

# Shady and Woodland Areas

Most gardens have a piece of shade somewhere. It may come from trees or shrubs or it may be on the north side of a building. There are some gardens that get very little sunlight at any time and depend entirely on a north light.

So often these areas are thought of as waste land and of no use whatsoever to the gardener, but whoever makes these assumptions would be wrong. You only have to consider the amount of flora that flourishes in woodlands to appreciate that there are bound to be some plants that will grow in these positions. And, indeed, there are a large number. Although many gardeners consider shade as a difficult area with which to cope (mainly because they cannot grow annuals there), most experienced gardeners will actually want to create some shade if they have not got any, so that they can grow many of the attractive plants that cannot be grown in the open.

## Types of shade

Shade can be classified by the degree of light it receives and by the soil's moisture content. Some areas receive little sun except possibly a few slanting rays at the beginning or end of the day, but still get a great deal of light from overhead. This kind of area is typified by those in the shadow of a building or fence. Other shady areas receive a dappled light where leaves of trees and bushes are constantly moving, allowing not only a certain amount of light to penetrate to the ground but also a degree of sunlight. As the foliage of the trees becomes denser so does the depth of shade, until eventually – under conifers, for example – the light becomes quite gloomy and very little will grow.

Another problem with shady areas is that they are often very dry. A tree with a dense

**Fig. 9.1** Remove some side branches to allow the light to reach the ground around the base of the tree.

canopy will shed much of the water it receives beyond the perimeter of its branches, allowing little to reach the soil beneath it. What little does penetrate is often eagerly lapped up by the tree itself, leaving little for other plants. The build-up of leafmould, however, does help preserve moisture. Under deciduous trees with a less dense canopy, where rain manages to penetrate, it is usually sufficient to grow quite a range of plants, especially in the early part of the year before the trees get going.

Undoubtedly dense, dry shade is a problem, but other shady areas should be treated as a bonus and exploited with the wide range of interesting flowering plants that will grow there.

To a certain extent it is possible to manipulate the amount of shade that is produced by a tree or shrub simply by thinning its branches. This can be done over the whole plant so that there is an increase in the light, or it can be achieved by removing the lower branches so that more light comes in from the sides (Fig. 9.1). This should be done with due care and attention to the shape of the tree or shrub. An oak tree (*Quercus*), for example, can have its lower branches lopped off without unduly upsetting its essential 'oakness', but try this with a weeping tree and the whole essence of it disappears.

Many trees and shrubs will lend themselves to thinning without upsetting their natural balance. One way to do it is to open up the crown in much the way that an apple tree is pruned, so that light can enter the centre of the tree (Fig. 9.2). Once this is done it will have to be pruned at regular intervals as the tree will try to replace its missing limbs and thickets of suckers will appear along the exposed branches.

Some trees are better at producing a dappled shade than others. Birch (*Betula*), for example, produces a good light shade, as does hazel (*Corylus*). Beech (*Fagus*) and horse chestnut (*Aesculus*), on the other hand, produce a very dense shade, often with branches that sweep right down to the ground. Some trees are more difficult to plant under because they have shallow and often very thirsty and hungry roots. Willow (*Salix*) has very shallow and thirsty roots (indeed, it is a good tree or shrub to plant in a boggy area to dry it up). Birch also has a shallow root system. Oak, on the hand, is quite deep rooted and is a good tree to underplant.

## Creating shade

If shade does not exist, it is possible to create it by planting trees and shrubs. The choice of suitable woody plants is very wide but in narrowing it down concentrate on those that will produce a dappled shade. Oak trees are probably the best choice but they will take a long time to mature to the desired size. Provided standard trees are chosen and not those on dwarfing stock, apple trees, particularly in the form of the

**Fig. 9.2** Thin the crown of the tree so that it produces a dappled light, suitable for many woodland plants.

'Bramley', make ideal shade; they will also grow quite quickly. The choice of shrubs is much wider but deciduous azaleas and smaller acers are perfect candidates. Before planting make certain that you are happy both with your choice of tree or shrub and its position, as there is nothing more annoying than discovering that a plant, which you have waited several if not many years to reach maturity, is in the wrong place.

Most plants that grow in a woodland situation do so in the leafy soil under deciduous trees or shrubs. This gives them a cool, moist root-run with plenty of nutrients from the rotting leaves, and moisture that is held in the humus. Before planting up any shady area the soil should be greatly improved so that it emulates, as near as possible, that of the woodland floor. Dig over the ground, incorporating as much organic material as you can. Leafmould and coir, or coarse peat, are the best materials as farmyard manure, used in quantity, will be too rich. It is a good idea to collect fallen leaves in the autumn and compost them in a wire cage (see page 39). This can be added to the soil every year to top up its reserves. Without this attention the soil will become too impoverished from the demands of the trees and shrubs to meet the requirements of perennials, which will languish and eventually fade away.

Borders that are constructed on the north side of buildings or fences can be prepared in the same way as any other border. Here it is only the light that is missing (and often the moisture caused by the rain shadow of the building), as there is no competition from hungry and thirsty woody plants.

## Plants for shade

There is a surprisingly large range of plants that can be grown in a shady position. Quite a number of those that grow in full sun can be persuaded to grow in shade but there is usually a penalty to pay: they will not flower as well and will often become drawn. The best plants to grow under these circumstances are plants that naturally grow in shade, especially woodland shade.

The main flush of woodland flowers is undoubtedly in the spring. Many will complete their whole seasonal cycle before the trees and shrubs come into life, put out their shading leaves and begin to suck up all available moisture through their roots. Wood anemones (*Anemone nemorosa*), for example, appears in late winter with the flowers and leaves unfurling at the same time. By mid-spring the flowers have died down, the seed has been formed and the leaves are beginning to die back. Thus they have made the most of the soil and light while there was little competition.

When planning a garden this is worth remembering, as it means that space under deciduous shrubs that is covered later in the year by foliage and low branches, can be used in the late winter and early spring for early-flowering plants. Here they can die back and rest, undisturbed until the following spring. This is making good use of space, as the soil under many of this type of shrub is too densely covered with foliage to be able to support any plants; and even if it could they would probably be obscured from view. There are literally hundreds of species to choose from. Many are bulbs such as bluebells (*Hyacinthoides*) or the delightful erythroniums. The trilliums are distinctive North American plants that, although slow to increase, are well worth seeking out from specialist nurseries.

Many plants are native woodlanders and are especially suited to the conditions. Bluebells and wood anemones have already been mentioned but there are dozens more, including primroses (*Primula vulgaris*), wood sorrel (*Oxalis acetosella*), wild daffodils (*Narcissus pseudonarcissus*), lily-of-the-valley (*Convallaria majalis*), woodruff (*Galium odoratum*) and so on. Nearly all of these will eventually make large drifts and are suitable for carpeting larger areas of shade.

Areas under taller trees and under north walls need to be planted with more care as they are visible for most if not all of the year. Not all plants die back and many, epimediums and pulmonarias being good examples, provide a display of leaves long after the flowers have died down, which not only provides an excellent ground cover but are interesting in their own right. Quite a number of these plants are taller and can be planted towards the back of a shady area. Solomon's seal (*Polygonatum*) or *Lamium orvala* are a good example of these. Several of the taller euphorbias, such as the wood spurge (*E. amygdaloides*), *E. griffithii* and *E. sikkimensis* will grow in light shade and provide interest over a long period.

Areas under trees and shrubs that allow quite a lot of light to reach the floor, either as dappled shade or slanting directly under the branches, are not confined to spring planting. There are many plants that will flower at other times of the year. Some of the most valuable are the toad lilies (*Tricyrtis*) which flower in the autumn. The native nettle-leaved bellflower (*Campanula trachelium*) flowers in the summer. Astilbes will readily grow in light shade as long as there is enough moisture. They will produce a wide range of reds and creamy white flowers during the summer. The uncommon *Kirengeshoma* is a good plant for the autumn, while the lamiums, although common, are useful during most seasons.

There are many unusual and interesting plants that can be grown in shady areas. Children (and adults) are always intrigued by the mouse plant (*Arisarum proboscideum*), whose flowers are protected by a brown hood ending in a long tail, the whole reminiscent of a mouse's hind quarters. Closely related to these are the arisaema which, as a result of increasing popularity, are becoming more available. These have curious flowering spikes that are encased in very decorative spathes, which look like hooded leaves, much in the manner of the wild lords-and-ladies (*Arum maculatum*). Another intriguing plant is the parasitic plant *Lathraea clandestina*, which has purple flowers but none of the usual green parts. It grows mainly on the roots of willow and poplar. One of the most stunning spring flowers is the double Canadian bloodroot, *Sanguinaria canadensis* 'Plena'. The golf ball-sized flower heads are a mass of glisteningly white petals forming a perfect sphere and backed by a glaucous grey leaf.

Borders that are in the shade because of a building or a garden wall or fence, are more adaptable and will take quite a number of plants that one would never think of planting under trees. *Geranium psilostemon*, for example, flowers well in open shade in spite of not seeing the sun. In fact quite a number of the geraniums, which we normally think of as sun lovers, will grow well in this position. *G. sanguineum* does well here as will *G. phaeum*. *G. pratense* 'Mrs Kendall Clark' is especially good as the silvery, pale blue flowers stand out well in the comparative gloom of the north light. *G. macrorrhizum* is one of the best as its fragrant leaves form a good ground cover.

One of my favourite plants for such areas is *Phuopsis stylosa*, a low-growing perennial that tends to ramp over and between other plants. It is covered with golf ball-sized heads of pink flowers from late spring until the end of summer. Although it does become rampant, rooting where it touches the ground, I do not consider it a nuisance, nor do I object to the foxy smell that the foliage exudes when it is wet. Daylilies (*Hemerocallis*) do well, as do astilbes, if the soil is not too dry. Many woodlanders do well in the open position under a north wall. Solomon's seals, smilacina and hellebores are superb plants for such a position, as are the lower pulmonarias, violas and many of the primulas. There are many, many more plants that can be tried and there is little excuse for not having a very good display of perennials throughout most of the year in this kind of shade.

Autumn colour is mainly the province of the more woody plants but there are several perennials that are useful at that time of year. The leaves of *Polygonum affine* (now called *Persicaria affinis*) turn a wonderful rust-brown and their flowering spikes change from pink to a similar rust colour. The spikes of astilbe make good autumn and winter decoration. Some plants produce attractive berries. One of the favourites is *Arum italicum marmoratum* which has creamy veined leaves in the winter and spring and naked spikes of vivid orange-red berries in autumn. Less commonly seen plants, but not difficult to grow, are the baneberries: *Actaea alba* having white berries and *A. rubra* having red ones.

The most difficult shady areas in which to grow plants are those that are parched, either through there being a naturally dry soil or because the shade is created by trees that are thirsty and constantly drain the soil of its moisture. Before planting anything it is essential to try and improve the soil as mentioned above. It is possible that some areas under the tree are relatively moister than others. For example, you will often find that rain water will always run down and away from the trunk along the same line, sometimes forming a slight gully. The soil here will be wetter and if moisture-retentive compost or leafmould is added, it could improve the conditions a lot.

There are a few plants, but not many alas, that will take dry shady conditions. The most celebrated is *Cyclamen hederifolium* which will grow under a horse chestnut tree, even close to the trunk, where nothing else will grow. The small flowers of this cyclamen appear in the autumn, followed closely by its leaves which last well into the following year, creating an attractive ground cover. A somewhat bigger plant that will grow in dry shade, although it will not become its normal rampant self, is *Euphorbia amygdaloides robbiae*. This also remains attractive for quite a long season, well after its insignificant flowers have finished.

Damp shade is much easier to cope with, especially if there is a stream or wettish area in light shade with some sun reaching it. There are plenty of suitable plants; the main worry will be keeping it weeded as all kinds of grasses and other pests are likely to crop up. The range of plants runs from carpeters, such as the bugles (*Ajuga*) and creeping Jenny (*Lysimachia nummularia*) through the taller kingcups (*Caltha*), candelabra primulas and mints (*Mentha*), to the vast *Gunnera manicata*. Damper areas are also the preferred homes of many of the ferns but be warned, do not introduce bracken (*Pteridium aquilinum*), however pretty you might think it looks, else you will soon find that your whole garden has been overrun.

Shade-loving plants are not as commonly available as border plants and are not frequently seen in garden centres. However, nurseries that specialize in perennials usually stock quite a number and most cited in this chapter are widely available.

Shady areas should not be ignored but turned to the gardener's advantage by growing unusual plants that will give plenty of pleasure and contrast well with the sunnier borders. If the garden is big enough then a small wood, perhaps only comprising one or two large trees, will make a wonderful retreat on a hot summer's day, or even as a refuge from a light shower. If the garden is too small for trees, then a few shrubs will provide more than adequate shade to grow some of the more interesting and decorative shade-loving plants.

# CHAPTER 10
# *Water Gardens*

Lucky is the gardener who has a stream running through his or her garden. Water contributes another dimension to gardening, not only in the number of plants that can be grown, but also in that its sounds and reflections add greatly to the atmosphere.

Water can be present in basically three forms. It can be a pond, either formal or informal in shape; it can be running in the form of a natural or artificial stream or cascade; or it can be virtually unseen in the form of a bog garden. Some gardens are big enough to accommodate all three alternatives; others are more limited and a choice is needed.

## Ponds

Probably the easiest to create and maintain is a pond or pool. The simplest of ponds can be created by digging a hole in the ground and lining it with a rigid, preformed plastic liner. Unfortunately these are limited in size and they rarely look other than what they are, namely plastic. Concrete used to be a widely used material in pool construction but it has been generally superseded by the use of butyl liners. However it is still used for small decorative ponds, especially ones that have a regular shape, and is particularly useful for creating pools on terraces and patios. Alternatively these can be built from brick or concrete blocks and then faced with a waterproof cement or lined with a plastic liner. The most popular way of constructing a pond is to line a hole in the ground with a butyl liner, which is commonly available from garden centres. The final way is to use the traditional method of creating a pond, namely to puddle it with clay. This is very hard and messy work but it does create a natural pond with no ugly liners to be seen or punctured.

## Construction

The site for the pond must be considered carefully as once it is constructed it will be a tremendous disappointment if it is in the wrong place. Look at the site carefully from all different directions, and try and visualize what it will be like once it has matured into its surroundings. A flat site is obviously easier to cope with than a sloping one, although it is possible, with effort, to create one on the latter. Try to avoid areas where there will be a large fall of autumn leaves. Also avoid a shady position as most water-plants prefer sun. It is important, too, to think of the safety aspects if there are young children about. Can the area be easily and securely cordoned off?

The size and shape of the pond should be decided by visual considerations, but there is the question of the spoil and what to do with it and this may influence how adventurous you are going to be. The top layer should be kept and used elsewhere in the garden, but the subsoil may well be useless and require disposing of; not the easiest of tasks if it is a large pond. It is surprising how much soil comes out of a hole and several skipfuls may be involved, which can get expensive. It is not only the disposal of spoil from a large pool that is a problem, it is the actual removal in the first place. Digging by hand may well temper the size and depth of the pool. It is possible to use a mechanical digger, either a full-sized one that will do the job quickly, or one of the miniature ones that can be manoeuvred into position without wrecking the rest of the garden. If a driver is hired along with the digger, be certain that he does exactly as you require and make sure he understands that the topsoil and the subsoil must be kept separate.

If the ground slopes it may be necessary to build up one end to allow the top of the pond to be level all the way round (Fig. 10.1). Subsoil can be used for this as long as it is covered with a generous layer of topsoil. This artificial bank should be well rammed down so that it cannot move under the pressure of the water. This is especially important if the pond is to be puddled with clay.

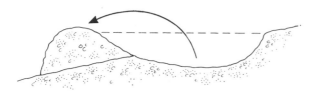

**Fig. 10.1** On sloping sites it may be necessary to build up the banks to ensure that the rim of the pond is level.

It is advisable to have deep and shallow areas within the pond. The maximum depth of water should be about 75 cm (30 in) which allows the fish protection during the winter and, at the same time, is not too deep for plants such as water lilies. It is a good idea to create ledges round the edge of the pool (Fig. 10.2) so that there are different planting depths to meet the requirements of individual plants.

**Fig. 10.2** Create ledges around the edge of the pond so that plants with different depth requirements can be accommodated.

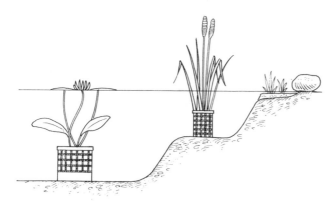

The rigid, preformed pools are relatively easy to install, requiring little more than a hole to be dug. Their only requirement is that the top should be level. Make the hole slightly larger than the pool and once the latter is in place fill in the gap with sand, tamping it well down. Paving slabs or some other form of stonework will be needed to go round the edge of the pond, to cover the plastic lip.

Concrete pools are more complicated to install, but if done well they will outlast most other forms of pond. Obviously the hole should be larger than the finished pool to allow for the thickness of the concrete. Again the top should be level. The concrete can be laboriously mixed by hand or bought ready-mixed. If the latter, get a team of people to help as the work will need to be carried out swiftly and accurately. The problem with ready-mixed is that you have to wait between the stages mentioned below for the concrete to harden partially. To ensure the pool is watertight it is possible to add a waterproofing agent to the mixture. Alternatively the walls and floor can be painted with a rubber or plastic sealant once it is dry.

The bottom of the pool is first covered with a layer of about 10–13 cm (4–5 in) of concrete, which is well tamped down. For large ponds the bottom will need reinforcing with steel mesh. Wooden shuttering is then erected around the sides of the pool, leaving a gap of about the same amount between it and the earth. Fill in the space with concrete and tamp well down. If ledges are required, then the pool is built one step at a time (Fig. 10.3). As can be seen from this method of construction, concrete pools are best suited to formal shapes, for which shuttering can be easily made.

The most effective way of making a pond for most gardeners is to line the hole with a flexible plastic or butyl liner. Once again a hole is dug to the final shape and profile of the pond. The whole of it is then covered with a 5 cm (2 in) layer of sand to prevent any stones penetrating the liner. On vertical surfaces, where the sand will not adhere, place several layers of newspaper. The

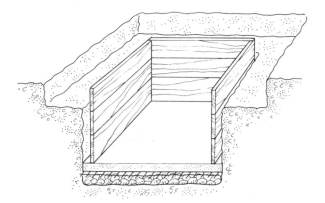

**Fig. 10.3** Concrete pools will need to be constructed one section at a time, using wooden shuttering.

length of the liner should be the length of the pool × twice its depth, and its width should be the width of the pool × twice its depth, plus about 45 cm (18 in) in either direction for overlap round the edge of the pool.

Stretch the liner horizontally across the pool, holding it level with a number of paving slabs or stones. Place the nozzle of a hose pipe in the centre and allow the liner to fill with water, sinking into the hole as it does so (Fig. 10.4). The stone weights slowly move inwards, keeping the liner taut. This is a much better and easier method than trying to line the pool with a dry liner. Once the pool is full and the liner in place, a trench can be dug just beyond the rim of the pond and the edge of the liner buried in it.

Unfortunately the liner is not a very attractive addition to the garden so the margins must be disguised in some way. The easiest way to do this is lay paving slabs around the pond so that they project slightly over the water (Fig. 10.5). Alternatively turfs can be laid round the edge but these will turn brown and shrink unless they are actually touching the surface of the water to provide them with sustaining moisture. This in turn brings problems of how to mow the grass in this position. Yet another possibility is to turn the liner over at 30 cm (12 in) or so below the level of the bank and bring it up further inland (Fig. 10.6). This has the advantage that there is a band of moist soil around the pond in which you can grow marginal plants, but you must beware

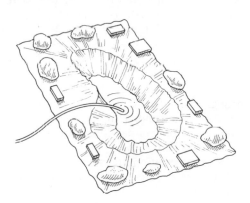

**Fig. 10.4** Stretch the liner across the pond, holding it taut with stones. Fill the pond from a hosepipe, allowing it to sink into position.

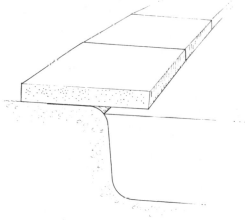

**Fig. 10.5** Hide the edge of a polythene liner with stones or concrete paving stones.

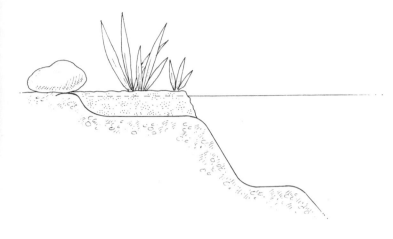

**Fig. 10.6** The liner can also be hidden by burying it in the bank and then overplanting it with grass or herbaceous plants.

of puncturing the liner with a fork while tending them, otherwise the level in the pond will drop and once again reveal the liner.

Puddled ponds are not so common as they once were, when every farm had several. If you have a clay subsoil it is perfectly feasible to produce one as long as you do not mind getting very muddy. It is not essential to be on clay, but if it is not available in the garden you will have to import it which may be expensive. The idea is to line the pond with good, stone-free, plastic clay. If the pond is on clay then only a few inches will be needed, but if it is on a lighter soil then 30 cm (12 in) or more may be needed to make a watertight lining. Wet the clay down and apply the resulting sticky 'goo' to the floor and walls of the pond, stamping and punching it into one continuous mass. I used the traditional method of putting a flock of sheep into my clay pond to trample it well down, but this is not a very practical method for those that live in towns – although the local playgroup might make a good alternative!

All ponds need a supply of water to keep them topped up. This can come from the mains supply if only a little is required, and as long as there are no water restrictions in force. An alternative is to channel all the rain water off roofs and paved areas into the pond. In most years this should provide an adequate supply as long as the pond is not leaking. It may be desirable to install an overflow pipe at the desired water level so that any excess water can drain off into a soakaway or ditch.

**Planting**

Plants for ponds are of three types. There are the deep-water floating ones such as waterlilies (*Nymphaea*). Next there are the marginals which grow in the shallow water near the edge of the pond. These are typified by the rushes and by water irises. Finally there are the plants that grow in the boggy soil around the edge of the pond. There are a great number of plants that will grow in these conditions, including kingcups (*Caltha*) and candelabra primulas. These will be discussed in more detail under the section on bogs (see page 100).

One of the problems of introducing plants to ponds that are lined with concrete or plastic is that there is no earth in which they can grow. This is easily overcome by growing the plants in containers. Special lattice pots have been devised for aquatic plants that allow their roots to pass through the sides into the water. These pots are filled with a soil-less compost and the plants planted in the normal way. The compost is then covered with gravel to stop it floating away. Those that like the shallower water can easily be placed near the edges of the pond, on the ledges that have been provided, just below water level. Those that require deeper water need a bit more ingenuity as they should not be simply thrown in. Two long strings are passed through the sides of the latticework so that the pot is suspended in the middle. Two people, on one either side of the pond, manoeuvre the pot above the water until it is in the right position and then they lower it in (Fig. 10.7). One person lets go of the string ends, while the other pulls them through and out of the positioned pot.

Puddled ponds have the advantage that plants can be planted directly into the bottom and left to fend for themselves.

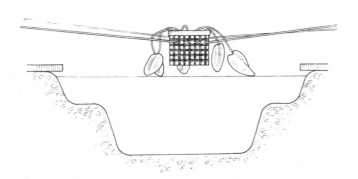

**Fig. 10.7** A lattice pot can be lowered into the centre of a pond using two strings which are withdrawn once the plant is in place.

Floating plants are difficult to root as they are likely to float away. These can be anchored by wrapping a small piece of lead round them.

### Wildlife

Most ponds will soon start teeming with wildlife without the intervention of man. Water beetles and pond skaters seem to appear from nowhere and it is not long before dragonflies and damselflies are skimming over the surface. Frogs also seem to smell the water and soon put in a quiet appearance. The only wildlife that the gardener will have to introduce is fish. Whether to have fish or not, and what sort to have, is up to the individual. Many feel that fish introduces an imbalance to a pond as they eat so much of the other type of wildlife.

Whatever you wish to see in the pond, you will have to include some oxygenating plants, such as the Canadian pondweed (*Lodea canadensis*). This will not only help provide oxygen for the aquatic wildlife but also help keep the pond clear.

### Maintenance

The main requirement of ponds and pools is that they remain topped up with water, as already mentioned (previous page). If the pond is well-balanced with oxygenating and other plants it is likely to remain clean and fresh. However, before the plants have become established there is always the risk of algae growth in ponds. This can be cleared up by the use of chemical algaecides, but it is essential to get plants into growth as quickly as possible as they will help to restrict the algae.

The other major problem with ponds is when the water goes black and smells foul when stirred up. This is due to an excess of rotting vegetation, usually leaves. The answer is to clean the pond out and start again. Autumn leaves can be a nuisance. It is possible to put a net over the pond until all have fallen. Again, a good healthy growth of plants in the pond will produce an environment that will be able to cope with leaves falling in it, as long as it is not overhung or surrounded by trees.

Weeds develop around the margin of the pond and will need to be regularly removed to prevent them crowding out the more desirable plants. Similarly reeds and rushes should not be allowed to become too prolific. Reedmace (*Typha*), particularly in a natural pond, will romp away and will need regular removal.

Any operations that involve work in the pond should be undertaken with utmost care, particularly if it is lined with butyl or plastic as it is easy to puncture the liner.

### Streams

Moving water is a joy to have in a garden. The sounds and the coolness it seems to impart can become an important part of summer. Very few gardeners are blessed with a natural stream, but it is perfectly possible to create an artificial one with a bit of ingenuity. It should be constructed in such a way that it is possible to locate plants that like moist soil and a moist atmosphere along its length.

An artificial stream can be constructed from concrete or from strips of butyl liner. In order to induce a flow there must be a fall from one end of the stream to the other. If this does not exist then it must be constructed, perhaps building a large rock garden through which it can flow. Water can be lifted from the bottom to the top by an electric pump which is readily available from most garden centres and specialist stores. If you are in doubt about its installation, call in a qualified electrician as water and electricity can be a lethal mix.

There are many plants that will enjoy growing beside a stream, many of which are similar to those plants discussed in the next section on bog gardens. However, it must be remembered that if the stream has been constructed properly it will be watertight. This means that the ground immediately adjacent to it will be as dry as the rest of the garden and not necessarily moist enough to grow waterside plants. The answer to this is to arrange for the water to splash over at certain points, or occasionally to flood over the sides to soak the surrounding area. The soil here should contain a lot of organic material in the form of leafmould, coir or peat so that it becomes moisture-retentive.

Choose the plants with care and do not grow too many tall or wide-spreading ones, as these will swamp the stream and make it invisible. This is not a bad thing for short sections but it is undesirable to lose it altogether, particularly as a similar planting can be achieved in a bog garden without the trouble and expense of constructing a stream.

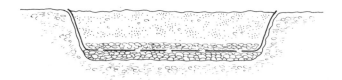

**Fig. 10.8** Diagram showing the construction of a bog garden, the details of which are described in the text.

## Bog gardens

Bog gardens are always exciting places as the plants that grow there always seem to produce brightly coloured flowers that contrast well with the lush greenness of the foliage and stems. They also exhibit a rich range of shapes and textures, from the spiky leaves of the irises to the gigantic umbrellas of the gunneras. Throughout the summer they always appear to be places of liveliness and freshness.

Boggy areas can be associated with the margins of ponds or streams, or can be constructed completely separately. However, it must be said that they do look more at home if they are near water. Although there are many moisture-loving plants that will grow in light shade, it is best to create such an area in full sun.

### Construction

The easiest way to create a bog garden is to line a hole with a liner and then backfill it with soil. While many plants will tolerate moist conditions, they do not like stagnant water and so in this case the liner should be pierced to allow excess water to drain away. A shallow basin about 30 cm (12 in) deep should be dug, keeping any good topsoil for re-use and disposing of any heavy subsoils. This should be covered with a layer of grit to help with drainage and the liner laid on top of it. A few holes should be made at the lowest points to allow excess water to pass through. This can be helped by a further layer of gravel on the inside of the liner, especially around the holes to prevent them clogging. The liner should then be filled with a mixture of the soil plus organic material, which will help to retain sufficient water for the plants use without the whole area becoming waterlogged (Fig. 10.8).

Depending on the amount and the frequency of the local rainfall, the bog garden will need watering. This can be done with a hose-pipe if water restrictions allow. Another valuable source of water supply is from roofs and paved areas which, if the fall of the land allows, can be connected by pipes or gullies into the boggy area.

As already suggested, association with a

pond or stream is the ideal as these can supply the water as well as a moist atmosphere which most bog plants enjoy. An overflow pipe can be placed between the pond and the boggy ground or the liner in one short section of the bank can be lower so that water can flow over the top into the bog whenever the pond becomes overfull (Fig. 10.9). With plenty of organic material in the soil and with a liner to prevent the surrounding soil from sucking out too much moisture, the occasional overflow from a pond should be sufficient to keep it moist. In times of drought, either the pond can be topped up to overflowing or the bog garden can be watered directly.

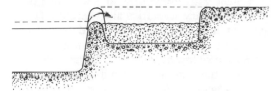

**Fig. 10.9** To create a bog garden adjacent to a pool, continue the liner over a gap in the bank to create an independent basin, into which overflow water from the pond spills.

### Planting

There is an incredible range of very attractive plants that can be grown in a boggy area. Some such as rushes and the large gunneras are grown for their foliage but others are included for the colour of their flowers. Some, such as irises, provide both colourful flowers and interesting foliage. Quite a number of plants do much better in areas such as the coasts of Scotland, where the climate is not only cooler but also moister, often reflecting the atmosphere of their own native haunts. In warmer, drier regions a bog garden provides a microclimate in which many of these plants will grow. Thus primulas will do very well, the candelabra primulas in particular. Similarly, as long as it is not too wet or too hot, meconopsis will enjoy these conditions, making it possible for everybody to be able to grow these delightful blue poppies.

Cheerful mimulus with their brightly coloured flowers find these conditions emi-nently suitable, as do the bright yellow kingcups (*Caltha*) which are a 'must' for plantings near water. Closely related to the latter are the globe flowers (*Trollius*), which have large yellow or orange flowers, in the style of overblown buttercups. Taller plants that form large clumps and colonies are the purple and yellow loosestrifes (*Lythrum* and *Lysimachia*). The latter can be somewhat rampant and should only be planted where there is plenty of space. Astilbes enjoy a moist soil and their feathery flower heads add splashes of purples, reds and creamy whites.

If you have space there are some really spectacular plants for wet areas. The gunneras, *G. manicata* in particular, are gigantic plants with large rhubarb-like leaves. On a smaller scale but none-the-less spectacular are the lysichiton, often known as skunk cabbage, whose giant leaves are accompanied by fascinating white or yellow hoods surrounded by green flower spikes. Probably the most spectacular of all moisture-loving plants are the arum lilies (*Zantedescia aethiopica*), with their pure white spathes that surround the yellow flower spikes. There are many plants to explore, both large and small, and quite a number are given in the alphabetical section of this book.

Unfortunately it is not only the plants that the gardener likes that flourish well in boggy soil. Many weeds and rushes also do well – too well – and need constant attention to prevent them from overtaking the whole area. Try and get them while they are still young, as once they have put their fibrous roots down they will remove great lumps of soil when they are cleared from the ground.

Apart from weeding, the only regular attention that a bog requires is to ensure that it is kept moist in dry periods. Since many of the plants are gross feeders it is essential to feed the bog every year with farmyard manure or compost. This should be applied in winter or early spring before the plants start stirring. Some of the water plants are vigorous growing since they have ideal conditions, and plants like astilbe need to be divided regularly every few years to keep them healthy and vigorous.

# CHAPTER 11

# *Wildflower Gardening*

All garden flowers derive originally from wildflowers and what may be considered the wildflowers of one country are often the garden flowers of another. Thus in effect all the plants mentioned in this book are native to somewhere or other. When referring to a wildflower garden one is writing about those flowers native to just one country; the country of the gardener or garden. In the chapter that follows one country (Britain) has been selected as a sample. The principles hold true for all other countries, although naturally the plants will vary.

In recent times the use of wildflowers in the garden has become very fashionable. This sudden interest stems partly through the desire to preserve wildflowers, setting up small colonies in the garden, and partly through the appreciation of the simple beauty of so many of our native flora. Many have always been part of our garden heritage, with such plants as primroses (*Primula vulgaris*) and cowslips (*P. veris*) having long been appreciated and treasured.

In spite of great interest in conservation and the countryside, wildflowers seem to be ever decreasing for a variety of reasons. It is rare to see fields ablaze with colour and even their boundaries and the hedgerows, which were a welcome refuge, have become quite barren. Roadside verges were another area that were once a colourful spectacle. Now they have taken on a drab, uniform green colour. Many people see creating wildflower gardens as one way in which they can contribute to their conservation. Not only does this conserve the native flora but it also helps to look after the native fauna that goes with it. Although our gardens are alive with insects and other wildlife, more will visit them if we add an element of the plants that naturally grow in the area.

There are several ways of growing such plants. The first is to treat them as ordinary border plants and mix them in with other, cultivated plants. I grow large quantities of foxgloves (*Digitalis purpurea*) in various borders, as well as viper's bugloss (*Echium vulgare*), as if they were cultivated plants. One snag with growing wild plants in this way is that they are native and therefore feel quite at home in the garden and begin to ramp away at what can be a terrifying speed. Introduce yellow archangel (*Lamium galeobdolon*), the bulbous English bluebell (*Hyacinthoides non-scripta*) or ramsons (*Allium ursinum*), and they will be travelling through the cultivated ground at such a rapid rate, that you will probably be rueing the day you thought of the idea.

Many wildflower gardeners would object to this way of growing their plants as it is not a natural way. They prefer to grow the plants in as naturalistic setting as possible. Unfortunately, if nature is left alone it will often let the thugs and the villains take over and before long what set out to be a beautiful flowery meadow turns into a weed patch and an eyesore. Interference becomes necessary to allow flowers to thrive. Even in the wild a certain amount of interference (such as grazing cattle or cutting down scrub) is needed to keep herbaceous plants happy, otherwise things get out of hand and the vegetation moves towards its climax, the forest.

## Meadow gardens

It is possible to have a flowery meadow in the garden but be warned, it is a lot of hard work and certainly not the soft option. The first task is to grow the meadow. The ground should be prepared as for any other aspect of gardening, with attention paid to the removal of perennial weeds, especially the coarse grasses which will swamp any attempt at establishing flowering plants. Once this has been achieved, it can be sown with soft grass seed. An existing lawn can be used and the gardener may well be surprised at how many species of flowering plants are already there just waiting for the mower to cease passing just over their heads. If a meadow is to be created out of rough grass or a field, then the coarser grasses will have to be removed otherwise they will too dominant to allow the establishment of wildflowers. To achieve this the grass must be regularly cut as a lawn for several seasons. This will reduce the coarser grasses strength and they will eventually give up.

Having achieved a 'meadow' the next task is to introduce the plants. They can be sown as seed but the competition will be fierce and not many will succeed. A much better way is to sow the seed in pans, prick out into individual pots and grow on until healthy young plants have been established. At this stage they can be planted out into the grass. Once these have become established they will seed themselves around and the few seedlings that succeed will add to the colony. The individual species can be planted in groups to give a greater impact and to give the impression of a slowly spreading colony, or they can be spread around so that many individual colonies build up, creating a patchwork of colour.

It should be emphasized that the conservation of wild plants is of paramount importance and plants should be grown from seed and not dug up from the wild. There are several firms that sell wildflower seed and many that supply ready-grown plants in pots. Seed may be collected from wild plants as long as there are a large number of plants in the vicinity. If there are only a few, then the seed should be left to reinforce the colony.

A natural meadow is grazed by animals or cut for hay. In this way the coarser grasses and the more dominant plants such as shrubs and trees are prevented from taking over. In the meadow garden this can be copied by mowing it after the flowers have died down, preferably after they have seeded. This means that the meadow is predominantly spring- or early summer-flowering. The first cut is made in late summer and subsequent cuts are carried out at monthly intervals until the late autumn. If there are autumn-flowering bulbs, such as colchicums, the cutting must cease earlier. It is often a good idea to concentrate these in one area so that mowing can continue elsewhere.

Which plants are used is a matter of personal choice (as, indeed, it should be in all planting schemes). It might be tactful to avoid growing pestilent plants, such as thistles that produce masses of seed and will colonize any neighbouring gardens. Plants that spread as easily as these are usually under no threat in the wild. No meadow would be complete without buttercup (*Ranunculus*), but mind that the creeping types do not spread into other parts of the garden. One solution to this is to grow the bulbous form, *R. bulbosus*. There are plenty of members of the daisy family that should be included, of which oxeye daisy (*Leucanthemum vulgare*) is one of the most important.

Colour can be added by the introduction of the purple meadow cranesbill (*Geranium pratense*) and in damper areas the pink ragged robin (*Lychnis flos-cuculi*). Red clover (*Trifolium pratense*) will also provide a bright accent. On chalky soils the clustered bell-flower (*Campanula glomerata*) and greater knapweed (*Centaurea scabiosa*) will colour the meadow respectively a blue-purple and red-purple. A shell pink can be added to the palette by growing the delightful musk mallow (*Malva moschata*). The list is endless and it can be great fun to sit down on a winter's night with an illustrated book of wildflowers and plan what you will include.

## Hedgerows

Another approach to wildflower gardening is to make use of a hedgerow and create a reserve under it of plants that like a little bit of shade. If the garden has no hedge then a couple of shrubs planted next to each other will create a similar habitat. The wild nature of the hedgerow is enhanced if the shrubs that comprise it are natives such as hawthorn (*Crataegus monogyna*) or hazel (*Corylus avellana*). Many of these species will provide autumn colour either with their leaves or with their fruit.

The best time for flowers in the hedgerow is in the spring when primroses (*Primula vulgaris*), lesser celandines (*Ranunculus ficaria*), campions, both red (*Silene dioica*) and white (*S. alba*), herb robert (*Geranium robertianum*), and many more can be seen. Later in the year taller plants, such as hedge woundwort (*Stachys sylvatica*) or hogweed (*Hieracium sphondylium*), or scramblers such as tufted vetch (*Vicia cracca*) can be used as these are able to compete with the grasses.

A further development of the hedgerow garden is to go the whole way and create a woodland garden as described in Chapter 9 (see page 90). Here larger colonies of plants can be grown, including some that will grow in quite dense shade. Again, a full-scale wood is not required; a few shrubs or a couple of trees will provide space for a surprising number of plants. Here it would be possible to grow bluebells (*Hyacinthoides non-scripta*), lily-of-the-valley (*Convallaria majalis*), the delightful wood anemones (*Anemone nemorosa*), sweet woodruff (*Galium odoratum*) and other species that form quite large drifts. Clump-forming plants such as wood spurge (*Euphorbia amygdaloides*) and wood cranesbill (*Geranium sylvaticum*) can also be grown.

## Damp areas

Water and bog gardens have already been covered in a previous chapter but it is worth mentioning here that many of the native waterplants can be grown in a garden. A ditch, not necessarily one that carries water all the year, as long as it is moist will provide an ideal habitat for many plants and will be a useful addition to the wild garden. If none exists then one can be created as described on page 100.

One of the most attractive wildflowers of wet areas is the yellow flag (*Iris pseudacorus*) which will soon develop into quite a large colony. Another yellow is the yellow loosestrife (*Lysimachia vulgaris*). Similar in name, but not related, is the purple loosestrife (*Lythrum salicaria*), which is one of the most colourful of the wetland plants. Of a softer colour and adding a perfume to the air is the water mint (*Mentha aquatica*). Another plant well-endowed with perfume is the meadowsweet (*Filipendula ulmaria*), whose frothy heads of cream flowers are produced in late summer. Also a late flowerer is the purple hemp agrimony (*Eupatorium cannabinum*), which is one of the tallest of the damp-loving plants.

## Arable wildflowers

One area of wildflower gardening that is often overlooked is that of annuals (which is strictly speaking outside the scope of this book). Anyone that is keen on this type of gardening would do well to use a piece of ground that is dug over every year to grow some of the commoner and rarer weeds that have vanished from cornfields and other arable land. Many of these will flower later than the flowers of the meadow, giving a welcome continuance of colour. Here poppies (*Papaver*) will add a good splash of colour, which will contrast well with the blue of cornflowers (*Centaurea cyanus*). The other primary colour, yellow, can be represented by the bright colour of the corn marigolds (*Chrysanthemum segetum*). White can be added to the mix by the introduction of mayweed or chamomile (*Matricaria recutita*).

There are many more annuals, often of less visual significance but none the less of interest, that can be used, perhaps as underplanting to their taller relations.

## Wildlife

Closely allied to native plants are the native animals. There is no doubt that if a wildflower garden is created it will attract a greater number of animals, in particular insects, to the garden. These have a greater affinity to native plants than to the introduced cultivated ones and there will always be more butterflies and moths about, as well as hoverflies and ladybirds, and many more beneficial bugs of all sorts. Wild hedgerows are particularly important and not only provide food but also protection in the form of homes and corridors, along which animals can safely pass. Birdlife will increase, not only because of the rich supply of food in the form of seed heads, but also because of the increase in the number of insects.

Wildflower gardening is not a simple matter of scattering a few seeds and letting nature take charge. It needs as much attention as conventional gardening, otherwise the coarser grasses and weeds get the upper hand. However, the effort is worth while as this is an interesting and even exciting way of growing plants.

# CHAPTER 12

# *Reserve Beds*

If the garden is big enough it is very useful to designate one area for reserve beds. These are beds in which plants that are not immediately required for use in the main borders can be lodged. In larger gardens they may be a separate area, away from the main flower gardens, perhaps next to the kitchen or vegetable garden. In smaller gardens, part of the vegetable garden may be used or even a small area out of sight at the back of a border.

While not essential, reserve beds are very useful for a variety of purposes. The most obvious perhaps is for the storing of plants that are not in flower. Many gardeners dislike the way daffodils (*Narcissus*), for example, refuse to die back gracefully. After flowering they can be dug up from the borders and replaced in the reserve beds until they have died down.

Conversely plants may be kept in reserve beds until they flower and then moved out into the borders. There are quite a number of fibrous-rooted plants that can be moved in full flower, as long as they are given a good soaking before and after removal. Michaelmas daisies (*Aster novae-angliae* and *A. novi-belgii*) are classic examples of this. They can be moved in the autumn into spaces between plants that have had their season and died back or have been cut down. It is a very good way of rejuvenating an end-of-season border.

Another use along the same lines is to row out young plants that are not yet mature enough to flower. Many plants, especially bulbous ones, take many years to reach maturity and, rather than have them take up valuable space in the border, they can be grown on in the reserve beds. Similarly these beds can be used to house plants that are being built up into sufficient numbers to

plant out. For example if only one plant of a particular species has been bought or otherwise acquired, but a minimum of five is required to make a decent planting in the border, it can be planted in the reserve bed until it is big enough to divide.

Gardeners are always acquiring plants that they are not certain what to do with. Rather than put it into an inappropriate position in the borders it can be placed in reserve until a proper decision has been made about its future. One advantage of this is that you can wait until it is in flower and then take a sprig of it round the garden to see how its colour fits in with the existing plantings, until the perfect position is found. It frequently happens that a gardener receives a plant that is a complete mystery, and it is useful to have somewhere to plant it in order to discover how big it grows and what colour flowers it has and so on.

When it is time to renovate a border and divide up many of its incumbents, it is surprising how many spare plants are produced. For example, when replanting a large clump of *Helenium* only a quarter or less of the original plant may be required. Rather than throw the rest away, something that most gardeners hate doing, the excess may be given away to friends or to plant sales. While in the process of working on a border it is a nuisance to have to break off in order to pot up some plants, especially if there are a lot of them. It is much easier to plant them in a reserve bed until you have time to deal with them. It is also a useful place to keep plants that are no longer required in one part of the garden but may be needed later elsewhere. If you have ever had clumps of plants lying around and wilting as they await future attention (and what gardener hasn't?) then you will more than appreciate the benefits of a reserve bed.

Finally, a good use of the reserve bed is to grow extra plants from which flowers can be cut for the house. For example, to pinch a few stems of a delphinium from the border, in order to take inside, can upset the visual effect of the border, but it will not matter in a reserve bed. Similarly there are some plants that you may not like in the border but like as cut flowers. Dahlias often fall into this category. One advantage of growing cut flowers in the reserve bed is that they can be given individual attention, perhaps rubbing out buds so that the terminal flower develops fully, or staking individual stems to keep them straight – something that would be ugly in a border.

Not all plants are suitable for keeping in reserve beds as they do not like to be transplanted. Tap-rooted plants, such as the sea hollies (*Eryngium*), should be placed in their final position as young as possible. Another warning is that some plants with thicker roots may be difficult to remove totally. Any scrap of comfrey (*Symphytum*) root left behind after the plant is removed, will produce a new plant. This can become a nuisance, especially on heavy soils where it is not so easy to sift through the soil to remove every last piece.

Reserve beds should be prepared and tended as one would the vegetable garden, with the plants laid out in rows where they can easily be reached and where they have ample space, free from competition, for them to grow and clump up. They should be kept weed-free and watered. Plants that are left there for several years should be divided if necessary, just as if they were in a border, or they will lose their vitality and vigour.

For any gardener a reserve bed is worth having if space can be found, even if it is only big enough for a few plants.

# CHAPTER 13

# *Perennials as Container Plants*

Hardy perennials are usually thought of as being plants for the border but many of them also make good plants for containers, to be used alone or in conjunction with other plants.

The advantage of growing plants in containers is that they can be moved to any position that is desired, even while in full flower. Indeed they need only be displayed when they are in this condition, making it possible to have a constant show of colour on the terrace or next to the front door. It also means that it is possible to grow plants that are marginally tender, agapanthus for example, keeping them inside until the frosts have passed. Perennials have the advantage over conventional annual container plants in that they do not need renewing every year.

Hardy perennials are valuable as container plants not only because of their flowers but also because of their foliage Hostas, bergenias and ferns are particularly useful. Taller, more upright shapes can be provided by the various grasses.

Plants in containers need a lot of attention. They need regular watering, sometimes more than once a day in very hot dry weather. Because of the amount of water that passes through the container, food is quickly leached away so that they also need a regular liquid feed. The containers should have drainage holes in them so that they do not become waterlogged. The compost can be any good potting compost, either soil-based or soil-less, depending on your preference. Plants can be left permanently in the containers until they have filled it with their roots and then they should be divided and replanted in new soil. For plants that cannot be divided, it may be necessary to provide them with a larger container.

The container can be of any size or shape that the gardener desires, as long as there is room for the plant to grow in it. Many still feel that terracotta pots take a lot of beating as they set off the plants so well, but they do allow water to evaporate from their surfaces and so may need extra water.

Whilst most plants will take a light frost without damage, they object to being frozen solid and this is what can happen to containers in a very cold winter. This can be avoided by wrapping insulation around the container and plant or by moving it inside. An alternative is to bury the pot in the garden so that the plant's roots are protected by the surrounding earth in the same way as if it were a border plant. Do not leave the pots too long in the ground in spring, otherwise the roots might start to come out through the drainage holes in search of moisture and nourishment.

## Selecting plants

There are a large number of plants that can be used in pots. Those that run, spreading by stolons or underground roots, tend to be unhappy as they have very little room to spread and soon become congested and unhappy. Those that are clump forming or form a single plant are usually quite happy as long as they are fed and watered.

While perennials can be mixed in containers, as usually happens with annuals, they usually look better if kept to a single species. Many can make quite a dramatic effect. A large container of bear's breeches (*Acanthus mollis*) for example, can look very spectacular. These tend to have a long season, but it is equally possible to grow lilies in pots, for example, which can simply be brought out for the short while they are in flower. Grouping several containers together, perhaps in the corner of a terrace or paved area, can be very effective and makes a good substitute for a border in a small garden where there is no space for one. Such plantings are also valuable for those that only have a roof garden.

It is not essential to place only one type of plant in each container and if it is big enough several species or cultivars can be effectively mixed, perhaps contrasting the shape and texture of the foliage and flowers. For plants that die back below ground, i.e. herbaceous plants, it is possible to provide these with more interest in the earlier part of the year by underplanting them with small bulbs or some sort. Snowdrops (*Galanthus*) or crocuses are particularly effective. There is no reason why larger bulbs such as daffodils (*Narcissus*) and tulips should not be used with other plants in containers that are big enough. In fact the combination of plants is only limited by the number that the container will support, and the willingness of the gardener to tend to their needs.

Perennials in containers can be a very versatile and useful way of growing them, particularly for gardeners who have paved areas or very small gardens. They take a bit more looking after than those planted in the open border but the effort is well worth it.

# CHAPTER 14

# Cottage Gardens

Of all the forms of gardening, that of cottage gardening is thought by many to be the most romantic. The chocolate box image of a thatched cottage with roses round the door and windows, and with a garden full of flowers spilling out over the path, is something that many wish to emulate. Whether we can create a true cottage garden now is open to debate as one of the qualities that owners of such gardens had was a simple naivety that did not take into consideration such things as design; these gardens just happened. New plants were put where there were gaps and annuals were left to sow themselves wherever they liked. The result was a patchwork of colour with no apparent order to it. Perhaps, nowadays, we know too much and strive too consciously towards a particular design to create such a work of art.

Having said that, there are still many gardens that come close to the original and great fun and pleasure can be had in creating a cottage garden effect. One of the pleasures of this sort of garden is the type of plants that are used. Old-fashioned flowers had a simplicity and beauty that many modern cultivars cannot touch. It is very difficult to know why, but this type of plant has a quality that makes them stand out. Grannies bonnets or columbines (*Aquilegia vulgaris*) are old fashioned and definitely belong to the cottage garden. We know that from written accounts and from pictures, but they also have an indefinable look that immediately marks them out.

Most of the plants grown were tough: cottage gardeners had no recourse to modern chemical sprays and if a plant could not survive then it died or was thrown away. This toughness is why so many of them have come down to us and one of the reasons why cottage gardening is popular today. A simple, but not always infallible test, as to whether a plant belongs in an old-fashioned cottage garden is to see whether it has a vernacular name or not; those with purely Latin names are unlikely to have been grown (not because they had Latin names but because if they had been grown it is likely that an English name of some sort would have been given to them).

Another characteristic of these old plants is that they are easy to propagate. The cottager had little time or facilities for complicated procedures. Most came readily from seed or were clump-forming plants that could be easily divided. Increasing plants by cutting was often confined to breaking off a piece of the plant and pushing it into the ground. Only the most amenable and toughest of plants would survive.

Having already said that cottage gardens were not designed it is difficult to go on now and tell you how to design one. I can only repeat that in essence the attraction of a cottage garden lies in its overall appearance as a wonderful jumble of plants, often planted so close together that there is no need to stake plants as they hold each other up. To designers' eyes many of the colours clash violently but somehow this enhances rather than detracts from the overall appearance.

I live in a very old cottage and the large front garden is very much a cottagey one, but when I think back to its origins I cannot remember how I first laid it out. Certainly I went for plants that had an old-fashioned feel about them. I certainly did not set out to make clashing combinations or other combinations that one would not normally put together; nature eventually takes care of that by self-sowing plants. Quite a number of annuals and biennials, such as foxgloves (*Digitalis purpurea*) and antirrhinums, were introduced in the first place and thereafter they looked after themselves. In traditional fashion, new plants were introduced into existing gaps rather than redoing the whole borders. Gradually this built up into a wonderful *mêlée* of flowers.

One of the characteristics of many cottage gardens was that there was no strict delimitation between flowers and vegetables, the two merged and often overlapped. Thus chrysanthemums could be found growing next to cabbages. Fruit trees and bushes have been popular in such gardens since the middle ages.

Plants were allowed to flop over the front paths, especially pinks (*Dianthus*) and rock roses (*Helianthemum*). As a rule paths leading to front doors were straight; curves were left for lesser paths amongst the flowers.

Cottage garden paths were always made of local materials, often stone or brick. The subsidiary paths would often consist of beaten earth covered with ashes from the fire, or perhaps gravel or small stones if they were available. Gates and fences were usually of wood; iron could only be afforded by the larger houses.

## Cottage-garden plants

The season in the cottage garden starts early with crocuses and daffodils (*Narcissus*), moving onto primroses (*Primula vulgaris*) and the cheerful polyanthus in many colours. Spring would be a gay time with bluebells (*Hyancinthoides non-scripta*), wallflowers (*Cheiranthus*), and surprisingly perhaps, crown imperials (*Fritillaria imperialis*) all adding their colours to the patchwork.

As spring moved on towards and into summer, the garden would really come into its own with lily-of-the-valley (*Convallaria majalis*), violas, lupins, dame's violet (*Hesperis matrionalis*), lady's mantle (*Alchemilla mollis*), poached egg-flower (*Limnanthes douglasii*), peonies, delphiniums, pinks (*Dianthus*) and many others. Summer would continue with the many white, yellow and orange daisies, as well as hollyhocks, phlox and geraniums.

Autumn would see the garden still colourful with michaelmas daisies (*Aster novi-belgii*), Japanese anemones (*Anemone* × *hybrida*) and fuchsias that had flowered throughout the summer.

The list is as endless as the cottage garden is timeless.

# CHAPTER 15

# *Herb Gardens*

Many herbs are perennials and they represent one of the oldest forms of gardening there is. They can be treated in one of three ways. In the first they can be treated as any other hardy perennials and be mixed into the borders along with plants that are solely decorative. Thus there may be a clump of chives (*Allium schoenoprasum*) at the front of a border nestling amongst geraniums or silver-leaved plants, or a stately plant of angelica towards the back. In the second place they can be planted in the vegetable garden either as individual plants or in rows. But since they are decorative plants, it is often the third method that appeals to most gardeners; that of making a separate herb garden or border.

The concept of herb gardens suggests a romantic setting to most people, but alas, unless they are done well they can become a sprawling, overgrown mess. Some gardeners prefer it this way and produce a herb garden, much in the style of an old-fashioned cottage garden with herbs tightly mixed in together. This type of gardening has been described in Chapter 14 and little more need be said about it.

Another approach to herb gardening is no less romantic but it is a much more formal approach. Here different herbs are kept separate in individual plots, sometimes surrounded by miniature box (*Buxus sempervirens* 'Suffruticosa') hedges or brick paths. The different plots can be arranged in a

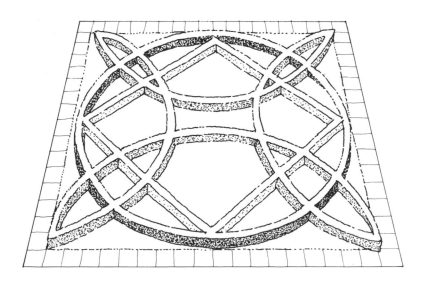

**Fig. 15.1** Herbs can be grown in patterns created by low box hedges or simply paths, in the form of a knot garden.

variety of patterns, perhaps based on the old knot gardens, or simpler patterns based on segments of the circle (Fig. 15.1). One popular device is to grow the herbs between the spokes of an old cart-wheel (Fig. 15.2). The advantage of keeping herbs in small separate compartments, divided or surrounded by paths, is that they are easy to get at; it must be remembered that herbs are for use as well as to look at. Since herbs are required for cooking and other purposes, whatever the weather, it is a good idea to use solid paths rather than grass ones. In appearance gravel and brick are the most sympathetic. In winter few herbs are above ground and if concrete or even paving slabs are used, the garden can look a pale barren waste.

Herbs are difficult to keep tidy and many attempts to create a garden of such plants are given up in despair at the resulting chaos. At the younger stages of their growth many look compact and under control, but somewhere around mid-summer, many get leggy and start to flop over each other. The key to successful herb gardening is not to pack the various compartments too close to each other; any that the design needs to be small or closely packed should contain only the lower-growing plants. Get to know your plants and keep those that do become tall and floppy, lemon balm (*Melissa officinalis*) for example, in areas where they will not smother other plants. An alternative is to cut down the stems once they have passed their prime so that the plant puts on a new flush of young growth.

This is not the place to go into the uses of herbs – there are many specialist books that cover the subject – but suffice it to say that they can be used in the kitchen and for medicinal purposes, as well as for scented potpourris, dyeing and many other household applications. Not all herbs are visually attractive – indeed some are quite dull – but most emit a fragrance if touched or bruised, and much enjoyment can be had from just wandering through such a garden, trailing fingers through the plants.

Herbs are likely to attract many bees and other insects to the garden and one of the many pleasing aspects about this is the constant sound of buzzing as the bees go about their business. If one or more hives are kept, then the herbs provide a very useful back-up to the other plants in the area, for supplying nectar and pollen, particularly late in the season when the bees are stocking up for winter.

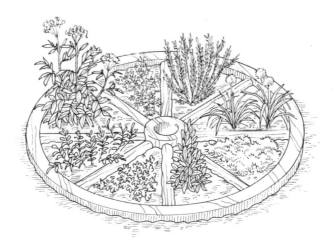

**Fig. 15.2** A simple decorative device for herbs is to grow them in the sections created by the spokes of a cart-wheel.

# PART IV
## A–Z OF HARDY PERENNIALS

# CHAPTER 16

# *List of Hardy Perennials*

The number of perennials that are suitable for including in a garden is well beyond the scope of one book, and so the list that follows has to be, by necessity, a selective one. I have tried to include all the basic plants that one would expect to find, plus a few unusual ones of which I am rather fond. It is difficult to be objective about plants, as any gardener knows, and so this is very much a personal list. Doubtless there are some plants omitted, for which I apologize, but I hope readers will find some unexpected and new plants with which to furnish their gardens.

## Plant names

Naming of plants is fraught with difficulties. It is remarkable how unstable Latin names are when their intention is to present a plant with an unequivocal name throughout the world. There are good reasons why changes occur, of course, but they are still a nuisance. I have tried to use the latest forms of name in this book, so that it will hold its validity for many years to come. Unfortunately, this has meant that I have had to acknowledge the passing of such genera as *Chrysanthemum* and *Polygonum* and include new tongue-twisters in their place.

I have only partially embraced the breakdown of the family of Liliaceae and have included both the new and the old names which have been indicated thus: **Polygonatum** (Convallariaceae/Liliaceae).

The giving of cultivar names is getting a bit out of hand. While it is justifiable, indeed essential, to give names to new forms that are worthy of introduction, too many nurseries and individuals seem to be giving names to every seedling that they raise. This means that plant lists are becoming overburdened with names for plants that are so similar in appearance that the names become meaningless. The sad thing now is that many of the larger commercial organizations, both plant and seed distributors, are giving cultivar names to the species in the attempt either to appear to have their own better form or to make the name appear easier or more catchy to the purchaser. In the lists that follow, although cultivars and hybrids are often referred to by name, emphasis has been given to the species, often with just a blanket reference to the different colours available as cultivars.

While many genera have vernacular names (*Eryngium* – sea hollies, for example) it has also been custom in recent years to refer to the Latin name as if it were English. This is not so strange, as for several generations we have referred to rhododendrons, chrysanthemums, delphiniums and so on; but now gardeners also refer to senecios and kniphofias as if they were everyday terms. In the list below only the true vernacular names have been given in the headings, but the alternative Latin version has often been used in the texts below.

## Height

The heights of the plants that are given are generally, unless otherwise stated, to the top of the plant when it is in flower – in other words it includes the height of the flowering stem. Similarly, unless otherwise stated, it can be assumed that the plants described below are generally hardy, down to $-15°C$ (5°F), with the majority to at least $-20°C$ ($-4°F$).

**ACANTHUS** (Acanthaceae) – Bear's breeches

There is no doubt that this is one of the cornerstones of any garden that contains decorative borders. It has all the qualities that one demands from a good herbaceous plant. The plant itself has a bold, statuesque appearance which is good for giving architectural emphasis to a border and, when cut, to the flower arrangement. The deeply cut foliage is a good dark glossy green, and this is surmounted by tall spikes of hooded flowers. The hoods are of a smoky-mauve colour, veined with green. The lower lips of the flower, which look more like floppy tongues than lips, are white. Each flower head is surrounded by spiny bracts. If one wanted to compare shape with that of a more familiar flower, then the foxglove would immediately spring to mind.

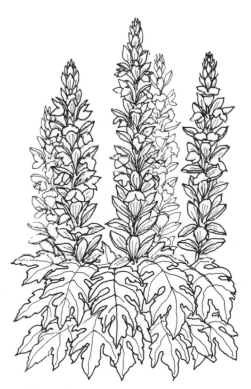

**Acanthus**

There are two species generally in cultivation, *Acanthus spinosus* and *A. mollis*. The 'spinosus' of the former refers to the leaves which are tipped with spines; in *A. mollis* the ends of the leaf segments are rounded. They are both about 90–120 cm (3–4 ft) tall and as much across when fully grown. The flowers of both species are similar but *A. spinosus* is probably the more free flowering of the two. Flowering commences in the late summer and continues into the autumn. Even before the flowers arrive the foliage of both species has much to commend it. *A. spinosus* has a variety *A.s. spinosissimus* which has more spiny leaves, the spines having a definite silvery-white sheen. *A. mollis* is more commonly represented in gardens by its variety *A.m. latifolius* which is larger and more robust than the type. If one has to choose between the two species, then *A. spinosus* is probably the better plant.

Acanthus has a history to compare with its stature, going back to Greek and Roman times and possibly beyond. The leaves are familiar to anyone who has examined classical Greek columns as it forms the main decorative element around the capital or top. The date of introduction into the British Isles is unknown but it was definitely here by the middle of the sixteenth century and could have been introduced as early as the beginning of the thirteenth.

Siting presents no problem as they are happy in both sun or light shade, although the former is preferred. There is no problem with hardiness as plants have locally survived temperatures of −15°C (5°F) with no adverse effects.

They are equally happy in most soils and will even grow on chalk. However, deep fertile soils suit them best and under such conditions they will quickly form a large colony.

Propagation is easily achieved from seed, division or root cuttings. Seed should be sown in the spring. Division and root cuttings can be undertaken any time during fine weather, from late autumn until the spring. It is one of the easiest of plants to propagate from root cuttings, as anyone removing an old plant by digging it out is likely to find (any portion of the roots left below ground will shoot and soon form a new plant). Plants raised in pots should be regularly potted on and planted out as soon as possible before the tap roots protrude through the bottom of the container.

## ACHILLEA (Compositae) – Yarrow

Yarrow is quite a contrast to the last plant in that the leaves are mainly light and feathery and the flowers held in flat heads. The main colour is also a contrast: it's yellow.

This is another mainstay of the herbaceous border giving good strong colours at the height of summer and beyond. These plants give enjoyment beyond their life in the border as they make fine cut stems for flower arranging and maintain their colour when dried for longer use.

In the border they quickly form large clumps of self-supporting stems, the height of which varies from a few inches to 150 cm (5 ft) or more. Except for *Achillea ptarmica*, the leaves have a much cut, feathery appearance, the colour varying from silver to dark green according to the species. The flower heads consist of many small daisy-like flowers arranged in a flat head. Most species produce yellow flowers, but a few produce white and in recent years there has been an increase in other, often garish, colours.

For the general border the tall and medium height plants are the most useful. *Achillea filipendulina* is one of the tallest, particularly in its fine form 'Gold Plate'. This and its slightly smaller but close relation 'Coronation Gold', are of a deep gold or mustard colour and are most useful for the warmer-coloured parts of the border. Of slightly cooler colours are *A.* 'Moonshine' and *A.* × *taygetea*. *A.* 'Moonshine' has a silvery-grey foliage which beautifully sets off the bright sulphur flowers. *A.* × *taygetea* is of a much softer yellow and is suitable for mixing into different colour schemes. The leaves are a grey-green. Both are about 60 cm (2 ft) tall and flower earlier than their taller relations.

Two of the white achilleas are derived from species native to England. *A. millefolium* is the wayside yarrow that can be a bit of a nuisance if it gets into the garden. It is sometimes introduced with lawn turf. However it is a splendid plant to have in the wild garden and it does produce a fine dark pink form, 'Cerise Queen'. This plant is best when it is still fresh, when it has a good rich colour; but as it fades it begins to look very drab. There is also a lilac-coloured cultivar, 'Lilac Beauty'.

The other white form is *A. ptarmica* (sneezewort). Unlike the other achilleas, this does not have feathery leaves and the flowers are more like small buttons than flat plates. It is best known in its double forms, of which 'The Pearl' is the best. It is a very good border plant, lightening up dark corners over quite a long period, and it makes a good cut flower. Unfortunately it does have the drawback that it is invasive and should not be introduced into a small border unless its rampant habit can be contained in some way.

In recent times new colour strains have been introduced in the form of 'Galaxy hybrids' which as well as the usual colours include pinks, reds and salmon colours. For my taste they look too much like bedding plants and for the moment, until some good forms have been raised, should be treated as such.

Some of the small species, such as *A. ageratifolia*, *argentea* and *tomentosa*, make good clump-forming plants for the front of the border. They mainly come from hot countries and therefore like a sunny position that is not overtopped by other plants. Their leaves are generally silvery and the first two above have white flowers and the third yellow.

*Achillea* will grow in any fertile soil but should be given full sun or it will quickly become leggy and flower poorly.

They can be propagated by division in the spring or by cuttings. When dividing a plant, throw away the old woody material in the centre and just use the newer growth found round the outside of the old plant. The silvery-leaved varieties such as *A.* 'Moonshine' need replacing every two or three years as they get very leggy and untidy.

**ACONITUM** (Ranunculaceae) –
Monkshood, wolfsbane

These attractive flowers are closely related to the delphinium and this relationship can clearly be seen in the tall spikes of blue flowers. The name monkshood is derived from the upper petal which closely resembles a hood, or to others who call it helmet flower, a helmet. Its other vernacular name, wolfsbane, derives from its use as a poison against wolves. Now that the days are gone when it was necessary to forage the hedgerows for food, the chances that someone will dig up a root and eat it are remote, but it is this part of the plant that is the most poisonous. Some people are alarmed at these and other poisonous plants and worry about putting them in the garden, but with the exception of those with poisonous berries which children might eat, there is little chance of accidentally eating parts of these plants and causing a fatal illness.

Aconitum are not as brash as delphiniums and do not make such a bold statement, but are none the less very valuable for the border. Different species flower at different times, giving a long flowering period from early summer into autumn. The blue flowers vary in intensity and there are white and yellow forms to add variety.

*Aconitum carmichaelii* (previously known as *A. fischeri*) is probably the best of all the species. It is a medium-sized plant, reaching up to 120 cm (4 ft) with dark green, deeply divided foliage. The flowers are a lovely light blue, often described as Wedgwood blue. One of the commonest and best of the cultivars is *A.c.* 'Arendsii' which has much darker blue flowers. A taller and more vigorous form is *A.c. wilsonii* which was introduced, as its name suggests, by E.H. Wilson from China. Its blue colour varies, but there is a particularly good form known as *A.c.w.* 'Barkers Variety' with violet blue flowers and another *A.c.w.* 'Kelmscott' which is richer in colour. *A. carmichaelii* and all its forms flower in the autumn and are useful for adding the colour blue to the border at that time of year.

*A. napellus* is the common monkshood, growing wild in Britain, from which many good garden forms have been derived. This is one of the earliest to flower in the year, usually in the early summer. It grows up to 150 cm (5 ft). Two interesting forms are *A.n.* 'Album' with white flowers and *A.n.* 'Carneum' with pink flowers. *A. vulparia* is the species from which the poison was extracted to kill wolves, hence its Latin as well as its English name. It is a slender-stemmed plant, reaching 150 cm (5 ft), with creamy-white flowers. While most of the aconitum are self-supporting, this is one that needs an extra bit of help. There are quite a number of other species and hybrids but I am only going to mention one more, *A.* × *bicolor*. This is a blanket name for a whole series of hybrid cultivars. Bressingham have introduced several of the most important. 'Bressingham Spire' is a good violet blue. 'Ivorine', a much shorter plant, is a very good creamy white. Others include 'Bicolor' and 'Blue Sceptre', both with violet-blue and white flowers. Probably the best form is 'Spark's Variety', which is now often listed under *A. henryi*, with its rich violet-blue flowers.

Aconitum prefer fertile moisture-retentive soils, but will tolerate most soils. They are a useful plant in that they will grow in either full sun or partial shade.

Propagation can be from seed, preferably sown fresh, or from division in the autumn or winter. The tuberous roots can be left *in situ* for many years but they seem to benefit from being split up and replanted every four or five years. Any pieces left behind when a plant is removed will usually throw up a new plant.

**ADONIS** (Ranunculaceae)

The perennial plants of this genus are exquisite and it is well worth while trying to acquire at least one, even if it does mean pawning your car to do it. The combination of the large golden flowers and the ferny leaves is truly beautiful. Like so many of the buttercup family, they flower in the spring.

One of the most exquisite is *A. vernalis*. This has the finest foliage of them all, the leaves are very narrow and silky to the touch. More commonly seen in nurseries and earlier to come into flower is *A. armurensis* from Japan. This is not quite such a refined plant as the previous, but still acquiring. This has a double form *A.a.* 'Plena' that is very popular.

These are plants of leafy soils that should never dry out completely. Ordinary soil with extra organic material should suffice. They prefer a shady position, but their appearance is even more enhanced if the late winter or spring sun occasionally catches the petals. Propagation is by careful division, or from seed if it is available.

## AGAPANTHUS (Alliaceae/Liliaceae) – African lily

A well-grown group of agapanthus can cause a great deal of delight. Suddenly to see the balls of blue flowers in late summer or autumn, can take the breath away. Because they originate in South Africa they were for many years considered to be tender plants and it was recommended that they were grown in tubs to be wheeled in and out of shelter each year. Fortunately there are now many hardy forms which can be left in the border where their hungry roots can become established. Although they can look magnificent in tubs and quite unlike anything else, a permanent planting needs far less attention and possibly produces better results.

Agapanthus belongs to the Alliaceae, which means it is closely related to the lily and amaryllis families. The arching, fleshy, strap-like leaves are beautiful in their own right. They form dense clumps from which rise leafless stems, which bear a round ball of small lily-like flowers. The colour varies from light to dark blue and there are white forms. Some are deciduous and others evergreen; it is the latter which are tender, the former usually coming through most winters. The white roots are very fleshy and form a tight mat just below the surface of the soil. They resent disturbance which makes weeding difficult, so this is a good case for mulching.

The nomenclature is in a bit of a mess. This is not only because the species are often difficult to tell apart, but because

**Agapanthus**

there has been a lot of hybridizing. This means that naming of the plant is not always accurate. I tend to favour seeing them in flower before selecting which ones I want to acquire.

The commonest available, but none the worst for that are the Headbourne hybrids, derived mainly from crosses with *A. campanulatus*. These were the forms that first made gardeners aware that agapanthus were hardier than previously thought. This is not one cultivar, but a whole series of them so there is quite a variation in the colour blue. If you are wanting to use several plants to form a clump all of the same shade, and the plants are just labelled 'Headbourne hybrids', then it is best to see them in flower. Some of the forms, however, have been

Blue and silver makes a pleasing association, although it is not something that should be overdone.

Yellows and blues can make a refreshing combination. The green holds the colours together, preventing them from being overpowering.

*Below:* The combination of hot colours can be visually very exciting, but avoid overdoing it otherwise the eye will become restless, with nowhere to settle.

Sometimes colours that would not normally be
put together, accidentally associate producing
bizarre but exciting effects.

*Above:* In the wilder part of the garden sudden splashes of colour contrast well with lush vegetation.

At other times accidental associations, such as this self-sown *Meconopsis cambrica* and *Euphorbia griffithii* 'Fireglow', work very well.

Texture and shapes can also create the interest in
the wild garden, particularly in shade where
bright flowers are likely to be lacking in summer.

*Oenothera stricta* is a short-lived perennial with flowers that only last for one day. It is scented.

*Helenium*
'Waldtraut'. The
heleniums are
wonderful clump-
forming plants
that are one of the
mainstays of the
summer border.

*Inula hookeri*
These delicately
cut flowers appear
on a somewhat
coarse plant that
likes a damp soil.
It can spread quite
quickly.

127

*Dactylorhiza foliosa.* Hardy orchids are not the easiest of plants to grow. However, this is one of the less difficult as well as one of the most striking.

selected and multiplied vegetatively under clonal names, giving a constant colour. One of the best is the dark blue 'Isis'. Other dark blues include 'Cherry Holly', 'Dorothy Palmer', 'Loch Hope', 'Midnight Blue', and 'Molly Howick'. Light blues include 'African Moon', 'Blue Moon', 'Lily'. The finest of the white hybrids is undoubtedly 'Alice Gloucester'.

If you get hooked on agapanthus, then there are many more species and hybrids to explore but they are nearly all variations on the same theme.

Agapanthus are happy in quite a range of soils. Some gardeners recommend rich, moisture-retentive soil, but I have them growing very well in dry stony soil above a soakaway. They must have plenty of sun.

Propagation is very easy either from seed or dividing up a clump in the spring. It grows well from seed sown in the spring, although it is a long process, taking up to three or even four years to get a decent-sized flowering plant. Copious amounts of seed are set, but in some years an early onset of winter might occur before it is ripe. Seed will give plants of varying shades; use division if you want to ensure the continuance of particular colours.

## AGASTACHE (Labiatae)
These are not plants to set the world alight, but they have a quiet presence that more than earns them their keep in the border.

*A. foeniculum* is a plant that I always enjoy. It looks a bit like a mint, with cylindrical spikes of mauve flowers that appear in summer and autumn. The whole plant has a soft appearance that would appeal to romantic gardeners. I am not certain about the fragrance though, as the leaves smell of aniseed when crushed. It does not run like mint, but it does seed itself rather generously. *S. mexicana* is the other main species that is seen. This is a similar bushy plant, but it has red flowers that can vary from pink to crimson. The flower spikes are more slender and lax. This plant is fragrant as well.

Both like a well-drained soil with plenty of sunshine.

Propagation is easily accomplished from seed, of which copious amounts are set.

## AJUGA (Labiatae) – Bugle
Ajuga is quite a large genus of about 40 perennials and annuals, but in spite of this *A. reptans* and its cultivars are virtually the only species in common cultivation. They are low-growing herbs that are valued mainly for their ground-covering qualities. The flowers are blue and are carried in spikes of up to 25 cm (10 in) high. It is mainly the foliage that gives the various cultivars their variation. Some are deep purple ('Atropurpurea') in colour; others are red ('Burgundy Glow'); others variegated ('Variegata'); while still further examples are marbled with three colours ('Multicolor' or 'Tricolor').

They are plants of light shade and moist soil, although they will tolerate a surprising amount of dryness. In the wild they are always seen at their best in damp ground where the sun can occasionally get through to them. They form a dense carpet and can become quite invasive given the right conditions.

They are very easy to propagate as they spread by runners, much in the manner of strawberries and the new plants can be easily split off from the mass. Of course it is also possible to grow them from seed but the cultivars are unlikely to come true.

## ALCEA (Malvaceae) – Hollyhocks
Latin names are supposed to be a stable form of identification of a plant that holds true in any country where the plant is spoken of. Unfortunately there is a tendency (usually for valid reasons) for names to change from time to time. *Alcea* was until recently, and still is in most nurseries and garden centres, known as *Althaea*, but to most English-speaking people they are known as hollyhocks – the epitome of the cottage garden. The tall spires of dish-shaped flowers seem to breathe peace and tranquillity – that is until the winds come and they start thrashing around and leaning at crazy angles. In spite of their height, sometimes up to 3 m (10 ft) or more, they

are in fact usually quite stable and really only need support in the more exposed positions.

Although strictly speaking perennials, they are best treated as biennials as they suffer rather badly from rust diseases which disfigure the leaves and saps the energy of the plant. They are perennial in the sense that they sow themselves around and one is rarely without plants once they have adopted your garden. This is the first year for 14 years that I have been without self-sown plants, all going back to two or three original plants, and this is probably due to over-zealous weeding on my part, although since writing this I have seen seedlings pushing up for next season.

By far the commonest species is *Alcea rosea* which in spite of its name comes in an incredible range of colours, varying from white and soft pastels to a red so dark that it is almost black. As well as singles there are doubles available that look like powder puffs. The flowers are held on tall straight stems with the buds and seedpods forming little balls above and below the current blooms. Some seed merchants sell seed of much shorter varieties, but these are a pale imitation of their stately brothers, in spite of their greater security against the weather.

Until recently *A. rosea* was the only species generally grown but in the past few years *A. rugosa* has gained in popularity amongst plantsmen. This is more of a shrubby plant with many branches sprouting from the base to form a plant 150 cm (5 ft) wide and up to the same height when mature. The flowers are all the same colour: a lovely pale yellow.

Hollyhocks are tolerant of most soils, but grow largest in rich, moisture-retentive soil. They prefer a sunny position, although I have grown them quite happily in a north-facing border with only partial sun.

Seed is the only method of propagation. These are held in round 'cheeses' resembling motor car tyres. It is always worth collecting your own seed just to see the extraordinary ways that nature has devised for packaging and dispersing them. It should be sown in the spring and planted out in their permanent positions as soon as possible as they resent disturbance.

## ALCHEMILLA (Rosaceae) – Lady's mantle

What a love-hate relationship one has with this plant! Love when it is where it should be and hate when it has wandered from the straight and narrow. In spite of its wayward tendency, it is a plant that no garden should be without. The lady's mantle of the name is derived from the shape of the leaves which are roughly circular with a wavy, toothed edge and veins, forming deep folds or pleats, radiating from the centre. The leaves are also hairy and this quality, plus the folds, often cause them to hold quicksilver droplets of water, which make them such an admirable target for photographers. The light green leaves are overtopped by froths of yellowish-green flowers. It is equally at home in a formal planting or a wild garden and combines well with a variety of colours. The light green colour of both leaves and flowers makes it a good plant for lightening up a dark corner. The flowers have a curious aromatic fragrance of which I am quite fond. It makes an excellent cut flower, especially with blue sweet peas.

One of its annoying habits is its tendency to self sow everywhere. With some plants this does not matter too much but with alchemilla it is often very difficult to weed them out, especially when they lodge themselves in cracks in the paving or, worse still, in the middle of another plant. If the whole plant is sheared over when flowering begins to go over then the problem is avoided. There is also the bonus, in that the plant immediately produces a new crop of leaves, which are more attractive than the ageing ones.

I have been writing all along about *Alchemilla mollis* which is the only member of a surprisingly large genus (over 200 species) that is large enough to be considered for the herbaceous border. There are however quite a lot suitable for the alpine garden and one of these, *A. conjuncta*, although low, is robust enough to be considered for the front of a border. It has darker green, more deeply cut leaves which are hairless except for the margins and the reverse, both of which are given a true silver appearance by the silky hairs. It does occasionally self sow, but very mildly compared to its bigger relation. It is at home in a wide range of conditions, but is probably happiest in damp or moisture-retentive soil. Beside a pool or stream is an ideal position. There is no problem with sun or shade as it will take both.

Propagation is all too readily achieved by seed. I have never actually heard of anybody deliberately sowing this plant; there are always more than enough self-sown seedlings around to provide for most of any gardener's needs.

## ALLIUM (Alliaceae/Liliaceae) – Onions

Although this is a book about hardy perennials it is impossible to ignore some of the bulbs (which are, after all, hardy perennials). They feature quite strongly in many mixed borders and are valuable in contributing unusual shapes to the plantings as their purple globes are quite unique. The taller species are usefully planted amongst other plants which disguise the rather tatty leaves that many of them sport at flowering time, and yet allows their round heads of flowers to float above the foliage of other plants awaiting their own turn in flowering.

Once we start on alliums we could go on with them for the rest of this book as there are about 450 species, with getting on for 200 species and cultivars in cultivation. It is probably the taller ones that are the most eye catching, with *A. christophii* (*A. albopilosum*) being the most spectacular. This has spherical heads that are up to 20–25 cm (8–10 in) wide and are carried on 30 cm (12 in) stems. They look marvellous in a grouping and have a second chance as they make excellent dried flowers for the house. These are best grown at or near the front of a border; further back can be planted *A. giganteum*, which have denser heads which shows up the colour.

Not so large in height, size of stem or flowers is *A. sphaerocephalon*. The flower heads are roughly spherical, about 5 cm (2 in) in diameter, and of a deep crimson red. With much looser heads is *A. pulchellum*. This has pink flowers and a bluish stem. It is extremely pretty, but there is a price to pay if the heads are not cut off before it seeds, in that it is one of the most rampant seedling plants around.

Of a smaller nature is the plant that is used a great deal as a herb, the chive, *A. schoenoprasum*. This has tufts of pink flowers. It is a plant that can be used in the front of a border as well as the herb garden, but there is a much larger form *A.s.* 'Forescate' which is better for this purpose.

Onions can be rampant plants to add to a border, but they do add a great deal both in the shape and colours of their flowers. I have only mentioned a few of the major ones; there are plenty of others to explore if the gardener gets hooked on them.

They all prefer a well-drained soil and full sun. They tend to propagate themselves but if you want to take a hand they can be raised from seed or by the divison of the bulbs.

## ALSTROEMERIA (Alstroemeriaceae/ Liliaceae) – Peruvian lilies

This is a genus that has increased enormously in popularity in recent years. Like the agapanthus and trilliums they inhabit a twilight zone between bulbs and herbaceous plants. The similarity with agapanthus does not end there; they too were considered generally too tender for the open garden until the hardy strain of hybrids were developed: the Ligtu hybrids. That their hardiness is now beyond dispute can be illustrated by a tale against myself of a polythene bag of donated tubers naughtily left lying, forgotten on the open ground, through one of the severe winters of late. In spite of the lack of protection I planted them out when I rediscovered them the following spring and they survived. This is not a recommended practice for any plant, but I suppose it is one way of selecting hardy forms.

Alstroemerias have lily-like flowers in a range of pastel and hot colours which are reminiscent of their South American home. The leaves are strange in that they appear to be worn upside-down, with the bottom uppermost. After flowering they produce curiously shaped seed pods borne on candelabra-like stems. They belong to that race of garden plants that include cyclamen and *Meconopsis cambrica*, that seem impossible to establish in a garden until one day they suddenly appear to be everywhere. The roots are rather brittle and can be easily damaged and any transplanting should be done with care. Pot grown plants are easiest to establish as, with care, there is no need to disturb the roots. Once established they are inclined to run about a bit, often popping up in unexpected places.

The first to become popular was *Alstroemeria aurantiaca*. In spite of being superseded by better plants it is still widely grown, although some gardeners consider it little better than a weed. As its name implies it has orange flowers, which are held on 100 cm (3 ft) stems. Their reputation as a weed comes from their tendency to run. 'Dover Orange' is the most popular of its cultivars. This is a good rich orange. 'Lutea' is a good yellow form and 'Aurea' is between the two, being a golden-yellow.

The Ligtu hybrids were developed in the 1920s. They produce their trumpets in a range of soft pastel pinks and apricots as well as some hotter oranges and reds, and white. As with all the alstroemerias, they make good cut flowers, lasting a long time in water. They are truly hardy.

*A. pulchella* has become popular of late. This has strangely marked red and green flowers. It is not so hardy as the other two and does need some protection.

They are not too fussy about the type of soil as long as it is free draining. A sunny position is preferred but some will tolerate a light shade. The protection of a wall might be appreciated in some of the colder areas and certainly this would be preferable for some of the more tender species that are available.

Since they can be difficult to establish the easiest way to propagate is by thinly sowing seed and then planting out the whole pot-ful of seedlings without disturbing them. To keep the true colours it is necessary to propagate vegetatively and this can be done by carefully dividing the plant and transplanting a piece of it with a large root ball, so that the brittle roots are not damaged.

## ANAPHALIS (Compositae) – Pearl everlasting

With anaphalis we enter into the field of silver plants, which are so popular these days. They are a good foil for so many colours and of course are extremely good in white and silver arrangements. The flowers are everlasting and consist of papery white bracts which rustle when they are touched. In this they are similar to helichrysums, to which they are related. They are quite small and are gathered together in large clusters. Like helichrysums they make good cut flowers and are suitable for drying. The leaves are more green or grey than some of the other 'silvers', but nonetheless the overall effect is of a silvery plant.

*Anaphalis cinnamomea*, previously known as *A. yedoensis*, is one of my favourites. It has willow-shaped, green leaves on which only the margins and the reverse are touched with silver hairs. The silver margins, contrasting with the green central part of the leaves, gives the plant a wonderfully fresh look. It is up to 75 cm (30 in) tall and has a spread which is constantly increasing due to its creeping roots. Spreading it might be, but it is not too invasive and is easy to control.

The other popular species is *A. triplinervis*. This is a shorter plant with similar papery-white flowers with a yellow centre. The leaves are woolly with hairs on both sides. *A. margaritacea* is very similar.

At the bottom end of the scale is *A. nubigena* which grows not much taller than 20–30 cm (8–9 in) and is useful for the front of a border.

Anaphalis are not too fussy as to the soil they require but can become a bit limp if conditions get too dry. They undoubtedly prefer the sun, but will put up with a little shade if not too dense. Silver-leaved plants normally hate any form of shade, which makes anaphalis particularly useful in such situations.

Propagation is simply by division in the spring. They all gently spread by underground rhizomes and it is easy to take off a piece to replant elsewhere. There is a tendency for the centres of the plants to die out after a few years, when the plant should be divided up and replanted, discarding the older central portion.

## ANCHUSA (Boraginaceae)

It is surpising how few plants have flowers that are true blue. There is usually a hint of red or purple lurking somewhere, or they are paled with white. The anchusa help to fill the gap as the forget-me-not-type flowers of several of the 40 or so species in the genus have deep, rich blue flowers. Unfortunately, and there always has to be a snag in gardening, they are only short-lived and should be treated as biennials.

The supreme one is *A. azurea*, sometimes still known as *A. italica* (which is odd as the plant in fact comes from the Caucasus). This is a tall plant growing to 150 cm (5 ft), but the bristly stems are a bit floppy so staking is usually required. In spite of this disadvantage, plus the fact that they are not very good after their first year as already mentioned, the intensity of their blue flowers make them very popular. Several cultivars have been selected as being the best forms, of which 'Loddon Royalist' and 'Royal Blue' have deep blue flowers and 'Opal' much lighter, almost sky-blue flowers. 'Little John' is a short form growing no more than 45 cm (18 in) while still retaining the deep blue flowers.

*A. leptophylla incana* (previously known under the simpler name *A. angustissima*) is a plant for the front of the border as it is no more than 30 cm (12 in) high. This also has dark blue flowers that appear over a very long period from late spring well into autumn. Again it is usually not long-lasting. One of the longest lived, *A. myosotidiflora* has been moved out of the genus into *Brunnera* as the well-known *B. macrophylla*. Another species, *A. sempervirens*, has also been moved away, this time to become *Pentaglottis sempervirens*.

Anchusas are not especially fussy as to their soil, but prefer it to be reinforced with some organic material. The taller ones need staking. Propagation is best done by taking root cuttings in winter, but they can also be grown from seed, indeed they may well self-sow if happy.

## ANEMONE (Ranunculaceae) – Wind flower

Undoubtedly this genus is one of my favourites. Anemones are a very diverse group of plants growing from just a few inches to several feet in height, and flowering at differing times from early spring to late autumn. For convenience of this book I will split them into two groups – the wood anemones and the Japanese anemones – and ignore the rest.

Wood anemones are one of the most delightful harbingers of spring. In its typical native woodland form, *Anemone nemorosa* is a delicate white-flowered plant that inhabits the woodland floor where it can catch the sun's rays before the trees put on too much leaf. It seeds immediately after flowering and then retires underground until the following spring. As well as seed it propagates itself by underground runners and once established it can get a bit invasive, but fortunately this does not generally cause a nuisance as it is unobtrusively below ground for most of the year. It is very good for planting in shady areas, particularly under deciduous trees and shrubs.

As well as its common wild form, *A. nemorosa* can be found in numerous other varieties. There are large ones like the legendary 'Leeds Variety' or those with more outer petals such as 'Hilda'. Others have wonderful double flowers like 'Vestal' or no flowers at all, or rather the flowers have been replaced by a whirl of green feathery bracts as in 'Virescens'. Even more pleasing to those that know them are the delicate blue forms such as 'Robinsoniana', 'Allenii' 'Royal Blue' and 'Blue Bonnet' – all worth looking out for.

Another great favourite of mine is the little *A. ranunculoides* which, while roughly similar in size and shape to *A. nemorosa*, is a buttercup yellow. There is a hybrid pro-

133

**Anemone**

duced between the two species called *Anemone* × *seemannii* which has delicate pale yellow flowers. *A. ranunculoides* has a beautiful double form *A.r.* 'Flore Pleno' that is well worth seeking out.

Wood anemones like the moist leafmould of the woodland floor but will thrive in any good soil. They are happy in sun or shade. Increase is easily achieved by division or from seed which should be sown soon after it has ripened. The former is, of course, the only way to propagate the named forms.

There are many more anemones of the woodland floor, such as *A. blanda* and *appennina*, but as delightful as they are, they lack the grace of those already mentioned.

Moving to the other end of the scale we now look at the Japanese anemones which to many people have more of a rightful claim to be in an herbaceous border. That they have a claim to be there I would not dispute, but I would certainly like to see their smaller brethren grown more frequently.

The naming of the Japanese anemones is in great confusion. *A. japonica*, *A. hupehensis* and *A.* × *hybrida* will be seen on garden centre labels and in the literature, but while the first two exist they are relatively rare plants, available only from specialist nurseries, and it is to *A.* × *hybrida* that most of the common cultivars of what are known as 'Japanese anemones' belong.

These are wonderfully graceful plants growing up to 150 cm (5 ft) high with thin stems which bend in the wind, but need no staking. The flowers are saucers of pink or white with yellow centres. There are quite a number of good-named forms to choose from, such as the pure white 'Honorine Jobert' and the dark pink 'Prinz Heinrich'. They all flower from the late summer through the autumn. There is no problem with soil as they will tolerate quite a good range of types. Although flowers of the sun, they will take a bit of light shade which adds to their versatility.

The Japanese anemone is one of those plants that belong to that intriguing group that can be propagated by root cuttings taken in the winter. They can also be increased by sowing seed while it is still fresh or by division in the spring. They sometimes take a while to establish themselves but once happy they will naturally increase. They are difficult to eradicate should you want to clear them from a particular piece of ground, as any piece of root inadvertently left in the ground will shoot up as a new plant.

There are many other wonderful species of anemones, but space and, to a certain extent, lack of availability, precludes any mention of them here.

**ANTHEMIS** (Compositae)
Both *Achillea* and *Anaphalis* belong to the daisy family, Compositae, but this is the first of the genus that we have come to that has big bold daisy-like flowers. There are three species contending for favouritism; one white, one yellow and one orange.

The white is an old garden favourite. *Anthemis punctata cupaniana* (all their names seem a bit of a mouthful until you get used to them) has much-cut silver foliage that forms spreading hummocks only a few inches high. The large white daisies (about 5 cm/ 2 in) across are held on thin stems 30 cm (12 in) or so above the leaves. The main flush of flowers is in the late spring, but they go on throughout the summer and well into autumn. The odd flower is even found during the winter. It can look a stunning plant; it can also look dreadful, particularly at the end of a wet season. It is best to keep it cut back and to replant it every year to prevent it getting too straggly and dying out at the cenre. It is a marvellous plant for softening the edge of a border, where it will flop out onto the path or lawn. It will often kill the grass on the latter by excluding the light. Slugs love to encamp beneath it.

There seems to be no restriction on the type of soil it likes, as long as it is reasonably free draining. A sunny position is preferred. It is extremely easy to propagate as virtually any stem that is broken off from the parent plant will root if bedded into the ground and kept moist.

*Anthemis tinctoria* 'Golden Marguerite' is a popular border plant. The flowers are yellow and are borne throughout the summer and often into the autumn. They make excellent cut flowers. This is the tallest of the three species, being up to 90 cm (3 ft) high. There are quite a number of different cultivars giving a range of yellows. Possibly the best is 'E.C.Buxton' which is a lemon yellow. A more creamy colour is 'Wargrave Variety'. For a brighter colour 'Grallach Gold' is one of the best. All of them can be a bit weak in the leg and require some sort of support to prevent them flopping. They all thrive in ordinary garden soil in a sunny position.

Propagation is by division in the spring. The newer, outside growth should be used and the middle discarded. Life of the plant is prolonged by dead-heading.

*A. sancti-johannis* has a good hot, orange colour which makes it a useful plant for the border, but at the same time a difficult plant to place. It flowers for quite a long season during the summer and into the autumn. It is a shorter plant than the preceding and has a tendency to be short-lived, but it comes readily from seed and can be divided. If there are other anthemis around, the plants might not come true from seed and paler colours might be introduced. Unless they are particularly good forms, discard any of these paler hybrids and retain the true darker-flowered plants. It likes a well-drained soil in full sun.

**AQUILEGIA** (Ranunculaceae) –
Columbine, granny's bonnet
Along with hollyhocks this is one of those plants that is most evocative of the cottage garden. The flowers are a curious shape and perhaps granny's bonnet is as good a description as any. The best way of describing it is by imagining a ballerina standing on tip-toe with her arms in the air. The stamens form the legs, the inner petals the main skirt, the divided sepals the outer twirling skirt and her raised arms and inward bent hands the strange spurs that surmount the flower. Perhaps not all ballerinas would thank me for this description as although some species are elegant, in others the overall appearance of the flower is rather dumpy. The height of the plants varies considerably according to species, but even the tallest are strong enough not to need support.

The one grown in cottage gardens that acquired the name granny's bonnet was *Aquilegia vulgaris*, which, in its typical form varies from a rich dark blue to a deep plum colour, with the occasional white one to lighten up a dark spot. Also popular with the cottagers was the double-flowered form of the same deep colours. It is happy growing in the more formal setting of a border or in the less controlled surroundings of a wild or woodland garden. They tend to self-sow themselves around but rarely become a nuisance; dead-heading will prevent this if more control is required.

*A. vulgaris* has produced some named cultivars which, mercifully, nearly always come true from seed. 'Munstead White' is a good white form. 'Adelaide Addison' is a double-flowered form in white and dark blue. Another double, but with a unique character is 'Norah Barlow'. Its many petals are made up of red, pink, green and cream.

The other group of aquilegias that are frequently seen in gardens are the Long Spurred and McKana hybrids which are large-flowered varieties that come in a mixture of reds, yellows and blues. These are grown from seed which is available from most seed houses. They are not long lived; a sunny and well-drained situation helps to prolong their life.

Among the species there are many that make very attractive garden plants. *A. canadensis* and *A. formosa* are very similar with dainty red and yellow flowers. *A. alpina* is a good blue and *A. chrysantha* has varying shades of yellow.

Aquilegias grow well on most soils but preferably one that is free draining. They will happily grow in full sun or partial shade. The latter is rather fortunate as they look good growing amongst shrubs and in woodland settings.

Propagation is generally from seed although it is also possible to divide the plants. Unless you only grow one species, or at least only species that flower at different times, there is great difficulty in keeping the seed pure as aquilegias are most promiscuous, helped by eager, itinerant bees. For best germination, sow the seed while it is still fresh.

## ARGYRANTHEMUM (Compositae)
This is the refuge of several of the more tender of the *Chrysanthemum*, of which I am going to mention one which is becoming an increasingly popular border plant. This plant was *C. frutescens* and is now known as *Argyranthemum frutescens*. It forms low bushes of yellow, pink or white typical daisy flowers. These are more delicate-looking flowers than most other chrysanthemum and look good when planted towards the front of a border or in tubs. There are a good number of named forms from which to choose. They have a very long flowering season, from summer well into autumn, but unfortunately they are not very hardy except in the milder areas and must be perpetuated by cuttings taken every year in the autumn; an effort well worth making.

*A. maderense* is another species that should perhaps be mentioned. This is a good clear yellow daisy that, again, has been increasing in popularity amongst gardeners. It is also tender.

They like a reasonably well-drained soil, although they dislike being totally dry. A warm sunny position is important.

## ARISAEMA (Aracea)
This is a large genus of hooded plants that has recently taken on a popularity of cult status. They are not plants for the open border, so I will not dwell on them for too long. They are shade lovers and make ideal plants for growing under shrubs or trees, or even in a shady border against a north wall. Arisaema are typical of the Araceae in that the flower spike, the spadix, is surrounded with a hood, the spathe, similar to the British native lords-and-ladies (*Arum maculatum*). Their beauty is as individuals rather than the effect of mass planting.

One of the oldest in cultivation and still one of the most popular is *A. candidissimum*. This has a 30 cm (12 in) spathe that is pure white, striped with pink on the inside and pale green on the outside. Another popular species is *A. triphyllum*. This has a green spathe with brown stripes. This is more hooded than the previous species. Many of the species are variations on the brown and green theme, some exquisitely beautiful.

Arisaemas must have a soil that does not dry out. A leafy woodland soil would be ideal. They prefer to be in light shade rather than in the open. Arisaema are often very late coming above ground and care should be taken not to disturb or overplant them accidentally. Propagation is by seed or careful division.

## ARNEBIA (Boraginaceae) – Prophet flower
*Arnebia pulchra* is a curious flower rather than a beautiful one, although it can hold its own as a front-of-border plant. Its curiosity

value lies in the fact that when the yellow flowers first open they have five black blotches at their base. These are supposed to be the Prophet's fingerprints. As the flower ages so these spots disappear, leaving a pure yellow flower. The plant grows to about 30 cm (12 in) in height. I have not found it to be long-lived but it can be renewed from seed or from root cuttings. Until recently it was called *A. echioides*. There are a number of other species in this genus but none are in general cultivation.

It likes a well-drained position in full sun.

## ARTEMISIA (Compositae) – Wormwood

In recent years silver plants have become *de rigueur* and none more so than artemisias. The genus is large, over 400 species, and those that have been introduced into gardens have mainly been selected because of their silver or grey foliage. Foliage of this colour is extremely useful in a border. It is restful to the eye and is particularly good as a go-between between two plants of contrasting or clashing colours. There are very few colours with which they will not happily sit and, of course, they really come into their own in the fashionable white and silver gardens. Some are floppy, giving a carpeting effect (often untidily so), while others have a more erect habit, giving a good block of silver.

These are plants of the sun; nothing can look more miserable in a damp wet summer than artemisias turned to mush on the border. It is not only damp that they hate, shade will also quickly send the plants into decline. Still it is not difficult in most gardens to provide the conditions they like: sun and a free-draining soil. Heavy soils should be lightened with gravel, or better still, a raised bed built to accommodate these and the many other plants that like these conditions.

Just to be perverse I will start with the one plant that does not at all fit the general description as it has green leaves and is grown for its flowers. This is *Artemisia lactiflora*. It is by far the tallest of the genus, growing up to 180 cm (6 ft), carrying plumes of creamy-white flowers from late summer into autumn. The strong stems need no support and, when cut, are very useful in flower arrangements. It is more moisture-tolerant than other members of the family.

Returning now to the more typical members of the genus, perhaps *A.* 'Powis Castle' is my favourite. This has very fine filigree foliage of pure silver. Flowers on plants grown purely for foliage can be a nuisance, but 'Powis Castle' has solved this by not flowering, or at least not doing it very often. It grows to about 90 cm (3 ft) in height and will stand most winters. One of its parents is *A. arborescens*, from which it gets its silky fine-cut foliage. This is a magnificent plant, but is a bit on the tender side and needs overwinter protection in many areas.

The other parent of *A.* 'Powis Castle' is *A. absinthium* which is the British native plant wormwood. Its contribution to the partnership is hardiness. It is not such a fine plant as *A. arborescens*, but it will stand the weather better, and it nonetheless has the fine form 'Lambrook Silver', selected by Margery Fish for her garden at East Lambrook Manor.

A tall species with a tendency for flopping over is *A. ludoviciana*. The leaves are broader than many of the others and undivided, making it an excellent plant for the grey and silver garden. It has a cultivar 'Silver Queen' which does have more delicate leaves and a variety, *latiloba*, which is a shorter or more stocky plant with jagged edges to the leaves. *A. ludoviciana* has a tendency to run, soon forming a large clump, but can easily be controlled before it gets out of hand.

Another runner is *A. stelleriana*, which soon forms a low carpet of white felted leaves. This one is reasonably hardy and is often grown in exposed positions such as in gardens by the sea.

Propagation of all the clump-formers can be easily achieved by division in the spring, preferably using the younger material from round the edge of older plants. The shrubby species such as *A. arborescens* and *A. absinthium* should be increased by taking cuttings in late spring.

137

**ARUNCUS** (Rosaceae) – Goat's beard

For anyone that has the space, as it will grow up to 180 cm (6 ft) high, *A. runcus dioicus* is a perennial that you ought to try and grow. It makes a large clump of attractive pinnate, almost fern-like foliage for all of the summer and autumn, and plumes of tiny creamy flowers for a short while around midsummer. These, perhaps unfortunately, soon turn brown, spoiling their effect, but the foliage remains.

It is a plant that can be used in a variety of positions as it is bold enough to stand alone as a specimen plant or to be included in a border as part of a general scene. Although

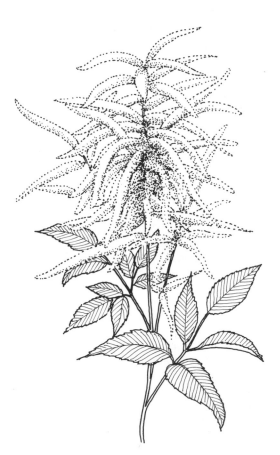

**Aruncus**

it will grow in most soils (except really dry ones) it relishes moist ones: it thrives and looks especially good when planted near streams or ponds. Confusion can occur over the name as it has been known as both *Spiraea aruncus* and *Aruncus sylvester* in the past.

The variety *A.d.* 'Kneiffii' is a very attractive variant that does not grow as large as the type (up to about 90 cm/3 ft in height) and has very finely cut leaves, making it a more delicate-looking plant. Another similar small form is *A.d. astilboides*, although this is not now so frequently seen.

Aruncus is not a difficult plant to grow. It prefers a moisture-retentive soil but will take a degree of dryness. A position in either sun or light shade will do. For those that are strong enough, propagation is by division, but it can also be grown from seed.

**ARUNDO** (Gramineae) – Giant reed

*Arundo donax* is a grass to be reckoned with. It will grow up to 3 m (10 ft) or more, making it one of the tallest perennials in the garden. Fortunately, it is clump-forming and not a fiercely running grass, otherwise many gardens would have been turned into jungles. It is a very stately, upright-growing plant that can either be used as a feature or at the back of a large border. It also mixes well with trees and shrubs. It rarely flowers in Britain, but is grown for its leaves and tall stems.

There is a variegated form, with striped leaves, but this is smaller and more liable to succumb to a cold winter. It will do well in most soils although it prefers a moisture-retentive one. A sunny, warm spot, with some winter protection should be allocated to it. Propagation is by division in spring or by taking stem cuttings.

**ASCELPIAS** (Asclepiadaceae) – Milkweed, silkweed

This is quite a large genus of plants but most are too tender for temperate gardens. However, there are two or three that are worth attempting to grow as they seem to survive most winters and their contribution to the border makes the effort worthwhile.

*A. tuberosa* injects a note of bright orange into the border in a way that few other plants can. This has flat heads of small flowers that reach up to about 45 cm (18 in) above the ground. Beware of its tendency to be a late starter in appearing above ground, so avoid accidentally overplanting it or otherwise destroying it. It is not entirely tender, but planting it in a warm sheltered spot helps and should bring it through most winters.

*A. speciosa* is a much taller plant, often reaching 150 cm (5 ft) or more, and has a tendency to spread. This has looser heads of pinkish-purple flowers. It is more reliably hardy.

*A. incarnata* is another pink variety, but it has stiffer flower heads. This grows to about the same height as the previous species.

Milkweeds like a moisture-retentive soil and a sunny position. They can be increased by division or from seed.

## ASPHODELINE (Asphodelaceae/ Liliaceae) – Yellow asphodel

This is a small genus of plants mainly from around the Mediterranean, two of which are grown in gardens. They are tall spiky plants with thin, grass-like leaves that flower from late spring into early summer.

The commoner of the two is *A. lutea*, sometimes known as king's spear, which carries yellow stars on its 90 cm (3 ft) stem that emerges from the clump of untidy foliage. This is not a front-line plant but it does add interest with its vertical emphasis and its large starry flower.

There is another similar species, *A. liburnica*, which is occasionally grown. The flowers are paler and carried on more slender stems that may need staking. The leaves are similarly clump-forming at the base of the plant but they are finer. This is a plant that is late in opening its flowers; they appear slightly later in the year than *A. lutea*.

They both can be easily grown in any well-drained soil in a sunny position. They can be propagated by division in the autumn or from seed. In the right position, they will often self-sow.

## ASPHODELUS (Asphodelaceae/Liliaceae) – Asphodel

This small genus is very closely related to the previous, but is not so frequently seen in cultivation. The difference between the two can easily be seen as this one has basal clumps of leaves which are much stiffer and erect, as opposed to the floppy nature of the *Asphodeline* (except early in the season before the stems appear).

*A. albus*, as the name suggests, has white flower spikes, but with brownish bracts which softens the whiteness. *A. ramosus* (sometimes called *A. cerasifolius*) is the only other one that is generally grown as a border plant. Again the flowers are white warmed with brown, but this time they are carried on divided flower stems. Perhaps one other should be mentioned, although it is really an annual or a short-lived perennial. This is *A. fistulosus*. Its flowers are again white, but this time with a distinct pink or brown central stripe on each of its petals. This is probably the most popular of the genus.

Asphodels like a well-drained soil and a sunny position. Propagation can be carried out by division or by sowing seed.

## ASTER (Asteraceae/Compositae) – Michaelmas daisy

What I knew as asters as a boy (and still refer to them as such for that matter) are in fact called Chinese asters and belong to another genus entirely, *Callistephus*. What the genus *Aster* contains are those tall, small-flowered plants that are generally known as michaelmas daisies — a name that derives from the fact that they are usually in flower around Michaelmas.

For some reason people either love or hate michaelmas daisies. I find it very difficult to hate them as they flower at a time when so little else is available and they do so with colours that are sympathetic to autumn. One of the big advantages of the true michaelmas daisy (*A. novi-belgii*) is that it can be grown in a reserve bed, vegetable garden or at the back of a large border and moved out into a vacant spot at any time, even when it is in full flower, and it does not turn a hair. If the plant's fibrous roots are given a good soaking before lifting and then lifted with a good root ball, they can be placed where instant colour is required. This is immensely valuable at a time of year when so much is going over and bare patches are appearing in the borders.

There are a tremendous number of cultivars of *Aster novi-belgii* (perhaps this is why some people look down their noses at it), giving an enormous range of colours and sizes. They do seem to suffer from a large number of diseases but are still worth growing.

Closely allied is *A. novae-angliae* which is a taller, more robust version of the previous plant. The colour range is more restricted. They make excellent plants for the back of a border.

There are a lot of species of *Aster* beside the michaelmas daisy and I think it is worth a quick trot through them to get some idea of the range of plants available. One of the most valuable for late flowering in the garden is *A. × frikartii* 'Mönch'. This produces cartwheels of blue petals over a long period. One of its parents is *A. amellus* and although it is not as good as 'Mönch,' this is a plant worth growing in its own right. There are quite a number of good cultivars in shades of blue and pink, of which 'King George' (violet-blue) is one of the best. Moving to smaller-headed flowers. *A. sedifolius* (*A. acris*) has masses of lavender-blue flowers. It tends to flop rather badly and needs some form of support. A virtue can be made of its flopping nature if it is planted behind an earlier-flowering plant on which it can lean, thus filling a gap. Even smaller still are the flowers of *A. ericoides*, but this is a plant of quite different appearance. The flowers are held on strong wiry stems that give the plant an airy appearance. They are long lasting and come in a variety of soft colours. 'Pink Cloud' is one of my favourites, but there are many other delightful varieties from which to choose. *A. divaricatus* is another small-flowered species, this time with white flowers. Interest in this plant begins earlier than flowering time as it has attractive dark brown, almost black stems. Unfortunately these often prove incapable of supporting the flowers and need staking in some way. Finally I must mention *A. tradescantii*, with small white flowers held airily on tall stems. This species has the virtue of flowering very late in the autumn with me. It is reasonably self-supporting, but a high wind will knock it in all directions.

Asters seem to be happy on most soils as long as they are not excessively dry. They prefer sun, but will take a little light shade. An open airy position will help to control mildew to which many seem prone.

Although many will come from seed, the best way to multiply asters is by division or by planting out individual rooted shoots from the outside of the clump. They do need replacing every few years to keep the plants vigorous.

## ASTILBE (Saxifragaceae) – False goat's beard

If you are lucky enough to have a damp garden astilbes will grow well. I can just about keep them happy but I have to keep a good eye on them in order to give them plenty of extra water should they need it. Rightly or wrongly, I use them as an indicator in some of my borders, because the leaves immediately show signs of distress if the soil begins to dry out and I then know it is time to turn on the hose.

Astilbes are very good garden plants given moist conditions. The flower heads consist of tapering foaming plumes of small flowers, coloured white, pink, red and purple. After the flowers are over they are replaced by rusty-coloured seedheads which maintain the plant's attractiveness throughout the autumn and even into winter. The foliage is deeply cut and very attractive. If planted in full sun and allowed to get too dry this foliage becomes easily scorched, with large brown patches appearing.

There are quite a number of species of astilbe in cultivation, but it is the cultivars that are most readily available. These are very popular in Europe, where many new varieties have been raised. Most of these are listed under *A. × arendsii*. These vary from the white 'Bridal Veil', through the pink

'Rheinland' to the deep vivid red (too red for my taste) of 'Red Sentinel'. There is a colour for all tastes and all situations. As I have already stated at length, astilbes prefer a moist soil and one of the best positions to see them is next to water. They also like a little shade, so are ideal plants to group amongst shrubs or trees, preferably planted in large drifts.

For the front of the border there are some smaller hybrids of *A.* × *arendsii* such as 'Sprite', but I prefer the dwarf form of *A. chinensis*, *A.c. pumila*, with its compact heads and long flowering season.

Unless you are attempting to grow new cultivars the best way to propagate astilbes is by division, which is easily accomplished during the autumn or spring.

**ASTRANTIA** (Umbelliferae) – Masterwort
What curious flowers these are! Surprisingly they are related to the cow parsley of the hedgerows and the fennel of the garden. Surprising that is, until one looks at it more closely and realizes the green 'petals' are in fact a shallow cup of bracts and the true flowers are inside arranged in the familiar dome of the Umbelliferae. These little pincushions of flowers are most exquisite in shape and delicate in colour, the common forms being green with touches of pink. They are much loved by flower arrangers.

Their pale colour allows them to fit in with many colour schemes, particularly white gardens or those which need cooling down. They will tolerate full sun but do best in a light shade where dapple light makes their colour and shape even more intriguing in the interplay of light and shadow. Any good garden soil will be adequate but they do best in a moisture-retentive one.

Nomenclature is in a bit of a mess and some authorities will say that *Astrantia major* is the only one in cultivation with all the others being forms of it. Be that as it may, there are three recognized species in general cultivation. The already mentioned *A. major* is the commonest with several good cultivars to its name. 'Shaggy', or 'Margery Fish' as it is sometimes called, is one of the most spectacular, with a particularly large and shaggy collar of bracts around the flower. 'Sunningdale Variegated' has variegated leaves as its name suggests. These are at their best in the spring, losing the variegation as the year progresses. This is best placed in full sun. *A.m. rubra* is distinct for its rich plum-coloured flowers.

The only other species that concerns us here is *A. maxima* which has quite large flower heads which are a good solid pink. I say 'solid' because in *A. major* the bracts always seem semi-transparent whereas in *A. maxima* I always get the impression that the bracts have been painted in with pink paint. This is a curious notion, but it always occurs for some reason. A more botanical distinction is that *A. maxima* has leaves that have been divided into three sections whereas its brother has more.

There is usually no need to propagate this plant as there is normally enough self-sown seedlings around to supply one's needs. However, it is also easily increased by division or by sowing the seed yourself if you want to remain the plant's master.

**BAPTISIA** (Leguminosae) – False indigo
This is quite a large genus from North America, but only one of them is in general cultivation. This is *B. australis*. It is one of those plants that gives you value for money, because, although it flowers in early summer, its fresh-looking foliage continues until well into the autumn. These leaves are a bluish-green and are carried on a plant that reaches up to 120 cm (4 ft) tall. The flowers are typical pea flowers, are blue and are held in loose, lupin-like spikes.

Baptisia like a rich, moisture-retentive soil. They prefer a sunny position, although they will tolerate a little light shade. Propagation is from seed or by division.

**BERGENIA** (Saxifragaceae) – Megasea
Bergenia is one of those good all-the-year round genera that are the cornerstone of so many gardens and, indeed, of many flower arrangements. The main reason for their continuing popularity is the evergreen foliage. This consists of large paddle-shaped leaves which in several of the species is

glossy. Foliage of this sort has several advantages for the gardener. The rounded shape and overall size is useful for softening straight lines, particularly the edge of borders, and yet are bold enough to make a statement of their own. Wherever it is grown, it makes excellent ground cover through which weeds have difficulty penetrating. They also happen to be perfectly designed for setting off the dumpy spikes of pink or magenta flowers that appear during spring.

It is difficult to find more accommodating plants as they are happy in any type of soil, will grow in either sun or shade and once planted need no further attention; they will happily look after themselves for years.

Most commonly seen is *Bergenia cordifolia* with its crinkly-edged, rounded leaves. The solid heads of flowers are held above the leathery foliage on reddish-purple stems. They are of various shades of pale pink to magenta. There is a cultivar 'Purpurea' whose leaves take on a distinct purplish hue during the winter.

*B. crassifolia* is a similar plant except that the leaves are more spoon-shaped. Another similar plant is *B. ciliata*, but in this case both sides of the large leaves are covered in hairs. Although an attractive plant, it is on the tender side and should be avoided in cold or exposed gardens. The flowers are a pale pink, surrounded by a reddish calyx. It has an interesting variety, *B.c. ligulata*, which has the hairs restricted to the margins of the leaves.

The tallest of the species is *B. purpurascens*, again to be recommended for its leaves. These are green in summer, but take on a deep beetroot colour in the late autumn. Unlike most other species, the leaves are held upright, showing off both top and underside of the leaves.

Before looking at the modern hybrids and cultivars, mention should be made of the smallest of the species which has been gaining in popularity in recent years. This is *B. stracheyi*. Again the leaves are held more upright and it has very pale, usually white flowers.

As bergenias have grown in popularity in recent years, so has there been a great increase in the number of hybrids. There are many to chose from but I shall just list a few of my favourites. 'Silberlicht' is one of the best, not only of the cultivars, but of the whole genus. It has white flowers that turn pink with age, supported all the while from brown calyces. The foliage remains green. 'Morgenröte' as a contrast, had deep reddish purple flowers. Moving from morning to evening 'Abendglut' also has deep red-purple flowers, but has rosettes of foliage that turn a maroon colour in winter.

Division is the easiest way to increase one's stock, in autumn or spring. Taking cuttings from the rhizomes is also an easy method. The species can also be grown from seed.

## BRUNNERA (Boraginaceae)

Brunnera is a small genus of three species or so, of which only one, *B. macrophylla* is in general cultivation. Its beauty lays in the floating sprays of small blue flowers, which look like airy forget-me-nots, floating 45 cm (18 in) above the ground. The blue is a light colour, but seems more brilliant than forget-me-nots – more in keeping with some of the anchusas to which it used to belong (known as *Anchusa myosotidiflora* and still listed as such in some catalogues). The flowers appear in spring when the blue is set off well against the heart-shaped, green leaves. After flowering the leaves remain, increasing in size to give an effective ground cover.

The flowers are particularly useful for brightening up a shady corner as brunnera will tolerate quite a deal of shade and are hence useful for planting amongst shrubs and under trees. They will also take sun, although their preference is undoubtedly light shade. Similarly they have a preference for moisture-retentive soils although any good garden soil will suffice.

There are quite a number of cultivars around, all dependent on leaf variations rather than differences in the flower. *B.m.* 'Dawson's White' (known as *B.m.* 'Variegata') has white edges to the leaves and *A.m.* 'Hadspen Cream' which is similarly variegated but this time with creamy white

**Brunnera**

margins. 'Langtrees' has silvery-white, spotted markings on the leaves.

Propagation is by division in the autumn or spring, but seed can be used for the straightforward species. It is another of those plants that can be increased by taking root cuttings in the late autumn or winter.

## BUPTHALMUM (Asteraceae/ Compositae) – Yellow oxeye daisy

This is a small genus of yellow daisy-flowered plants of which only one is in general cultivation (there were two, but *B. speciosum* has been moved off to become *Telekia speciosa*). This is *B. salicifolium*, its specific name means 'willow leaved' and, indeed, it has narrow willow-like leaves that

appear on 60 cm (2 ft) stems. The typical daisy-like flower appears over a long period during the summer and into autumn. It is a good plant for positions that have a little shade, such as the edge of woodland gardens. Some of the other species may be worth exploring, but they are not in general cultivation.

It will tolerate most soils and although preferring sun will also grow in light shade. It can be easily propagated by division or from seed.

## CALAMINTHA (Labiatae) – Calamint

This is a sad little genus as most of the species have moved off to such genera as *Acinos* and *Clinopodium*, the latter taking the lion's share. *C. nepeta*, the most interesting of the genus, has passed through *C. nepetoides* and *Satureja grandiflora* has now been dispatched to *Clinopodium calamintha*. Nothing of merit remains.

## CALTHA (Ranunculaceae) – Marsh marigold, kingcup

To see the shining golden-yellow petals of a marsh marigold beside a stream or in a boggy place, even amongst trees, in the early spring is a truly uplifting sight. I am fond of all the Ranunculaceae, but this is one that really stirs my heart, particularly when I come across it unexpectedly while out walking. The distribution in the wild is very widespread; not only is it native to both Britain and North America but it can be seen in most of the world, including the Himalaya and New Zealand. In cultivation it likes a similar habitat to that in the wild: wet or damp soil, preferably by water.

It is the glowing yellow of the petals set off against round, shiny green leaves that makes this plant so attractive during the spring. The flowers are quite large, up to 5 cm (2 in) in diameter, on plants which reach up to 30 cm (12 in) or more. Unfortunately, after its spring flowering the plant does not offer much else for the rest of the season, but there are usually many other waterside plants to divert the eye.

There are quite a number of species of *Caltha* but it is *C. palustris* (a native British

143

**Caltha**

plant) that is the most widespread. It was probably introduced into gardens at a very early period – certainly the double form 'Flore Pleno' was around in the early seventeenth century. The double form makes a very attractive garden plant, but I think it loses the purity and simplicity of the single form. Purity is what the white form 'Alba' has in plenty. This form has a longer flowering period than the others.

*Caltha polypetala* is another species that is often seen in gardens. This has a more limited distribution, coming from the Caucasus mountains. Both in leaf and flower it is a larger version of *C. palustris* but it

differs in habit. Whereas the latter is a clump-forming plant, *C. polypetala* tends to sprawl and run over the surface with rooting stems. It will even run out onto the surface of water. It has a long flowering season.

Both of these species, as well as the few others that are occasionally found in cultivation, like a damp soil or at least a moisture-retentive one. If the soil is on the dryish side then the plants must have light shade, otherwise they do best in a sunny site.

Propagation is by division or from seed. Division can be in spring or autumn. As with all the Ranunculaceae, seed germinates best if it is sown while it is still fresh, but spring-sown seed will still give a reasonable germination rate.

**CAMPANULA** (Campanulaceae) – Bellflower
Remove bellflowers from the garden and one of the mainstays of an 'English Garden' would disappear. They help to conjure up the image of romantic, sunny borders that typify both the small cottage garden and the large expanses of a country house with sweeping herbaceous borders.

The flowers are typically blue, often a soft blue, with occasional white and even pink forms, and two eccentric yellow species. The name 'bellflower', as indeed the Latin *Campanula*, comes from the bell-like shape of the flower, although in one or two species the bell is so flared that it almost becomes more of a shallow dish. They vary considerably in stature from ground-hugging plants, more suitable for the rockery, to statuesque plants several feet high. There are one or two thugs, such as *Campanula punctata* and *C. rapunculoides*, which, however pretty they may appear, should be avoided or else they will take over the whole garden.

*C. pyramidalis* is one of the tallest species, throwing up a great spire of 150 cm (5 ft) or more of blue or white flowers. These last for a long time, particularly if grown as a pot plant and bees are prevented from carrying out their work of pollination. As a pot plant it is most spectacular.

Moving down to 120–150 cm (4–5 ft) or so we find *C. lactiflora* which some would argue, with much justification, is the best of the bellflowers. Its pale blue flowers are born in profusion from summer through to the autumn. It is one of the mainstays of herbaceous borders. The individual flowers are not very big but they appear in abundance. The petals form an open bell, giving a starry effect. There are several named forms. 'Loddon Anna' is a mauvy pink, but is too muddy a colour for my taste. 'Pritchard's Variety' is a strong plant in a good blue. There is a shorter form, 'Pouffe', with pale blue flowers.

*C. latifolia* has a confusingly similar name and similar height, but there the similarity ends. The flowers are not in large panicles but are borne on the upright stems. *C. persicifolia*, the peach-leaved bellflower, is another upright plant of slightly smaller stature. It is a graceful plant with spikes of blue or white flowers. There are double forms around, but they are more difficult to find. It seeds itself gently around the garden and will take a surprising amount of shade.

*CC. lactiflora* and *latifolia* are both clump formers as is *C. alliariifolia* with heart-shaped leaves interspersed on the upright stems with white bell-shaped flowers. Shorter still at 30 cm (12 in) is *C. glomerata*, a British native, with purple-blue flowers clustered into balls at the end of its stems.

There are many dwarf forms that really are only suitable for the rockery, but some are robust enough to withstand life in an herbaceous border and make good subjects for the front or edgings. *C. carpatica*, particularly in the form *turbinata*, has large cup-shaped flowers in various shades of blue and white. It is about 23 cm (9 in) tall and has a long flowering season. While *C. carpatica* is a compact plant, *CC. portenschlagiana* and *poscharskyana* (what horrible names to get the tongue round!) are both sprawling, mat-forming plants. The latter is particularly rampant, but can be easily weeded out if necessary. It has the virtue of growing in shade and can be a valuable ground cover between shrubs or other plants. Its starry flowers appear over a long season and look very fine flowing down a bank.

There are a lot more that I have not mentioned and I can perfectly see how people can become addicted to them; if one wants to specialize in any one plant then you could do worse than choose campanulas. One specialist nurseryman has well over 200 and he still thinks he is only just scraping the surface!

Campanulas come fairly easily from seed sown in the spring. The clump-forming varieties can be divided in the autumn or spring. They will thrive in any good garden soil and although most prefer full sun, many will take a little light shade.

**CARDAMINE** (Cruciferae) – Cuckoo flower, lady's smock
Until recently this has mainly been known in gardening terms for the British native cuckoo flower *C. pratensis*, a delightful lilac or mauve flower that appears with all the freshness of the spring. The double form *C.p.* 'Flore Pleno' is the one that is normally grown. They will grow in any soil but prefer it to be on the moist side.

Recently *Dentaria* has been included in this genus and with it has brought two or three first-class woodland plants that flower in the spring. *C. kitaibelli* (previously *D. polyphylla*) has creamy white flowers, *C. heptaphylla* (*D. pinnata*) white, and *C.pentaphyllos* (*D. digitata*) has lilac-purple ones. All grow to about 30 cm (12 in) or more high and will soon make quite a large colony. They are ideal plants for a shady position that is not too dry.

Propagation is by division or from seed.

**CATANANCHE** (Compositae) – Blue cupidone, cupid's dart
Although only one species from this small genus is grown in gardens, it is nonetheless worthy of mention in this book. *C. caerulea*, from the Mediterranean, is its name. It looks like a plant that you might expect to find in hot places. The grass-like leaves are greyish-green, from which rise wiry stems carrying solitary flowers like cornflowers or chichory. They are a mauve-blue colour and have a papery calyx which rustles when rubbed through the fingers. It has a long

season from early summer through to the autumn.

*C. caerulea* 'Major' has larger and brighter flowers. There are also white and bicolor forms, but these are rarely met with.

The blooms make excellent, long-lasting cut flowers and can have even a longer life when dried.

The plant is not long lived, but given good drainage and a sunny site it will last several years before it needs replacing. It can be grown from seed, but if you are lucky enough to have one of the varieties, then root cuttings taken in the winter is the best method of ensuring that the plant stays true.

## CENTAUREA (Compositae) – Cornflower, knapweed

This is the family to which the cornflower, *Centaurea cyanus* belongs, but since it is only biennial, it has no place in this book. There are, however, a number of others that are worthy of our attention, although in no way am I attempting to cover all the 600 species that are present in the wild.

The commonest one seen in gardens is *C. montana*, the mountain knapweed. It is rather a floppy plant, but it has the most marvellous purplish-blue flowers with a reddish centre. The flowers are a typical cornflower shape but much larger than the common one, 6 cm (2½ in) or more. They flower typically in the spring, but some continue into the summer. The plants however get a big straggly as the year progresses and wants cutting back; if this is done immediately after the first flowering, a second flush can be induced later in the season. It has a tendency to run so should not be planted next to choice plants which it might invade. In a good garden soil it is easy to control by pulling up the spreading rhizomes. However it is determined to spread and so seeds itself around as well, but this can be prevented if the plant is cut back early enough. In spite of its invasiveness by root and seed, it is still a plant well worth growing.

There are several forms of *C. montana*, although personally I think the type itself takes a lot of beating. *C.m.* 'Alba' has white

flowers as its name suggests. 'Carnea' (sometimes called 'Rosea') has pink, while 'Rubra' has a deeper pink. 'Parham Variety' has a deep amethyst colour and is probably the best of the forms.

*Centaurea dealbata*, often called the perennial cornflower, has fine pink flowers, carried in the summer months. The finely dissected leaves are pale green on their upper surface and grey beneath. As with the previous species, it tends to be floppy and needs some form of support. There is a much richer, rosy-crimson form, *C.d.* 'Steenbergii' which is commonly available. This is a more vigorous plant and its questing root system can become invasive.

A plant somewhat like the previous species, although bolder and with foliage that is a bit coarser is *C. hypoleuca*. It is mainly grown in the form 'John Coutts'. This has deep pink flowers. The plant spreads but it is not difficult to control.

*C. macrocephala* is the tallest of the commonly grown species, growing to over 90 cm (3 ft) in favourable conditions. This is a coarser, stronger plant that can support itself. Unlike the others it produces a deep yellow flower encased in brown papery scales. It makes a good dried flower. There is a more refined version with smaller yellow flowers in *C. glastifolia*, but it is nowhere near as common.

Knapweeds do well in a well-drained garden soil. Although they do not like it too dry, most will grow well on chalk. They prefer a sunny situation.

Propagation is easily achieved from division in autumn or spring, or from seed in the spring.

## CENTRANTHUS (Valerianaceae) – Red valerian

The only member of this genus that appears in general cultivation is *C. ruber*. It has become naturalized throughout Britain and can frequently be seen growing on walls and banks, especially near the sea. It was often grown in cottage gardens. The leaves and stems are pale green, glaucous and rather fleshy. The flowers are held as rounded heads up to 75 cm (30 in) above the ground, and are red. There are also white and pink forms. Basically they flower in summer, but young plants can often be found in flower later in the year. They can run and form small colonies.

They like a well-drained soil in full sun. Propagation can be from seed or from basal cuttings taken in the spring.

## CEPHALARIA (Dipsacaceae)

*Cephalaria gigantea* is a refuge from *Scabiosa*, where it was known as *S. tartarica*. It is the only one of a rather larger genus of plants that is in general cultivation. It is a magnificent plant, growing to 2.4 m (8 ft) or more, with spreading branches carrying yellow flowers. It is an obvious candidate for the back of a border.

Being such a large plant it likes a reasonably rich diet and should be planted in a soil that has had plenty of organic material added to it. It likes a sunny position. In spite of its height it seems to be able to cope without support.

It comes very easily from seed and will self sow unless it has been deadheaded. It can also be divided.

## CHELONE (Scrophulariaceae) –
Turtlehead

Chelone is a very small genus of four species. The one that is commonly seen in gardens is *Chelone obliqua*, which, like its companions, comes from the United States. It is a medium-height plant reaching 90 cm (3 ft), and of an upright habit that rarely needs staking. The flowers are carried in autumn in a terminal spike and resemble its near relative, the penstemon. The flattened tubes of the flower give the appearance of a turtle's head, hence one of its vernacular names. They are a warm rose-pink and last well into the autumn. Although the plant flowers late, the dark green leaves still manage to look presentable and act as a foil to the opening spikes of flowers.

There are two forms that can be found with a bit of searching. *C.o. alba* is distinguished by having white flowers, while *C.o.* 'Praecox Nana' is a much earlier-flowering plant and is more dwarf in habit.

**Chelone**

Moisture-retentive, or even damp soil is required to grow chelone well. It will take full sun or partial shade.

Propagation is from division in spring or autumn, or from seed sown in the spring.

## CHRYSANTHEMOPSIS (Compositae)

A new genus that has been derived from the break up of *Chrysanthemum*. It is also the final resting place of what was known as

*Leucanthemum hosmariense* (*Chrysanthemum hosmariense*), but is now to be known as *Chrysanthemopsis hosmariense*. Whatever the name, and I expect it will change again next week, it is a very good plant. It is relatively short, only reaching about 20 cm (8 in) in height. The flowers are large white daisies with a golden centre. This is not uncommon in what were the chrysanthemums, but what is more unusual are the superb silver or pewter leaves that keep their neatness and freshness throughout the year. It is a choice plant for the front of a border.

*C. hosmariense* likes a well-drained soil in a sunny position to perform of its best. The best means of increase is by taking cuttings.

## CHRYSANTHEMUM (Compositae) – Chrysanthemum

In writing about this well-known genus I am writing an obituary, as to all intents and purposes, it no longer exists. Over the years species have constantly come and gone, but now there seems to be a general agreement amongst botanists that the genus should be totally split up and redistributed.

Many of the more tender species have gone into *Argyranthemum*. The species that arrived as refugees from *Pyrethrum* have been moved on yet again, this time to *Tanacetum*, as have such plants as feverfew (*C. parthenium*). The shasta daisy (*C. maximum*) and the oxeye daisy (*C. leucanthemum*) have been moved to *Leucanthemum maximum* and *L. vulgare* respectively. *Chrysanthemum hosmariense* (also known as *Leucanthemum hosmariense*) has finally settled, one hopes, as *Chrysanthemopsis hosmariense*. Other genera that have appeared include *Arctanthemum*, *Balsamita*, *Dendranthema*, *Leucanthemella*, *Leucanthemopsis*, and *Nipponanthemum*. The typical 'chrysanths' of flower shows are now part of *Dendranthema*.

Bearing in mind that we are still calling *Pelargonium* 'geraniums' a hundred years after they were removed from that genus, it must be a matter of speculation as to how long is it going to take us to get used to this upheaval.

## CIMIFUGA (Ranunculaceae) – Bugbane

Now this is an attractive group of plants. The spikes of tiny white or cream flowers look just like rockets going off – slightly erratic rockets as the tall spike often has a small curve to it. They look best against a dark background or in a dull corner where the flower heads seem to become disembodied from the plant and look even more like fireworks shooting off. They look well in a variety of positions. Groups amongst shrubs look very dramatic, but a more subtle approach is to use them with pink Japanese anemones. The flowering period varies from species to species, covering overall a period from midsummer to late autumn.

It is not only the flowers that are good, the foliage is equally attractive, especially in those with purple leaves and stems.

Undoubtedly one of the greatest attractions must be *C. ramosa* 'Atropurpurea', which has the most beautiful deep purple foliage and stems which are touched with bronze. This colour sets off well the tall spikes of white flowers (purple in bud), which can reach up to 2 m (6½ ft) high and appear in the autumn. The species itself is also attractive, but has green leaves. Another attractive species with which the last is often confused, is the similarly named *C. racemosa*. This again has white flowers but they appear earlier, in the summer. The plant is also smaller, reaching about 1.8 m (6 ft).

The last of the season to flower, and very useful for that reason, is *C. simplex*. This is shorter still at about 1.2 m (4 ft), but again the flowers are white. There is a very good variety called 'Elstead' which is purple in bud before it opens to a pure white, the two colours making a good contrast. *C. americana*, with cream flowers, is one of the earliest to flower. There are several more species in cultivation that those with a large garden might like to explore.

Cimifugas like a cool, moisture-retentive soil, preferably in a lightly shaded position, although they will take sun if the soil is moist enough. They can easily be increased by division or from seed.

**CLEMATIS** (Ranunculaceae) – Clematis
This, to many people, may seem an unusual genus to find in a book on herbaceous plants but there are several species that are herbaceous and die back each year below the ground. They are not the big blousy cultivars that one sees hanging from garage walls but nonetheless, they still have quite a lot to add to the border.

One of the earliest to flower is *Clematis recta*. This is a very garden-worthy plant as it gives you three bites at the cherry. First the young foliage can give colour and freshness to the border if the purple form 'Purpurea' has been selected. This is followed by clouds of frothy, fragrant flowers, and finally the seed heads contribute to the autumn scene. It is a very floppy plant and needs support.

*C. heracleifolia* in its form *davidiana* is one of the most commonly seen in gardens. It is a rather coarse, sprawling plant that, surprisingly, has blue flowers similar to a hyacinth's and are strongly perfumed. There are several forms of which 'Wyevale', a good rich blue, is possibly the best. Another blue is *C. jouiniana:* this is also a tumbling sprawling plant that will ramp up through bushes or make an excellent ground cover. 'Praecox' is an earlier-flowering form that starts flowering in midsummer and goes on right into the autumn.

*C. durandii* is one of my favourites. It has more substantial flowers than the previous species. These appear over a long period from midsummer and are a deep purple-blue. Support is again needed and it is another that does well by draping itself over other plants.

There are several other species and hybrids which the keen gardener can pursue after what I hope is a glimpse into an unsuspected world.

Like all clematis, they have to have a cool root run in good garden soil, preferably moisture retentive. They also like a sunny position but will tolerate a little light shade.

They are probably the easiest of clematis to propagate as they can be divided in spring. Cuttings or layering can also be used.

**CLINOPODIUM** (Labiatae) – Calamint
This is a new genus made up from refugees from *Calamintha*. The main species of interest is *C. calamintha* (previously *Calamintha nepeta*). This is a delightfully aromatic plant with tiny white or lilac flowers, much in the manner of thyme. Bees love it. One of the joys of this plant is that it has a very long flowering season, from summer well into autumn. The other plant of interest is *C. grandiflorum* (previously *Calamintha grandiflora*) which is a similar plant but slightly taller (45 cm/18 in high), with pink sage-like flowers.

Both like a well-drained soil preferably in full sun, although they will take a little shade. They can be increased by division or from seed.

**CONVALLARIA** (Convallariaceae/
Liliaceae) – Lily-of-the-valley
This surely must be one of the most loved of all plants, yet surprisingly few people grow it. It has a reputation for being difficult, but once it is established it can become all too easy. In fact, it can turn into a thug, with its questing roots invading all parts of the border. The answer is to site it where it will not be a nuisance and then sit back and enjoy it.

Authorities disagree as to how many species there are, but for garden purposes there is really only one: *Convallaria majalis*. The charm of the plant lies in the strongly fragrant white bells that hang from the short (23 cm/9 in), swaying stems. The leaves form a natural backdrop to the white flowers.

The type is so perfect one wonders why anyone has bothered to produce any variants, but they have done so. 'Fortin's Giant', as its name implies, is a larger form whose only real benefit is that it flowers later than the type, prolonging the flowering season. 'Rosea' has pink flowers and 'Prolificans' has double ones. There is an interesting variegated form, 'Variegata', which has very fresh-looking leaves with distinct yellow stripes. It has a tendency to revert if left to its own devices, but this can be avoided by planting in full sun and

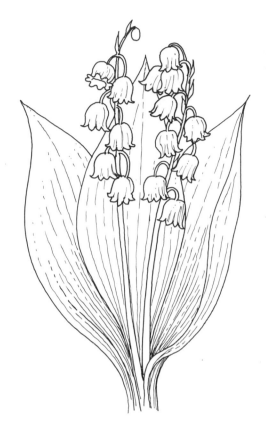

**Convallaria**

constant propagation from the better parts of the plant.

They are not difficult plants to grow and, once established in the right conditions, they will ramp away and could become a nuisance in some gardens. The conditions they like best are shade and a good friable soil, incorporating plenty of leafmould. The shade can be provided by trees or shrubs, or from a north-facing wall or fence.

A section of the tangled rhizomes can be dug up and divided to provide material for increasing the plant.

## COREOPSIS (Compositae)
There is yet another large genus of Compositae, of which only a few are in cultivation. The one mainly grown these days is *C.*

*verticillata*. This has thin wiry stems and narrow leaves which daintily set off the golden-orange flowers. The form 'Grandiflora' is a richer colour than the species and is the one usually grown. Of recent times its supremacy has been challenged by a pale yellow form called 'Moonbeam'. All are well worth growing. They need no staking and the flowers have a long season. They grow to about 60 cm (2 ft) in height.

The other species that is most frequently grown is *C. grandiflora*. This has a collection of cultivars, some shorter and some taller than the previous species. They all carry yellow daisies; some such as 'Sunray' and 'Sunburst' are double or semi-double. 'Goldfink' is a very short form at 23 cm (9 in), while 'Mayfield Giant' can be up to 90 cm (3 ft).

They like a well-drained soil in a sunny position. Propagation is by division.

## CORTADERIA (Gramineae) – Pampas grass
The pampas grasses are splendidly architectural plants that can be used as part of a large border or as special features in their own right. They look particularly well beside a large pond. They have stiff upright stems with large white plumes and cascades of narrow leaves. They vary in height, some getting up to 3 m (10 ft).

The main species in cultivation is *C. selloana*. This has a large number of cultivars, including several with variegated leaves. *C.s.* 'Pumila' is a smaller form that might be useful for those without much space.

They will grow in any fertile garden soil. Like most grasses they prefer a sunny position. Propagation is by division in spring.

## COSMOS (Compositae)
*Cosmos atrosanguineus* is a plant of great attraction. The flowers are of a deep velvety red; so deep is the colour that it is really a chocolate brown rather than red. The comparison with chocolate does not end with the colour, as on warm days it curiously has the smell of hot chocolate. The flowering period

150

is quite long, starting in the late summer and continuing well into autumn, the last flowers often being cut down by the frost. Related to the dahlia, it shares that plant's tendency towards tenderness. Away from very cold areas, it normally comes through the winter if it is given a good covering of bracken or straw. A word of warning: it is a very late riser, often not appearing above ground until the end of spring, so it is possible to think it has succumbed to the winter and to dig it out. Similarly it is easy to forget that it is there and overplant the supposed gap with something else. Many of the claims of non-hardiness are due to premature assumption that the plant has died. Once it does break the surface it quickly forms a plant 75 cm (30 in) high. In colder areas, it can be treated as a dahlia by digging it up and storing it in a frost-free place until it is planted out again in spring, when the harsh frosts have passed.

Good garden soil that does not get too dry is its preference, along with a good deal of sun. This plant once had great rarity value but now more nurseries are offering it for sale. In theory it is possible to grow it from seed, but this does not seem to set in this country. Cuttings are taken in early summer, when the shoots first appear. These should be struck immediately to get the maximum growing season. If it is possible to keep the cuttings in growth throughout the next winter in a greenhouse, then the chances of getting more plants is greatly increased. If allowed to die back, as it normally would in the autumn, then the new plant might not have made sufficient food stores to support regrowth in the next spring.

## CRAMBE (Cruciferae) – Seakale

The seakales are not plants commonly seen in gardens, but when they do put in an appearance they can cause quite a stir. Of the 20-odd species, only two are generally seen in gardens. *Crambe maritima* is a British native growing in shingle around the shores as its name 'maritima' suggests. This was probably first introduced into our gardens as a vegetable. The leaves them-

selves are very bitter and not at all appetizing, but the blanched stems, obtained by forcing or covering, have a delicate flavour of asparagus when cooked.

In the flower garden it is both useful for its foliage and flowers. The leaves are wide, wavy, very glaucous and blue in colour. The flowers erupt as a large dome of small, airy, white flowers, reaching up to 60 cm (24 in) in height. These smell sweetly of honey and appear at the end of spring or early summer.

The other species that one is likely to see is *Crambe cordifolia*. If it is present in flower one is hardly likely to miss it as it forms a massive cloud of white flowers 1.8–2.5 m (6–8 ft) high and 1.2 m (4 ft) or more across. It is a very impressive sight in midsummer, but after it passes over, as can be imagined, it leaves a big hole in the border. This can be filled by moving in some michaelmas daisies, having given them a good soak. Unlike *C. maritima*, the leaves of *C. cordifolia* are not particularly attractive and nothing is lost if these are masked by any plants in front. This is a big plant that needs a lot of space and is not really one for the small garden.

They are both happy in any good garden soil as long as it is reasonably well drained. Propagation is usually from root cuttings taken in the early winter, but can also be grown from seed. Plants that come readily from root cuttings can be difficult to eradicate should you so wish to do so. Any piece of root left in the ground when the plant is lifted is a potential new plant, so clear the ground with care.

## CREPIS (Compositae)

Few gardeners would like to grow many of the genus as they are generally very weedy, but there is one that makes a very good plant for the front of the border. This is *Crepis incana*, which looks exactly like a pink dandelion, except possibly that it carries more flowers. These come into bloom in summer and reach 30 cm (12 in) or so in height. It needs a well-drained soil in a sunny position. Propagate either from seed or by root cuttings.

**CROCOSMIA** (Iridaceae) – Montbretia
On the whole I have left bulbs out of this book, but no herbaceous garden would be complete without some of the crocosmias. One is constantly surprised that bulbs which emanate from South Africa will survive in cold British and North American winters, but the majority of crocosmias seem to be quite happy as long as they are not in too heavy a soil. They are valuable for their shape, colour, and the fact that they flower in autumn, giving the first hints of the blaze of autumn reds and oranges that are to come.

The flowers are held in flat, arching sprays of orange, red, or yellow. Sometimes the flowers point upwards, sometimes downwards from the spray. The leaves are grasslike, stiff and erect, sometimes reaching as high as 1.2 m (4 ft).

Of all the herbaceous plants, I have more problems with the specific names of crocosmias than any other genus. But in many ways names are unimportant; it is the flowers that one enjoys, not their names. However descriptions would be useless without names so one must make an attempt to sort them out. *Crocosmia × crocosmiiflora* is the commonest montbretia that everyone knows. It is in fact a hybrid between *C. aurea* and *C. pottsii*. The height varies between 60–90 cm (2–3 ft) and it typically has flowers which are orange-red on the outside and yellow within. However, there are many cultivars which vary in colour and size. It is impossible to list them all and, anyway, it is best for the gardener to go to autumn shows and select his own, but mention must be made of some of them. One of my favourites is 'Solfatare'. This is not one of the easiest to grow, but it has soft pinkish-yellow flowers set off beautifully against soft bronze-green leaves. At the other end of the scale is the brash 'Emily McKenzie', with her large orange flowers which are flared wide open to show bold brown markings. 'Canary Bird' and 'Citronella' are two very good yellows.

*C. masonorum* is a species well worth growing. The flowers point upwards from their arching sprays and are of a strong fiery colour that can be difficult to position. The leaves are much broader than other species and have a conspicuous deep veining running up their length. The corms have a tendency to rise to the surface and the weight of the flowering stems and large leaves can topple the plant over, so make certain that the corms are well planted and stake if necessary in windy areas. 'Firebird' is one of the best forms.

In recent years, some marvellous plants, with large brilliant flowers, that are a cross between *Crocosmia* and *Curtonus* have been introduced. The best known is 'Lucifer' with vivid flame-red flowers. Other good forms include 'Bressingham Blaze', 'Ember Glow' and 'Spitfire'.

They will grow in any good garden soil and are happy in either full sun or part shade. Propagation is no problem at all as the corms happily multiply without any help from the gardener and it is just a matter of dividing them. Some will self sow and if you want to keep the stand true to one cultivar, then any rogue plants should be removed.

**CYNARA** (Compositae) – Cardoon
This genus has about 14 members, but only one is generallly grown in the flower garden: *Cynara cardunculus*. This is a very imposing thistle that grows up to 1.8 m (6 ft) or so. It is grown mainly for its silvery-grey foliage, which is deeply divided, giving a filigree effect. In the border it is extremely useful for its architectural effect, as well as for its colour. The large flowers are borne on stiff erect stems over-topping the leaves and are in the form of a typical thistle flower, purple in colour.

These are plants for the large border as they not only need space to grow but need space to look their best. They will grow in any good garden soil as long as it is well drained. Like most thistles they prefer a sunny position and in spite of their strong stems, prefer a degree of shelter from high winds.

It is also occasionally found in the vegetable garden where its young leaves can be blanched for an addition to a salad. There is

**Cynara**

another cynara that is commonly grown, but which is usually restricted to the vegetable garden, and that is *C. scolymus*, the globe artichoke. Unlike the cardoon, it is the flower head that is eaten and, since it has very attractive leaves, it can be taken out of the vegetable plot and put into the flower border where the foliage can be appreciated even if the flower is removed to be eaten. It is a shorter plant than *C. cardunculus* and not so attractive, but with the bonus of the delicious, edible flower heads, it makes a good alternative for the smaller garden.

Propagation can be from seed, but it is better to take cuttings or offsets from existing plants to ensure that you get a good form, particularly for the globe artichoke.

## DACTYLORHIZA (Orchidaceae)
Orchids are a very difficult genus to grow and, generally speaking, should be left to the specialists. However, this is one genus that is not too difficult. They are attractive plants with very eye-catching large spikes of purple flowers.

There are several species that are similar in appearance and whose names seem, at least in the gardening world, to be in a bit of a muddle. The species that you are likely to find (at quite an expense you should be warned) are *DD. elata, foliosa, grandis,* and *mascula.*

The British native *D. fuchsii* does very well in the garden. This is a pale pink with crimson spots. The spikes are not so large and it is nowhere as flamboyant as those already mentioned. It is available from specialist nurseries, so do not dig up plants from the wild.

Orchids like a reasonably moisture-retentive soil and seem to like a light shade. Propagation is by very careful division. *D. fuchsii* will self sow if happy.

## DELPHINIUM (Ranunculaceae)
Think of a traditional English herbaceous border and one of the first plants that must spring to mind are the stately delphiniums. In their varying shades of blue, the large spires grouped together can give a border a strong focal point or, at least, some form of architectural substance. Delphiniums can become obsessive and there are many people who grow them as show plants which are never exposed to the vagaries of the open flower border. More is the pity, as that is where they truly belong. Along with many people, I find some of the show delphiniums a bit vulgar; they are too big and brash. The garden hybrid delphiniums are typically blue, varying in shade between pale and dark, but now there are many more colours from which to chose: white, cream, yellow, pink, mauve, purple and now at last red. Some of these colours, particularly the red, comes as a surprise to many gardeners, but they are all to be found in one or other of the 250 species that exists in nature. Given time and patience it has been possible to hybridize the existing garden hybrids with the wild species and introduce these other colours. The centre part of the flower, the 'bee', contains the petals; the coloured outer

'petals' are in fact the calyx which encloses the flower.

The garden hybrids have *D. elatum* as their main parent and there are now hundreds from which to choose. In order that these hybrids should remain true they must be propagated from basal cuttings taken in spring, but if all that is required is 'typical' blue delphiniums, then they can be grown from seed. The problem here is that you will get plants of varying shades of blue and, since it always looks better to have a clump restricted to one colour, you will have to be ruthless and throw away, or plant elsewhere, those that do not match your chosen colour. *D. elatum* hybrids produce large plants up to 1.8 m (6 ft) or more in height, the flower spike often being several feet long. If planted thickly they may be self-supporting but it is always wise to stake them if there is the slightest risk of wind damage.

There are many more species that the average gardener rarely comes across, any of them are very garden worthy, but are usually restricted to the rock garden. However there are one or two that are good for the herbaceous border. One of my favourites is *D. tatsienense*, from China, which grows only up to about 60 cm (24 in). The deep blue flowers are airily carried on wiry stems. It is unfortunately short-lived and, although a perennial, really needs replacing every year from seed.

A similar species is *D. grandiflorum* (sometimes known as *D. chinensis*) which grows to about 60 cm (24 in) rich blue flowers. There are several cultivars available, of which 'Blue Butterfly' is the best known. Again it is not long lived and fresh plants should be propagated every year to ensure against loss.

*D. nudicaule* is an American species with red flowers. It is from this plant that the red has been introduced into modern hybrids. It is only about 30 cm (12 in) high and again needs to be renewed regularly from seed. It also has yellow forms, but it is *D. zalil*, from Iran, that has provided the yellow of modern hybrids. It is a plant worth growing for its own sake, with its bright yellow flowers.

It is not an easy plant, but with good drainage and a sunny spot it is worth the attempt.

## DENDRANTHEMA (Compositae) – Chrysanthemum (see also page 148)

I wonder how many gardeners would associate the name *Dendranthema* with the genus which is one of the most popular of all plants. Well this is the latest form of name for chrysanthemums. When talking about 'chrysanths' one immediately thinks of the flowers that bloom in the autumn, or rather *did* bloom in the autumn as it is now possible to buy them as pot plants or cut flowers at any time of the year. The masses of different cultivars are well worth growing, but really fall outside the remit of this book as they are not really hardy plants. Instead, they should be treated as annuals by buying fresh plants each year or by taking cuttings from plants overwintered indoors. Some of the smaller varieties, especially those of the *rubellum* group, are hardy and can be treated as perennials. One of the best of these is the pink 'Clara Curtis'. Another two worth acquiring are 'Mary Stoker', which has a curious salmony-yellow colour, and 'Emperor of China', which is a good rosy-pink.

Chrysanthemums can be grown in any good soil and should be given a sunny position. By the autumn they can become top-heavy with blooms and are likely to require staking. They are best increased by taking basal cuttings in the spring, but can also be propagated by division.

## DIANTHUS (Caryophyllaceae) – Carnations, pinks

Who could garden without pinks? They are an essential ingredient in any garden, but are particularly associated with cottage gardens where they can easily evoke nostalgia for times past. Dianthus must be one of our earliest garden plants: it has a history stretching back to medieval times and beyond. The oldest pinks had very strong perfumes which helped to disguise or at least distract from the bad odours of the day, and a strong clove flavour which was very much enjoyed in wine ('Sops in Wine', one of the oldest pinks, is still in existence today). Now they are grown as plants for the front of the border or as cut flowers. When used in borders they look particularly good when they are flopping out over paving stones of paths or terraces. This is an appropriate place to grow them as their scent can then be easily appreciated.

Pinks today are arranged into two basic groups, 'old-fashioned' and 'modern', with several subgroups which need not trouble us too much here. 'Old-fashioned' refer to those that were in existence before the twentieth century, some going back into history, others bred in Victorian times, and those modern ones that resemble them. They tend to be looser and more informal looking than the moderns, and they usually have a good perfume, often quite strong. Their one big disadvantage is that they only flower once, during late spring and early summer. Some have compact foliage and can be useful as silver foliage plants after flowering, but others are not so lucky and look straggly for the rest of the season.

One of the best-loved and most widely grown is the double white 'Mrs Sinkins'. It is untidy both in flower and habit but it has a gorgeous scent and I would hate to be without its Victorian presence, flopping over the garden path. 'Inchmery' is a wonderful silvery shell-pink. This is a semi-double and again has a wonderful fragrance. 'Charles Musgrave' is a single white with an intriguing green centre or eye. The fragrant flowers are borne on a nice compact plant. 'Sops in Wine' is one of the oldest varieties known. There are several claimants to the name, but they are generally all double white with a dark red, almost black, centre. The scent is very strong indeed and is reminiscent of cloves. 'Sam Barlow' is very similar. 'Fimbriata' dates from Elizabethan times and is a creamy white double with a strong perfume.

Modern pinks have the big advantage in that they are repeat flowers, producing blooms from late spring right through to the late autumn frosts. They have the disadvantage that they look 'modern' i.e. they seem to have clean, regular lines and look too formal. The other major disadvantage for many, but not all, is that they have lost most if not all of their fragrance. The modern equivalent of 'Mrs Sinkins' is 'Haytor White', a fine upright, double white with a good fragrance and a long season. But its neat, almost military appearance is very different to its Victorian predecessor.

Many of the modern pinks with a long season were bred by Messrs Allwood and are known generically as the 'Alwoodii pinks'. The best known of these is undoubtedly 'Doris' which is covered with a profusion of fragrant flowers all summer and autumn. It is a semi-double salmon pink with a reddish central eye. There are many other moderns: 'London Delight' is one of the series of 'London Pinks'. This one is mauve with a purple eye and a strong scent of cloves. There are many other modern varieties, which can be seen on specialist nursery stands at the various gardening shows. They are all worth looking at and making a selection to suit one's own choice.

Dianthus also, of course include the carnations. Again there are several different groups, but only one – the border carnation – is worth considering in our context. Even this group is mainly grown for cutting and showing rather than as an integral part of the border's display. There is a long tradition of these carnations and over the years a large number of varieties have been bred.

Pinks like a well-drained soil and detest the wet. They also need the sun. Propagation is easily achieved by taking cuttings during the summer. Layering can be considered as an alternative, and is the preferred method for increasing border carnations. Pinks and carnations can be grown from seed, but there it little control over the progeny and the results are decidedly inferior to vegetative propagation.

## DIASCIA (Scrophulariaceae)

Diascias have been around since the last century, but it is only in recent years that they have been reintroduced from South Africa and become very popular. This

155

popularity stems both from their appearance and long flowering period, but also from the ease with which nurserymen can propagate them. They are all similar in general appearance: low prostrate plants with rising stems of pink flowers which look at their best when associated with other plants, especially if they are climbing through or over them. They were used as bedding plants at Wisley one year, where *en masse*, they looked particularly vulgar.

**Diascia**

*Diascia rigescens* was the first to catch the public's attention and in a matter of a couple of years it was growing everywhere. Popularity of this species has waned a little, partly because of its tendency towards tenderness and partly because it has been replaced by better forms. It is strong growing and more heavily featured than the other species, but still worth growing as a border plant.

*D. vigilis* is one of the best species. It has soft pink flowers and vigorous growth. It seems to come through the winter quite well. *D. barberae* is a salmon-pink but a bit on the tender side. A hybrid derived from this, 'Ruby Field', is much hardier and a rosy-pink. *D. fetcaniensis*, which masquerades under an enormous number of different names, is another very good species. It is very floriferous and vigorous and has come through some fairly hard winters with no protection.

All the diascias are of doubtful hardiness, although some are more tolerant than others. Young plants tend to come through the winter better than older ones. Hardiness does not really matter as it is very easy to take a few cuttings as assurance in the autumn, and overwinter them in a cold frame.

There can be no easier plant than this to propagate. Any piece of stem stripped of its lower leaves, will soon sprout roots if put into compost. Once it starts growing away the tips can be pinched out and also put into compost to provide even more cuttings.

Diascias dislike heavy soil, but on the other hand they do not like to dry out (they grow in wet places in the wild). They do well in any good garden soil that has humus in it. They will take a little shade, but are undoubtedly at their best in full sun.

**DICENTRA** (Fumariaceae) – Bleeding heart

Moving from a plant that likes a hot sunny position to one that prefers a cool, partially shaded one. Dicentra are graceful plants for dappled woodland shade. The flowers of all the species are held dangling from arching stems. The shape of these flowers has intrigued generations of gardeners and it has acquired a whole list of names besides bleeding heart and dicentra, which seem to be the current favourites. Dutchman's breeches, lady's locket and lyre plant, even lady-in-a-bath, are names that have been conjured up because of the images conveyed by the pouched, heart-shape of the flower. Doubtless there have been many more. It is not only the flowers that make these plants so attractive; the leaves are very finely dissected and in some species take on a wonderful silvery sheen, giving the plant value for its foliage when it is not in flower.

*Dicentra spectabile* is the showiest of the various species grown. It grows to about 60 cm (2 ft) in height, with long arching stems, from which dangle innumerable toy hearts. These flowers are quite large, up to 2.5 cm (1 in) across and in the typical plant are a rich pink with a white central tip. The flowering season is a long one, continuing from late spring right through until the autumn in some cases. The foliage is a brighter green and of a more coarse nature than the other lower-growing species. The pink form is the one most commonly seen and, beautiful as it is, can look a big vulgar to some eyes: There is also a refined white form, *D. spectabilis* 'Alba', which has a delightfully cool appearance and looks marvellous in a woodland setting, where it can lighten up a dark spot. A plant worth searching for.

*Dicentra eximia* is a plant that is gaining popularity in the garden. Even if this was not a beautiful plant it would have to be included because it adds some more bizarre names to this genus – turkey corn and staggerweed – both from its native America. This is much shorter than the previous species and has wonderful glaucous, fern-like foliage. This is surmounted by arching stems of pink to light purplish flowers. A similar plant with which it is often confused is *D. formosa*, also from America (the name 'formosa' has nothing to do with the island of that name but means 'beautiful' or 'handsome'). This has flowers of rich pinky mauve and glaucous foliage similar to the last species. It has a good subspecies *D. formosa oregana*, which has paler flowers. This in turn has a variety, 'Langtrees', with creamy-pink flowers. There are several other cultivars that some authorities claim belong to *D. eximia* and others to *D. formosa*. The matter is rather academic and does not really matter too much either way; the important thing, as always in these cases, is the plant.

'Adrian Bloom' is one of the best, with rich crimson flowers and grey foliage. 'Bountiful' is a rich red. 'Alba', of course, has white flowers, and 'Pearl Drops' has silvery, off-white lockets.

One species that is not seen very often, but when it is it causes a sensation, is *D. macrantha*. This is larger than the preceding and with coarser foliage, more like *D. spectabilis*. Unlike the others in cultivation, it has yellow flowers.

All the dicentras make very good border plants, but they do prefer partial shade from other plants or a north wall. Any good garden soil will do, but better plants will be obtained if it contains plenty of leafmould or other humus that will hold some moisture and provide a cool root run. And root run most of them need as they are rhizomatous and travel underground, although rarely to the point of being a nuisance.

They can be propagated from seed or from division or root cuttings. The roots are brittle and care must be taken when digging up a plant for division. The root cuttings succeed better if each cutting has the beginnings of a bud showing.

**DICTAMNUS** (Rutaceae) – Burning bush
There is only one species of this genus that is generally in cultivation, *Dictamnus albus* (previously known as *D. fraxinella*). It is not that frequently seen, possibly because it takes quite a while to work up a large clump of flowering plants. Once established, however, they are long-lived and need not be disturbed. They are a good conversation piece in a garden because on hot summer's days the seed pots emit a volatile oil which can be ignited without harming the plant by hold a lighted match beneath the stem. If you want to try this, choose a still evening after a hot day, preferably with a plant in shadow so that the flame is visible. And take care.

There are other reasons for growing this plant, besides its propensity to act as a cigar lighter. It is a very good garden plant. It grows to about 90 cm (3 ft) with ash-like, divided foliage that smells of lemon if bruised. The white flowers appear in erect spikes in the early summer. The type is pure

**Dictamnus**

white, but there is also a form, *D. a. purpureus* which has soft mauve flowers and darker purple veining.

Dictamnus like a good garden soil in a position where it gets the full sun. It will take a bit of shade but is happier in the open.

Propagation is from seed which should be sown fresh if possible. It can also be increased by division, but it takes a while for the resulting plants to settle down.

## DIGITALIS (Scrophulariaceae) –
Foxgloves

Although the common foxglove (*Digitalis purpurea*) is a biennial rather than a perennial, it still has a place in the herbaceous border. The technical details of its upbringing is of little consequence, it is the plant that matters. I love foxgloves and would never want to be without them in any garden. In mine I let them seed around at will and then remove the ones I do not want. In my woodland area they can roam as they wish, without restraint, building up large pools of dappled purple under the trees.

There is something endearing about the graceful spires of hooded flowers and certainly very reminiscent of the cottage garden. In my garden I prefer the wild foxglove without any improvements. There are many strains that one can purchase as seed; some of different pastel shades (Shirley strain); others (Excelsior strain) have flowers all round the stems instead of just down one side as in the wild plant. Certainly some of these spikes have more body to them, but I am quite content with my wild ones. In any batch of wild seedlings there will normally be several that will bear white flowers. Some gardeners rigorously reject any plants that produce the purple flowers so that eventually all seedlings produced in the garden are white.

So much for *Digitalis purpurea*, the wild foxglove. There are also quite a number of other species worth considering. Most of them are in theory perennials, but they are usually not long-lived and need regularly replacing from seed. One of the best is *D. grandiflora* which has soft-yellow flowers. Another yellow-flowered species is *D. lutea*, but this has much smaller flowers and smooth green leaves. Both these two are much shorter than the common foxglove, rising to only 60 cm (2 ft).

One of my favourites is *D. parviflorum*, the flower head of which is a solid mass of small tubular flowers of a rusty-brown colour. *D.* × *mertonensis* is like a shorter version of the common foxglove, except that it is a coarser plant, has larger, flatter flowers which are a rosy pink, and is perennial.

Foxgloves are happy in most soils and will grow in full sun or partial shade. They all come very readily from seed which can be sown in the spring.

**DISPORUM** (Convallareacea/Liliaceae)
These are generally plants for the plantsman rather than the general gardener as their collective appearance does little to enhance a summer border. They are related to the Solomon's seals and have inherited their cool appearance and like the same conditions.

The only species that does form an attractive colony is *D. sessile*, in its variegated cultivar 'Variegata'. This spreading plant produces a colony bearing green leaves striped with white, a very cool combination that looks very effective in light shade.

Another plant that is quite popular is *D. smithii*. This has small creamy bells followed by orange berries which are one of the reasons for growing this plant. *D. flavens* is rather like a large uvularia, with pale yellow bells.

They are an interesting group of plants with a lot of species to explore, particularly from China.

A moist, leafy soil in light shade is ideal for disporums, making them plants for the woodland garden. They can most easily be increased by division, but will also come from seed, especially *D. smithii*, which self sows.

**DORONICUM** (Compositae) – Leopard's bane
The few members of this genus that are grown in gardens make a cheerful contribution to the spring scene. They are rich yellow daisies, set off by fresh green leaves and can be guaranteed to brighten up any border, especially those in light shade. The only difficulty with doronicums is telling the various species apart, as they are very similar. The commonest is *D. orientale*, sometimes known as *D. caucasicum*, with its form 'Magnificum' being the one to go for if you have the choice. A common and similar plant is *D. plantagineum*, usually seen in its form 'Excelsum'. There is also a cultivar 'Miss Mason', of unknown origin, which again is similar to the preceding. Any of the above are worth obtaining but there being so little difference between them, one is enough unless you are a collector of daisies.

Doronicum will tolerate a wide range of soils and will grow in light shade, although they will not flower as well as they do in a more open position. Propagation is easily achieved by division in autumn.

**ECHINACEA** (Compositae) – Purple cone flower
Until relatively recently *Echinacea purpurea* was considered one of the rudbeckias (*R. purpurea*), from which it differs only in that it has purple flowers. It was introduced from America nearly two centuries ago and has served well in gardens ever since. The purple daisies come into flower in the summer and continue right into the autumn. It is the rays, or petals, that are a reddish-purple, the central disc being orange-brown, an odd combination that works very well. The rays droop slightly towards the hairy stems that hold the flowers stiffly erect. The plant is quite tall, about 1.2 m (4 ft) and clumps up well, needing no staking, thus making it a valuable plant for the back or middle of the border.

*Echinacea purpurea* is the only species that is widely grown in gardens but it does have several cultivars that are available. 'Robert Bloom' is one of the more popular with a very rich colouring of cerise-crimson. Another good crimson form is 'The King'. There are also white forms, such as 'White Lustre' and 'White Swan'. These are usually tinged, rather beautifully, with green. They like a good, moisture-retentive soil and prefer a position in a sunny border.

Propagation causes no problem as they can be easily divided in the spring or basal cuttings can be taken at the same time of year. They can also be grown from seed, but there is likely to be colour variation in the resulting plants.

**ECHINOPS** (Compositae) – Globe thistle
I love thistles and have a feeling that we are going to see many new ones in our gardens soon, introduced from such countries as Turkey, where they abound. Doubtless some will become a menace and will be immediately banished to the compost heap;

but others, like the globe thistle, will stand the test of time and become part of an established core of plants that we draw on for our borders.

The shape of the globe thistle's flower is unlike other thistles in that it is a complete sphere of florets (hence its name), each protected by its own spiny bracts to form a prickly ball. *Echinops ritro* is the plant that we are most familiar with and this has steely blue heads about 5 cm (2 in) in diameter, carried on grey stems over greenish-grey leaves, which are deeply lobed and have spines. They are plants that deserve a deep mulch so there is little reason to weed near them. There is a cultivar 'Veitch's Blue'

which is a richer blue than the type. *E. r. ruthenicus* is perhaps the star of the species. This has bright blue flowers over shining green foliage, which is deeply divided.

There are over 100 species of echinops and few of them other than *E. ritro* are seen in cultivation. *E. humilis* is occasionally seen, mainly in its form 'Taplow Blue'. This is very similar to *E. ritro*, but it is much taller, sometimes reaching 1.8 m (6 ft) and has less spines in the leaves. *E. exaltatus* has white or very pale blue flowers. Another white-flowered plant is *E. sphaerocephalus*. This is a large (1.8 m/6 ft) and coarse plant that needs a lot of space although it can look magnificent when in flower.

Echinops are sometimes confused with the eryngiums, the sea hollies, but these are quite separate plants that belong to another family, the Umbelliferae.

This is a plant that will tolerate most soils, but it must have a sunny position to look its best. There is quite a choice of propagation methods as this can be achieved from seed or by division and root cuttings.

**EPILOBIUM** (Onagraceae) – Willow-herbs
This is a very large genus and one that must be treated with respect as it contains some pernicious weeds.

The one that most people recognize is *E. angustifolium*, the rosebay willow-herb or fireweed. Certainly the species wants to be kept out of the garden as it spreads rapidly both underground and from seed. The white form 'Album' is reputedly less invasive, but unless you have plenty of space I would avoid this plant, however beautiful it may be.

One plant that I would grow is *E. glabellum*. This has creamy-white flowers and only grows to 30 cm (12 in) high. This is well behaved and a rather good-looking plant for the front of a border. A taller plant, a bit like the first-mentioned species in appearance, but better and also more well behaved is *E. dodonaei*.

Most of the cultivated willow-herbs like any good garden soil and a sunny position. They come easily from seed and can usually also be divided.

**Echinops**

*Above: Phygelius aequalis* 'Yellow Trumpet'. A shrubby perennial from South Africa that needs a sunny position.

*Omphalodes cappadocica*. A valuable plant for the front of borders that are in light shade. It flowers around mid summer.

*Lathyrus grandiflorum.* Perennial peas that like a low bush to scramble through. They spread quite quickly and can become a nuisance in the wrong place.

*Paeonia mollis.*
Single-flowered
peonies, such as
this, stand wet
weather better
than the brasher
double forms.

*Below: Echinacea
purpurea*
'Rosenberg'. A
very good form
of these
indispensable large
purple daisies.

*Opposite: Doronicum* 'Spring Beauty'. A vibrant yellow double daisy that stands out in the spring garden.

*Pulsatilla vulgaris*. A wonderful plant for the spring garden, especially when the sun lights up its golden boss of stamens.

*Artemisia ludoviciana latiloba.* A wonderful
foliage plant, whose silvery leaves act as a perfect
foil for so many other plants.

*Eremurus*. The foxtail lilies produce long, elegant spikes of flowers. They need a well-drained soil in a sunny position.

167

*Fritillaria imperialis*. The bulbous crown imperials are useful for growing amongst other plants as they retire below ground after flowering in spring.

## EPIMEDIUM (Berberidaceae) – Barrenwort

Epimediums have been used as garden plants for well over a century, but in recent years they have undergone a revival and have become very fashionable, with many new species being introduced, particularly from China. Their popularity stems from both their foliage and flowers. They are not very tall plants, rarely reaching above 30 cm (12 in) in height, but are useful both at the front of a border or as ground cover, particularly under trees and shrubs and other shady places. The leaves are especially attractive in the spring when they first unfurl, but they will earn their keep throughout the year. The flowers are very dainty, hanging from thin arching stems above the solid mass of leaves. Colours vary from yellow and white to red. They are a curious shape, many with spurs like horns.

*Epimedium grandiflorum* is one of the commonest seen. The flowers are some of the largest in the genus and vary in colour from red to white. It is usually found in one of its main three cultivars. 'Rose Queen' has deep pink flowers with white tips to the long spurs. 'White Queen', as its name suggests, is pure white and 'Violaceum' a dark violet. *E.* × *rubrum* also has red (crimson) flowers, but it is the foliage that is particularly eye-catching, with its bronzy-red tinted patterns. This is a cross of *E. grandiflorum* and *E. alpinum*. The latter comes from the European mountains and has red flowers with yellow spurs and tinted leaves that have passed on their enhanced colour to *E.* × *rubrum*.

*E. perralderianum* is another favourite that is easily obtained. It has large glossy leaves that give the plant a lot of its attraction, although the delicately hung yellow flowers give the plant an added passing attraction. The leaves are evergreen and should be cut back in the spring to allow a fresh flush to appear.

There are quite a lot more epimediums to explore if you can find them, particularly some of the newer ones. There is also a very closely allied genus, *Vancouveria*, that may be worth looking at. Epimediums are woodland plants that love cool root runs in moist leafmould. They will grow in any good garden soil, but dry soils should be avoided. They grow in partial shade although they will tolerate a good deal of sun as long as their roots are not too dry. They spread by underground runners, and can be a bit of a nuisance if planted amongst other choice plants.

They are easily divided up for propagation purposes.

## ERIGERON (Compositae) – Fleabane

Take away the daisies from our gardens and it would be surprising the hole that would be made. *Erigeron* alone has over 200 species, although admittedly not many of these are truly garden-worthy. Nonetheless it does provide us with quite a number of garden plants, mainly with mauvish petals, and a yellow central disc, although there are some that contribute yellow to the colour scheme. The majority of them come from America, although we do have some from Asia.

Erigerons are very similar to asters except that they have two or more layers of ray petals instead of one, and they generally flower earlier. Many of the taller species and hybrids unfortunately need supporting, but some of the shorter ones are quite happy to stand by themselves. It is the hybrids that are mainly grown these days. Probably the best is 'Dimity', which is a dwarf form with pink flowers that continue from early summer into the autumn. Another pink, but of tall disposition, is 'Charity'. 'Quakeress' is a much older cultivar with lilac-pink flowers, but it does need support.

Of the species, *E. glaucus* comes from a maritime habitat and is very useful in seaside gardens. The dense mats of evergreen leaves produce mauve flowers over a long period from early summer onward. 'Elstead Pink' is probably the best form of this species. *Erigeron aurantiacus*, as its name suggests, is an orange-coloured species. There is an old cultivar called 'Ava Gray' with yellower flowers. *Erigeron speciosus* has pale mauve flowers and its naturally occurring variety, *E.s. macranthus*, has rich blue or purple petals. This is one of the parents of some of the modern hybrids.

One erigeron that I would not like to be without is *E. karvinskianus* (previously known as *E. mucronatus*). This forms an airy bush of thin stems and small leaves and is covered with small white and pink daisies from late frost through to the winter. It only grows to 25 cm (10 in) or so, but is ideal for the front of border or in a wall. It self sows mildly but never becomes a nuisance as it can be easily removed.

Erigerons are happy in any good garden soil that is reasonably drained, as long as it has a sunny position.

## ERYNGIUM (Umbelliferae) – Sea holly

I would be hard put to make a short list of plants that I could never be without in a garden, but I suppose eryngiums would be bound to appear on such a list. They are the most wonderful garden plants, with both attractive foliage and flowers, both of which retain their fascination throughout the summer and, as an added bonus, can be dried for winter use. The flowers consist of a cone or in some cases a sphere of florets surrounded by a ruff of spiny bracts. They are blue, white or green. The stems and foliage often echo these colours. The foliage can be either deeply divided and prickly, or comprise strap-like leaves, edged with barbs, making it an awkward plant to weed near or to collect seed.

The shape and prickliness is reminiscent of the thistles but surprisingly this belongs to the cow parsley family, the Umbelliferae.

The name 'sea holly' is strictly reserved only for the British native, *Eryngium maritimum*, which, as its name implies, grows around the coast by the sea. Some of the others can be found in coastal districts, but grow inland as well. *E. maritimum* is not often seen as a garden plant but it is well worth growing. It has a pure blue flower, the colour of which diffuses down into the stem. The foliage is a good silvery-grey. It is not a very tall plant and will serve duty at the front of a border.

Two of the best are *E. alpinum* and *E. × oliverianum*. They are both very similar to each other with large, deep blue flowers cupped in a large whirl of spiny bracts. Again the colour is diffused down into the stems. They are of medium height (60 cm/ 2 ft), and are suitable for the middle of the border. The easiest way to tell them apart is bravely to run your hand over the spiny ruff: it is surprisingly soft and feathery in *E. alpinum* but stiff and prickly in *E. × oliverianum*.

Of a similar dark blue but with much smaller flowers that appear in great abundance is *E. tripartitum*. One plant of this gives the appearance of a small bush with wiry stems airily holding a profusion of these small prickly flowers in a haze of blue.

There are several similar species which are tall, up to 2.4 m (8 ft) or more. These have strap-like leaves with vicious teeth along the edges. These are undoubtedly the worst to weed around, so be warned. The flowers are usually smaller than the shorter forms, usually green or greenish-white in colour. They are very statuesque and are valuable for a feature or towards the back of the border. Probably the best is *E. decaisneanum* or *E. pandanifolium*, which it more easily used to be called.

*E. bourgatii* is an attractive evergreen plant grown for its very good foliage. The deep cut grey-green leaves have white veining. The flowers are small and greeny-blue in colour. A similar variegated plant with more rounded leaves is *E. variifolium*.

There are many more sea hollies that are worth exploring, but space precludes describing them. However, a final one should be mentioned. *Eryngium giganteum* is not strictly a perennial as it only flowers once, but it might take several years before it gets round to it. It grows to about 90 cm (3 ft) and has pale greenish-blue flowers and silver-white bracts. It sows itself around so that once a colony has been established it will look after itself and can be considered perennial. It is often known as 'Miss Willmott's Ghost' either because of the silvery bracts' ghost-like appearance at dusk, or because of the more romantic story that Miss Willmott was so enamoured by the plant that she surreptitiously used to drop

**Eryngium**

seeds in friends' gardens, where they flowered in her footsteps some years later.

Like most of the Umbelliferae, eryngiums have tap roots which mean they do not like disturbance; it is very difficult to move them once they have settled in. These long roots mean that the plant is able to delve deeply for moisture so they will tolerate dry soils, although they will do well in any garden soil as long as they have a sunny position.

Another advantage of these large roots is that they can be used for propagation in the form of root cuttings, which should be taken in the winter months. The other method of propagation is from seed, but the young plants should be planted out before the tap root becomes too big.

**ERYSIMUM** (Cruciferae) – Wallflowers
'But wallflowers are biennial?' people will object. Well, we treat many of them as biennial because we get a better and more reliable flowering that way, but in fact many wallflowers are perennials, albeit short-lived. There are basically two types of wallflowers, those that are used as bedding plants (and these are the ones that people consider biennial) and those that are used as single plants or in small groups. Some of these are very attractive and are a must in any border.

One of my all-time favourite plants is a variety called 'Wenlock Beauty'. It is a compact, low-growing form with spikes of a most beautiful patchwork of colours – basically a rich purply-red, with overtones of orange and mauve. It is hardy as it has come through two winters of temperatures down to −14°C (7°F) in my garden. In theory it is not long-lived and should be replaced every two years or so, but I have had plants that are still happily flowering after five or six years.

A different plant is 'Bowles Mauve' which forms a 60 cm (2 ft) or more rounded bush of rich mauve flowers on a silvery-grey framework of branches. It is one of the glories of the border and goes on flowering for most of the summer and often beyond. It is best to replant this every year as they can die over winter. I am doubtful as to whether this is due to hardiness in the cold, since I have had several plants growing in pure gravel that have survived several winters of the temperatures mentioned above. Plants in the open border suffer from wind-rock (a fault of many wallflowers) which causes a compacted cone-shaped hole to form round the stem which harbours water and causes the stem to rot. Another indication that this may be the cause of premature winter death in many wallflowers, is that the compact, ground-hugging forms seem, at least in my garden, to survive much better.

One ground-hugging form that does survive very well is the yellow 'Jubilee Gold' which has a long flowering period in the early summer. Another good yellow is 'Moonlight'.

171

There are many old-fashioned wallflowers, usually listed under *Cheiranthus*, which are worth growing. 'Harpur Crewe' (named after the Rev. David Harpur Crewe who 'rescued' it from disappearing) is a double yellow. 'Blood Warrior' is a very rich, double red. 'Rufus' is a good, light reddish-brown.

All the above are propagated by cuttings taken in early or mid-summer. These should be taken as a matter of course every year as a safeguard against loss. There are some however that can be propagated by seed. *Cheiranthus mutabilis* can be grown in this way. A variety of colours based on yellow, mauve, purple and red will be achieved, many attractively changing colour as the flowers begin to go over. It is a good idea to grow a batch from seed and then select those you like and continue them by cuttings.

Both *Erysimum* and *Cheiranthus* like well-drained soil (after all, their preferred habitat is on cliffs or walls) and should be given a good sunny position, preferably sheltered from the wind.

**EUPATORIUM** (Compositae) – Boneset, hemp agrimony
This is a vast genus of 1200 species, of which only a few are in cultivation and probably only one or two that are anything like widespread in gardens. This is either *E. purpureum*, a tall (2.1 m/7 ft) plant with a flat head of purplish-pink flowers carried on the purple stems, or the very similar *E. maculatum atropurpureum*. Both these flower late in the season and are much beloved by butterflies and bees. They are really plants for large borders because of their height and eventual spread. There are several others in cultivation, of which the British native *E. cannabium* should be mentioned. This is similar in general appearance, although the flowers are paler and the height more in the region of 1.2 m (4 ft). *E. rugosum* is somewhat different in that it has white flowers, whose flat head is more broken than those already mentioned.

Most of the eupatoriums prefer to have a moisture-retentive soil and do well in association with a stream or pond. They are usually seen in a sunny position although they will take light shade.

Propagation is by division or from seed.

**EUPHORBIA** (Euphorbiaceae) – Spurge
Euphorbias have, understandably, become very popular in recent years. They imbue the border with a freshness which is partly due to the foliage and partly to the yellow bracts that surround, in place of petals, the tiny flowers. It is an extraordinary genus that grows all over the world. We are familiar with the green herbaceous spurges, but who realizes that the poinsettia, that arrives as a Christmas present, or the pot plant that is known as the 'Crown of Thorns' are also euphorbias? They vary from tiny plants only a few inches high, to large tree-like succulents. However it is only the hardy herbaceous plants that concern us here, but even restricting ourselves to these leaves over a thousand species. More and more are being introduced into gardens, some of which, such as the tall, autumn-flowering *E. schillingii* are superb plants. Some are a bit rampant and there is always the worry that an aggressive weed might be introduced by mistake.

The flowers on the euphorbia are very distinct. They consist almost entirely of yellow or light-green bracts which surround the inconspicuous working-parts of the flower. As with so many plants with prominent bracts, they appear to be in flower for a very long period.

Starting in the spring, one of the best is *E. polychroma*, which forms a beautiful 45 cm (18 in) mound of fresh greenery topped by the radiant yellow bracts. The mound is continued throughout the summer, but is not so interesting once it has lost its freshness. Towards the end of the year it does briefly take on autumn tints.

*E. rigida* starts its interesting life in late winter or even earlier. It has whorls of pointed grey leaves that spiral up the stems. The flowers appear long before any other euphorbia and by late spring have turned a good shade of rust red, a colour they retain for most of the year. This plant needs a sunny spot in well-drained soil and is a fascinating plant to grow. *E. myrsinites* is a similar plant but its spiralled stems flop rather than stand upright as they do in *E. rigida*. It nonetheless makes an excellent plant for the front of a border.

*E. amygdaloides* is a British native, growing in light woodland. In the garden it is mainly represented by its form 'Purpurea', which puts on a fine display of dark purple leaves in the early spring. It gently seeds itself around, producing similarly coloured offspring. There is also a variegated form, 'Variegata', but this is not so interesting and difficult to keep going. *E. amygdaloides robbiae* is not over-distinguished in its own right but it does do well in shade, even quite dense shade, and is valuable as ground cover.

Other spring spurge include *E. characias*, which is a first-class garden plant, particularly in its variety *wulfenii*, which has huge broad yellowish heads.

*E. griffithii* flowers a little later. This has two good forms, 'Fireglow', with bright red bracts, and the superb 'Dixter', which is shorter and a darker colour. Both will run, given the right conditions.

There are several late summer and autumn-flowering species. *E. nicaeensis* is one growing to 60 cm (2ft) and *E. sikkimensis* is a taller species growing to 1.2 m (4 ft). This has a tendency to run a little.

Do not be talked into buying or accepting as a gift *E. cyparissias*. It has its moment in the right place, but it runs, or rather sprints, and can become a terrible weed. A similar, but larger plant, *E.* × *pseudovirgata* (sometimes *E. uralensis*), has the same tendencies and should also be avoided.

Euphorbias will grow in virtually any garden soil and many have the advantage of growing either in sun or partial shade. Those with a creeping rootstock can become invasive and are perhaps better in the wilder parts of the garden.

They can be increased by division or from seed. Those that do not have a running rootstock can be propagated vegetatively by taking basal cuttings in the spring or lateral cuttings later in the year.

One word of warning. The cut stems ooze a white juice which can be an irritant to some skins, so wear gloves when near the plants. At all costs avoid getting the sap in your eyes as it will produce an excruciating pain.

**FILIPENDULA** (Rosaceae) – Meadowsweet Many of the plants that we grow in our gardens also grow, or have relatives that grow, wild in the countryside. In many cases these plants have been introduced into the cottage garden either for their culinary, herbal or visual appeal. There are two native filipendula: meadowsweet (*F. ulmaria*), which grows in damp ground beside ditches, and dropwort, *F. vulgaris*, which

**Filipendula**

likes the opposite conditions: dry chalk downland. Both are represented in cultivation. Filipendula are tall plants with plumes of frothy white or pink flowers. The foliage consists of attractive pinnate leaves. One, *F. ulmaria* 'Aurea', is grown solely for the colour of its foliage, which is golden, the flowering stems being cut off before the plant seeds itself, producing green progeny throughout the garden.

The largest of the species, *Filipendula rubra*, grows up to 2.1 m (7 ft) and has very large leaves. It is a vigorous grower, soon making large colonies overtopped by the large plumes of pink flowers. The darkest pink form is called 'Venusta'. It is probably too vigorous for the normal border and would look good next to a large pond or in a woodland setting. There is a darker species, *Filipendula purpurea*, with carmine flowers. This is smaller than the previous plant, getting up to 1.2 m (4 ft). It needs more moisture than most of the others and looks particularly good by the waterside. There is a fine white form, 'Alba'.

One of the best is the similar-sized *F. palmata* which has soft pink flowers. Two selected forms are 'Elegantissima' and 'Rosea', both in different shades of pink.

*F. vulgaris* (dropwort) should be mentioned because, although it is not an outstanding plant, it is the only one that will grow in full sun in a dry soil.

All the other filipendulas like to have moist soil and partial shade. They will survive in full sun but only if the ground is not allowed to dry out.

Propagation is by division in the spring.

## FOENICULUM (Umbelliferae) – Fennel

Although there are a few species in this genus, only *F. vulgare* is grown in gardens. It is a tall plant with very fine filigree leaves that when touched produce a strong liquorice fragrance. The flowers are yellow and are held in very airy, flat heads. They are much liked by wasps and flies. It is a tall plant, growing 1.8–2.1 m (6–7 ft) high. The form that is generally grown is the bronze fennel (*F.v. purpureum*), whose leaves take on this very attractive colour.

Fennel can become a pest and self sow everywhere; and being tap-rooted it is not always easy to extract, especially when it is in the middle of a favourite plant, so cut it down immediately after flowering. It is happy in most soils and prefers a sunny position.

Seed is the easiest method of increase.

## GALEGA (Leguminosae) – Goat's rue

This is a small genus that has at least one species that makes a very good border plant and has been appreciated in our gardens for many generations. *G. officinalis* is tall (1.8 m/6 ft), with small spikes of mauve or white flowers in summer. These are set off well against the pinnate leaves, the whole plant having a lovely fresh look about it.

*G. orientalis* has good violet-blue flowers and is a very effective plant, but unfortunately it has the habit of running in suitable soils. It is shorter than the preceding.

Both plants are happy in any fertile garden soil. They prefer a sunny position.

Propagation can be from seed or by division.

## GAURA (Onagraceae)

This is a genus of about 18 species, of which *G. lindheimeri* is the only one in cultivation. Very few people know this plant, but when they see it in flower towards the end of the summer they are always impressed. The flowers are white, turning to pink as they age, and they seem to float above the plant, like butterflies, in the most charming manner. The whole plant grows to about 1.2 m (4 ft) in height and a little less in width, forming a nice bush. It is a plant that is well worth acquiring.

Gaura will tolerate most soils as long as they are reasonably well drained, and prefers a sunny position. It can be grown from seed.

## GENTIANA (Gentianaceae) – Gentian

Once seen, gentians are never forgotten; the blue of the flowers is so intense and distinct that it seems to burn a slot in the memory. Most of the several hundred species are low growing and only suitable for the rock or

**Gentiana**

peat garden, but there are some which will serve very well in the herbaceous or mixed border. They have the same deep blue trumpets as their shorter brethren, but they are borne on taller plants.

The most commonly seen is the willow gentian (*Gentiana asclepiadea*). This is quite a tall plant, growing up to 60 cm (2 ft) or more, with graceful arching stems of leaves resembling the willow, from which it gets its name. At the base of the leaves at the upper end of the stem are clusters of dark blue trumpets. The flowering time varies, but some will come into flower in the late summer, while others will wait until the autumn starts. There are several selected clones of varying shades of blue, as well as a

good white form, *G.a. alba*. It is a woodland plant and consequently is happiest in light shade and in a moist, leafy soil.

*G. septemfida* is a much shorter plant, reaching at best 30 cm (12 in), but it is still worthy of inclusion for the front of a border where its blue trumpets on floppy stems can be seen to their best advantage. It revels in a sunny position, but will also take a degree of shade.

It might come as a shock, but not all gentians are blue. In fact those of the southern hemisphere, from New Zealand for example, are all white, but there are also yellow ones. *G. lutea* is one such and is known as the yellow gentian – felwort or bitterwort in its native Europe. It does not immediately look like a gentian, with its tall stem reaching 1.2 m (4 ft) or more, each sheathed with clusters of yellow flowers held in the axils of the broad, ribbed leaves. This grows on the open mountainsides and prefers an open sunny position in the garden.

Having dismissed the rest of the genus as belonging to the rock garden, perhaps mention should still be made of one or two that would do well growing in any spot that does not become too dry, in the front of a border or other odd place where they will not get swamped by larger vegetation. *Gentiana sino-ornata* and its forms are probably the best and easiest to grow. They form a mass of blue trumpets emerging from a mat of green stems and leaves. They flower in the autumn, right through to Christmas. *G. acaulis* is the equivalent spring gentian, but it is more difficult to grow.

All are easy to propagate from seed, and the prostrate forms from division in the spring.

**GERANIUM** (Geraniaceae) – Hardy geranium, cranesbill

The first thing that any writer does when talking about geraniums is to define his subject. To many gardeners, geraniums mean the tender, brash red bedding plants that are strictly called pelargoniums. These briefly belonged to the genus *Geranium* way back in the last century and after over a hundred years the confusion over names still continues. Geraniums are the hardy, herbaceous plants, sometimes called cranesbills, which brighten any herbaceous or mixed border from spring round to the autumn. The colours are mainly purples and pinks and they vary in stature from a few inches to 1.2 m (4 ft) or more. They are one of the most important ingredients of the border and no garden should be without at least one, and you should find room, preferably, for a dozen or more; you will not regret it if you can. There would be no trouble in finding a dozen as they have grown enormously in popularity in recent years and there must be several hundred different species, hybrids and cultivars available. They are a most exciting genus and gardeners easily become hooked on them. Without realizing it, I have amassed 40 or 50 different ones in my garden and doubtless more will be added as the years pass.

It is difficult to know where to start with such a large genus. *Geranium pratense* is a native British plant, growing in meadows and beside the roads in the north of the country, and has been grown for a long time in gardens. It forms a good rounded clump of about 60 cm (2 ft) in height, covered in masses of violet-blue flowers during the summer. There are quite a number of cultivars, including the white *G.p.* 'Album'; a double white, a double lavender and a double violet: *G.p.* 'Album Plenum', 'Plenum Caeruleum' and 'Plenum Violaceum'. 'Striatum' has a curious bicoloured flower with violet petals striped with white. Mention should also be made of the wonderful 'Mrs Kendall Clark' with its silvery blue flowers and silver veins; a plant that needs support, but definitely worth growing. Another native of the same kind of habit is *G. sylvaticum*, which flowers earlier, in the spring. This is also violet-blue and has cultivars of white, pink and various shades of blue. It will tolerate some shade.

Staying with the larger ones, *G. phaeum* makes another good clump, this time with very dark maroon flowers and reflexed petals. The dark colour accounts for its vernacular name 'Mourning Widow'. It has a very good white form. Both will tolerate shade, but the dark flowers tend to get lost in the gloom, while the white form shines out in these conditions.

*G.* × *magificum* is a commonly seen plant (often called *G. ibericum*), forming a mass of soft leaves overtopped with large violet-blue flowers. A plant that typifies the herbaceous border for me. Slightly smaller and with divided leaves, but similar in colour is 'Johnson's Blue'. They both flower in early summer, as does *G. himalayense*, another blue-flowered member of the family. This has several cultivars including a good double form, 'Birch Double', and one with a reddish tinge, 'Gravetye'.

The tallest and one of the brightest is *G. psilostemon*. This forms a large clump 1.2 m (4 ft) tall and as much across, with vibrant magenta flowers that have black centres. It flowers throughout the summer and sometimes into the early autumn. By way of contrast, there is another geranium with the same intense magenta colour. This is *G. subcaulescens*. The contrast is in the height, as this one only reaches 5-7.5 cm (2–3 in). If it were not for the colour it would not be worth bothering with, but it can make an effective splash at the front of a border.

*G. renardii* is of intermediate height (30 cm/12 in) and is useful towards the front of a border. This has white flowers with a reddish-blue veining. The leaves are unusual in the geraniums in that they have a greyish-green and a wrinkled appearance and feel, a bit like wood-sage. This is a late spring and early summer plant, but is useful for its foliage for the rest of the summer.

Slightly taller, but with a tendency to flop, is another good garden plant: *G. clarkei* 'Kashmir White'. This has white flowers blushed with pink from the red veins. There is also a 'Kashmir Purple' along similar lines, but it is the former that I prefer.

Another white geranium, but one that is not frequently seen, is *G. lambertii*. This also has red marks but these are concentrated towards the centre of the flower, more in the way of an 'eye'. This is a bit of a sprawler and rambles through other plants. The sprawler *par excellence* is *G. procurrens*, which is a rampant plant that will quickly climb through other vegetation. It should be avoided in a small garden, but, where there is space, it can make a colourful sight with its mass of reddish-mauve, dark-centred flowers, which bloom from late summer through until late autumn. A much better sprawler that also flowers in the autumn is *G. wallichianum*, which is normally grown in the form 'Buxton's Variety'. This has blue flowers with a white centre.

A plant of refined habits, but which nonetheless is happy to climb through neighbours is *G.* 'Russell Prichard'. It has wonderful rose-magenta flowers over silvery-green foliage and is one of the geraniums I would never like to be without. In colour combinations it looks particularly fine growing through silver-leaved plants. One of its parents is *G. endressii*, which makes rather loose mounds of pink flowers throughout the summer and autumn. It can get a bit carried away, and soon seedlings appear to make great colonies, but if there is space then this can look marvellous. If it is shaved over in the spring, more compact plants are formed. 'Wargrave Pink' is probably the best form with bright salmon-pink flowers. 'Claridge Druce' is one of its hybrids, which is more vigorous than *G. endressi* itself. It makes good ground cover.

*G. macrorrhizum* also makes excellent ground cover – one of the best. The leaves that smother the ground are soft and very aromatic. They turn a nice shade of red in autumn. The flowers vary from pink to red depending on variety. There is also a white, but this is not very pure, tending towards pink.

One of the longest-flowered of the geraniums is *G. sanguineum*. It is a plant that should be in every garden. It forms dense tight hummocks about 30 cm (12 in) high and is covered in magenta flowers all summer and into the autumn. The finely cut leaves are a dark green, and colour attractively in the autumn. There are many forms including a white one, 'Album' which is not as floriferous as the type.

There are lots more for the keen gardener to explore, not only of the true border types but also the smaller ones which are usually grown on the rock garden. I will list just one of these which, with justification, often grow in the front of a border. This is *G. cinereum* 'Ballerina'. Its petals have a base colour of pink, which is overlaid with many reddish-purple veins coalescing in the centre to give a dark eye.

Geraniums are very accommodating in that they will thrive in any ordinary garden soil and many will tolerate a little shade. Most of the taller geraniums get very leggy, particularly after flowering, and they can be sheared over to get a new crop of fresher, compact leaves.

Propagation is very easy in most cases as they can be readily increased by division. Many will come easily from seed, but remember that the named cultivars might not come true. One can say 'might not' rather than 'will not' with geraniums, as many of the offspring resemble their parents quite closely, indeed with *G. wallichianum* 'Buxton's Blue', it is the only way to propagate it; any untypical plants being rejected.

## GEUM (Rosaceae) – Avens

When choosing plants for an herbaceous or mixed border, one can easily slip into the habit of selecting certain plants for impact and others as a supporting cast, with little more to do than fill in the background. Visitors will sweep their eyes straight past these plants without a second glance. Unfortunately geums seem to fall into this category, but they are very garden-worthy in their own right, particularly in the early summer when their bright colours suit the mood of the season before we settle down to the softer tones of high summer.

This is a group of plants in which the species are very rarely grown in gardens; one normally sees cultivars or hybrids. Many of these cultivars have double flowers borne on 60 cm (2 ft) stems above hairy pinnate leaves. The most common of these for use in the border are *G. chiloense* 'Mrs J. Bradshaw' and 'Lady Stratheden', which are a bright red and soft yellow respectively.

G. 'Borisii' is a smaller plant and has wonderful, pure orange flowers that glow in the border. Unlike the previous plants, this is a single flower, as is a similar plant with paler flowers, 'Georgenberg'.

One group of cultivars that are quite different in appearance is based on our native water avens, *Geum rivale*. In the species the petals are a pink or soft orange colour, with their bell-shaped flowers cupped by conspicuous sepals. This is quite widely grown, although many people prefer one or other of its forms. *G. rivale* 'Album' has petals that are not quite white, more a pale yellowish-green. 'Leonard's Variety' is the best of the hybrids with its soft coppery-pink flowers. A good yellow form is 'Lionel Cox'.

Geum seem happy in most soils and will tolerate a certain amount of partial shade, although most look at their best in the sun.

Propagation is usually by division in the autumn or spring. Plants can get untidy and straggly after their initial spring flowering and should be tidied up and divided at frequent intervals (every two or three years) to keep the plants young and compact.

## GILLENIA (Rosaceae)

*Gillenia* is another of the small genera in this book. It consists of only two species and only one of these is suitable for garden cultivation, *G. trifolia*. This is a plant that comes from eastern United States, where it is known as Indian physick or bowman's root. It was introduced from there as long ago as 1713 but even now, after more than two and a half centuries, it is not seen very frequently. This is a pity as it is a very pretty plant. The adjective 'pretty' was chosen carefully as this is a very airy, dainty plant and prettiness is its main attraction.

It forms a light airy bush of red-stemmed, starry flowers that look like a haze of white insects or butterflies at the height of summer. The red colour is carried through from the stems to the sepals which remain after the petals have dropped, giving the whole plant a red-and-white appearance. The leaves, as the name suggests, are made up of

three leaflets, each of which is sharply serrated. They colour well in the autumn. The plant grows to 90–120 cm (3–4 ft) high and may need a bit of support in a windy spot.

There is no problem with locating this plant as it will be happy in any garden soil and grow in either sun or partial shade. It is a marvellous plant to liven up a dark background.

Sowing seed is the best way of propagation, although they may be slow to germinate. Division in the spring is another method.

Its brother, *G. stipulata*, is very similar in appearance, except for variations in the leaf and its flowers are only half the size of *G. trifoliata*. Seed is occasionally seen and it might be worth having a try if you want to be different.

**Gillenia**

**GLAUCIDIUM** (Glaucidiaceae)

*Glaucidium palmatum* is the sole representative of this genus and is one of the glories of a shady garden. The species has large-cupped, lavender flowers, set against large, light green leaves. The general appearance is a very fresh one. The whole plant reaches about 45 cm (18 in). There is also a white form, which is also rather exquisite, but I think I prefer the straight species. If you have a shady garden this is a plant well worth acquiring.

They like a moist, leafy soil in a cool position.

Propagation can be by seed or by division.

**GUNNERA** (Gunneraceae)

Now for one of the giants of the garden. This is no plant for the small garden with its bristly umbrella-like leaves, each up to 1.8 m (6 ft) across, looking like a giant rhubarb. There are 50 of these southern-hemisphere plants and by no means are they all of this stature. Most gardeners would be surprised to see some that the alpine growers cultivate have leaves only 1 cm (¾ in) across and tightly hug the ground.

However it is the giants that interest us in the open garden. The best situation both from the growing point of view and for visual impact is beside water. It should have some protection from the wind. Planted beside a pond or lake the plant makes a gigantic mound of leaves and a curious flowering stem in the form of a rounded cone or club, about 60 cm (2 ft) or more long. The main two species grown in this country are not entirely hardy and their prominent crowns should be given a mulch of their own leaves and bracken in the winter, to protect them from the worsts of the frosts.

*Gunnera manicata* is the most frequently seen. This is the bigger of the two, sometimes reaching up to 2.4 m (8 ft) under favourable conditions. *G. tinctoria* is a very similar plant but is smaller and more compact.

They need a moist position or somewhere where they can be easily and frequently watered. One only has to look at the amount of growth put on each year to appreciate that a rich soil, regularly fed with manure, is required. They are happy in full sun or partial shade.

Propagation is not often undertaken as one does not require many of these plants but when it is, it is by division in the spring.

For the really small garden this is the ideal plant as one plant will entirely fill the garden, removing any necessity to weed or perform any other form of gardening activity. It will also provide shelter on wet or sunny days!

**GYPSOPHILA** (Caryophyllaceae) – Baby's breath

What a contrast this is to the last plant! From huge African elephant's ears we move to a dainty spray of flowers like a puff of smoke or a passing cloud. The tiny white flowers are borne in great profusion on wiry stems, creating the illusion of a puff of smoke or, as one of its vernacular names puts it, a baby's breath. The small narrow leaves play a definitely secondary role in this

**Gypsophila**

plant and are rarely noticed. It is a very popular plant for cutting, often used in wedding bouquets and decorations.

There are a large number of species, about 125 in all. Of these, quite a number are grown in the garden, although many are either annual or grown in the alpine garden rather than the herbaceous border. The one that is mainly grown for permanent borders is *Gypsophila paniculata*, which will form a mound of flowers in the summer up to 1.2 m (4 ft) high and the same across. The type plant is grown, when it produces single white flowers, but it is the cultivar 'Bristol Fairy' which is the most popular with its pure white, double flowers. 'Rosy Veil' has rose-pink double flowers, produced on a more compact plant, growing to about 30 cm (12 in). Another short form, 'Flamingo', produces a pale pink flower.

This is a plant for dry, sunny borders. It will not tolerate wet or damp conditions. As long as the soil is free-draining it is not too worried about what type it is; it will happily grow on chalk.

These are deep tap-rooted plants that can most easily be propagated from seed.

## HELENIUM (Compositae) – Helenium, sneezeweed

Heleniums are another of those plants that are vital to any border, but yet can be overlooked as the eye searches for more startling or interesting plants. They do not deserve to be put into the second rank as they tend to be quite colourful and their flowering extends over a long period during the summer and autumn. The name 'Helenium' comes from the legend that the plants so-called 'sprang' from the soil where Helen of Troy's tears fell. An interesting idea, but all the forms we grow in the garden originate in North America, which did not even form part of Ulysses' travels, let alone Helen's!

One of the reasons that heleniums are often relegated to the second division is because they belong to the daisy family and few of these seem to make it to the first. In this case the flowers are in a colour range from yellow to brown, sometimes with a dark centre and others with a yellow. These are borne on stems that vary in height up to about 1.5 m (5 ft). The dwarfer varieties tend to flower earlier in the season than the taller ones and if deadheaded can produce a second crop of flowers. The taller forms need staking except in the most sheltered of positions.

The parentage of the forms we grow in the garden is lost way back in gardening history, but one of the main influences, particularly with the taller cultivars, is *Helenium autumnale*. *H. bigelovii* is another one of the parents, this time mainly seen in the shorter cultivars.

One of the oldest cultivars is the medium height 'Moerheim Beauty', which has bronze-red petals and a dark brown centre. It has a long flowering period. Taller varieties include the yellow 'Riverton Beauty' and the reddish-brown 'Riverton Gem', both with maroon centres. 'Bruno' is a very good medium-height plant of a mahogany colour, but is a later flowerer. Other medium-height plants include 'Coppelia' with its orange petals, 'Butterpat', a good rich yellow and 'Pumilum Magnificum', a deep yellow. The shorter varieties derived from *H. bigelovii* include 'Aurantiacum', in which both the petals and centre are yellow, and 'Crimson Beauty' with bronze-red petals.

If there was space in a garden it would be an attractive idea to grow several of these cultivars in large clumps in different parts of the borders, where they would more than prove their worth as a pleasing mainstay.

Heleniums are happy in any fertile soil that is moisture retentive; they can look very sorry for themselves during dry weather unless watered. They prefer a sunny situation.

Propagation is by division and they should be divided every few years to keep the colony fresh and vital.

## HELIANTHUS (Compositae) – Sunflower

It is curious how many of the 'H's are members of the Compositae (daisy) family. Here is another and there would be more to come if I had decided to include *Helichry-*

*sum*. Again there is the Greek connection in that the name derives from the word 'Helios', sun, from which we also get its vernacular name 'sunflower'. These plants are not as attractive as the last genus, but nonetheless are an important part of the summer and autumn border. The genus is quite large with 110 members, all from the Americas, home of so many of our garden daisies. Some are annual, as indeed is the best-known of all sunflowers which has flowers the size of dinner plates. The perennial species do not grow anywhere near as large as this, although some of them are fairly tall. They are all yellow-rayed and they have rough, coarse leaves which rasp as you run your fingers over them.

They are useful in providing a splash of bright yellow at the back of a border, if this is what you're looking for, over quite a long period. In spite of their tough-looking stems they will need support in areas where they are liable to suffer from excessive wind.

*Helianthus decapetalus* is the most commonly available, particularly in its form 'Loddon Gold', which, as the name implies, has golden yellow flowers. An older form, 'Capenoch Star', is a much paler yellow. *H. atrorubens*, sometimes called *H. sparsifolius*, is a taller plant (up to 2.1 m/7 ft) with an invasive rootstock. It is mainly grown in the form 'Monarch', which is a semi-double with a dark centre. This is a characteristic of the species and accounts for its American name of 'dark-eye sunflower' It is not reliably hardy and in cold areas some of the rootstock should be lifted and overwintered in a frost-free place. It is not always a bad thing when an invasive plant is cut back occasionally by a deep frost.

*H. salicifolius*, or the willow-leaved sunflower, is occasionally seen. This also makes large clumps of very tall plants, sometimes stretching up to 2.4 m (8 ft) in height with smaller yellow flowers. It is not so coarse as some of the others in the genus and its stature makes it a good background for other plants.

Helianthus need a moisture-retentive soil in a position where they will get plenty of sun. Nearly all the sunflowers tend to run about a bit, some becoming a little invasive and, as with all plants that have this tendency, propagation is easily carried out by division.

**HELIOPSIS** (Compositae) – Sunflower
This is one of several genera that lay claim to the name 'sunflower' and like the others is an important plant for the autumn scene. Needless to say the flowers are yellow and usually carried on quite tall stems. *H. helianthoides* grows to about 1.5 m (5 ft) although many of the modern cultivars are much shorter. There are quite a number of these to choose from; some being semi-double or double, which 'Goldgefieder' ('Golden Plume')' is one of the best. If sunflowers have anything against them, it is their floppy nature which means they often require staking.

The soil for heliopsis is not critical, but they should have a sunny position. They are easy plants to increase, they simply need dividing.

**HELLEBORUS** (Ranunculaceae) –
Hellebore
If it were not for barren winter borders and lack of much else in bloom then perhaps hellebores would not be quite so popular as they are, but I must confess that they are one of my favourite genera. Their saucer shaped flowers, in a large range of colours from green through white and yellow, to purple so deep that it is almost black, appear from the beginning of the year through to mid-spring. The plants, so distinct during their flowering period, discreetly retire into the background for the rest of the year. As they will tolerate shade they can be grown amongst shrubs or under trees, thus utilizing space that otherwise might be wasted.

There are quite a number of species and hybrids that are widely available, but it is *Helleborus niger*, the Christmas rose – that appears on so many cards at that season – that most people think of when hellebores are mentioned. In spite of its name it rarely flowers before mid-winter, when it produces glistening white flowers with a boss of

**Helleborus**

yellow stamens in the centre. They often look much better on Christmas cards than they do in reality, as they often end up mud splashed and chewed by slugs; but precautions can be taken against both these and the perfect bloom can be a stunning sight.

*H. niger* is best propagated from seed.

Often earlier into flower is *H. foetidus* which has green bell-shaped flowers that are rimmed with red. This has some of the most attractive foliage of any of the hellebores; indeed, it could be grown purely as a foliage plant. The leaves are deeply divided like fingers on a hand, and of a very dark green, often tending towards black. The flowers are held high above the leaves in clusters.

In recent years the Lenten rose (*Helleborus orientalis*) has become more widely known and very popular. It is doubtful whether any of the plants known as this in cultivation are in fact true *H. orientalis*: they have been hybridized over the years and are now thoroughly mixed up. Not that this matters a jot; it is the resulting plant that matters, not its name. The typical plants have a greenish-plummy colour, often spotted with a rosy pink.

However there are now many much better forms with clearer colours, ranging from pure white to almost black. The spotting, where it is present, is also more refined in the better forms. Some of these forms bear cultivar names, but many do not, so it is best to choose them when they are in flower so that you can see what you are getting.

Similar in appearance to the last species, but appearing much earlier, often before Christmas, is *H. atrorubens*. This again is a name that covers the plants grown in the garden, the true species not being in cultivation. It has a dark purplish colour.

*H. argutifolius* (or *H. corsicus*, as it is still called in some catalogues) forms big plants 60–90 cm (2–3 ft) across, bearing large leaves with prominently serrated margins. The flowers are smaller than *H. orientalis*, more cup shaped and coloured a yellow-green. This makes a big bold splash in the spring border. It has to be crossed with the tender *H. lividus* to produce *H. × sternii*, which has the robustness of *H. argutifolius*, but the leaves and flowers take on the reddish tinge of *H. lividus*.

There are many other species to explore, including the delicate *H. torquatus*, with its gun-metal coloration, but this is left for the reader to do.

Hellebores are not fussy about the soil as long as it does not dry out excessively. They will take full sun or partial shade, probably looking their best in a woodland setting, or at least amongst shrubs. Propagation can be either by division in the spring or from seed. Some people have difficulty in germinating the seed, but if it is sown fresh it comes up like the proverbial mustard and cress.

**HEMEROCALLIS** (Hemerocallidaceae/ Liliaceae) – Day lilies, hemerocallis

From the winter and early spring we move to the height of summer and to a plant that is a regular feature of most large herbaceous and mixed borders. Early in the season it produces mounds of arching, grass-like leaves from which emerge leafless stems carrying the yellow, orange or brown trumpets of the day lily. As its name suggests, each flower only lasts a day, but fortunately each stem produces a number of buds which means that flowering is continuous. Different varieties flower at different times, so if there is sufficient space, a succession of flowers can be had over quite a long period in the summer.

I find that the cultivars that are of a single colour are more attractive than those that have their main colour concentrated inside the trumpet, where it can only be seen if the flower is looked at end on. Some of the mahogany-red cultivars, in particular, look very scrappy *en masse* and add nothing to the overall effect of a border, nor yet are interesting enough in their own right. The single-coloured flowers or even bicolours, where the colour is repeated on the outside of the trumpet, give a much more effective impression and make a better statement in a border. Another reason for preferring the simple colours is that nearly all the yellow varieties are scented, whereas most of the others are lacking this attribute.

Although there are some species grown, these tend to be found only in specialists' gardens. It is one or more of the many hybrids that will be found in the majority of gardens. I say 'many' because since the beginning of this century there have been several thousand named forms. Even today there are well over 300 available through commercial outlets in Britain alone, and many more in the United States where hemerocallis is a bit of a cult plant.

Of the species, *Hemerocallis flava* (now *H. lilio-asphodelus*) is one of the earliest to have been introduced, more than four centuries ago. It is not as tall as the modern cultivars, reaching only 75 cm (30 in), but it has clear yellow flowers and a superb scent.

It quickly forms a large clump from which it can easily be propagated. *H. citrina* is another yellow, this time with a bit more green in it. The big disadvantage of this species is that it tends to open more in the evenings. On the other hand it does have a good fragrance with which to scent the evening air.

*H. fulva* is another very old garden favourite, and although it has now been superseded by modern hybrids, it can still be seen in many gardens. The colour is none too special, a buff-orange with an apricot line down the middle of each petal, and it is without scent. It has a cultivar 'Kwanso', which is a semi-double, popular with some people but it has never done anything for me.

There are several other species, but it is the hybrids that demand more attention. There are so many that it would take the rest of the book just to list them and I can only hope to mention just a few of my own favourites. 'Corky' is one of the latest to flower. It has much smaller and more refined flowers than other hybrids (possibly showing it is derived from *H. multiflora*). The petals are yellow with a broad bronze stripe down the reverse of each. It has a very fresh appearance. Possibly of similar parentage is 'Golden Chimes' which has similar-sized flowers but with a deeper, golden-yellow petal and a broader mahogany stripe. Of the bigger forms 'Marion Vaughn' is mid-season with fresh lemon-yellow flowers. 'Stafford' is the best of the mahoganies with a yellow stripe down the middle of each segment. 'Cartwheels' is a good orange with wide petals that open well, showing the colour. 'Pink Damask' is a good old cultivar with a clear pink-salmon trumpet that is not a muddy colour like so many of the other pinks.

And so the list goes on. I can only recommend that the reader goes to a garden such as Wisley, where they have a large number of cultivars, and choose for themselves.

Day lilies will tolerate a large range of soils, although they do prefer them to be moisture retentive. They are at their best in full sun, but they will accept a little shade. They all grow on a relatively vigorous rootstock and this provides for a ready source of divisions, so propagation is easy. Only species will come true from seed.

**HEUCHERA** (Saxifragaceae) – Alum root, coral bells

Heuchera is one of those double-purpose plants that are useful in the border both for their flowers and their foliage. The latter form low clumps of rounded evergreen leaves, usually hairy and with a range of colours from bronze to marbled green. From these mounds spring thin, wiry stems bearing airy heads of small white, cream, pink or green flowers. The majority come from North America and have been around in gardens for a long time – the earliest being introduced over 300 years ago.

**Heuchera**

Although some plant names look very strange, they all have some purpose behind them. In this case *Heuchera*, which seems meaningless, is named after a Professor J. H. Heucher.

There are about 50 species in the wild, but only a handful are in cultivation. The most popular at the moment must be *Heuchera micrantha* 'Palace Purple', with its wonderful reddish-brown foliage that lasts most of the year, although there is a tendency for it to turn a lovat green towards autumn. It has cream flowers that are borne from the summer into autumn. Surprisingly, it comes reasonably true from seed, inferior forms being discarded. As a contrast *H. cylindrica* 'Greenfinch' has green leaves washed with a silver marbling, but it is the flowers from which the name is acquired. These are a soft yellowish-green.

Also grown mainly for its foliage is *H. americana*. Its lobed green leaves are coloured along the veins with coppery bronze, and covered with a silvery sheen. They darken with age, as do most of the heuchera. The flowers are greenish and appear in the early summer.

*H. sanguinea* is one of the most commonly grown species particularly in some of the forms that have come out of Bressingham. Called coral bells in its home country, the United States, it has flowers in shades of red. 'Bressingham Blaze' is one of the best.

There are quite a number of hybrids that are usually lumped under the name *H. × brizoides*, many of which are a result of crossing *HH. sanguinea* and *macrantha*. Again a lot of the best have come out of Bressingham with 'Bressingham hybrids' covering a number of them. These have pink to dark red bells. 'Pearl Drops' is a pinkish white and 'Coral Cloud', a coral crimson. 'Scintillation' is a good pink with red tips to the bells.

Finally mention should be made of *H. villosa*. This is much later flowering than other members of the genus, who all tend to flower in the earlier part of the summer, whereas this one enjoys the late summer and goes on into autumn. Its flowers are very tiny and appear as a cloud of white.

Well-drained soil that does not dry out too much is required to keep heucheras happy. They can be situated in either full sun or partial shade.

Propagation is by division, which should be undertaken regularly every few years to prevent the plant getting too old. Revitalization of the woody rootstock can also be achieved by digging up old plants and replanting them deeper, or by working compost into the crowns to get the same effect.

## HOSTA (Funkiaceae/Liliaceae) – Plantain lily

Here is a genus that has risen in popularity over the past few years, particularly in America and Japan where breeding programmes are introducing new cultivars so quickly that it is impossible to keep up with the flow. Although they do bear interesting flowers, it is for their foliage that hostas are mainly grown and it is easy to see why. The bold leaves make wonderful whorled clumps in a variety of greens, often contrasted with a yellow, cream or another green variegation. The leaves are prominently ribbed with veins and vary from a narrow willow-shape to a broad ovate outline. They make an excellent ground cover but should not be planted too close together as the appearance of the leaves will be spoilt by the overcrowding. The flowers, that are often overlooked, are borne on tall spikes and are either a lilac blue or white, mainly in late summer or early autumn.

My heart sinks when it comes to the descriptions of the various species and their cultivars. This is not so much because of the sheer quantity, although this is intimidating in itself, but because of the muddled nomenclature that surrounds this genus. As far as quantity is concerned, I suggest that readers keep their eyes open as they go round gardens and make notes on those hostas that appeal to them. I am going to mention some of my own preferences and those which will make up a basic framework for a garden.

Some people consider the straight forward green-leaved hostas a bit boring, but there are some fine plants. One of the best is *Hosta lancifolia*, with narrow shiny green leaves that taper to a point. It throws up 60 cm (2 ft) stems of deep violet trumpets late in the season and is one of the best for flowers. Another good green-leaved form is *H. ventricosa*. By contrast these shiny leaves are broadly heart-shaped with wavy margins. The plant is bigger in all its parts, the deep lavender flowers being carried on 90 cm (3 ft) stems and appearing in late summer. There are also fine variegated forms of this plant, in particular *H. v.* 'Variegata' with creamy-yellow margins to the leaves. Many believe that this is the best of the variegated hostas. The last of the green-leaved hostas we will consider is *H. undulata* 'Erromena'. This is a Japanese cultivar and one of the largest of the hostas, reaching up to 1.2 m (4 ft) with large clumps of broad green leaves.

Many of the hostas, while basically green, have a bloom to the leaves giving them a blue appearance. *Hosta sieboldiana* is the biggest of this group and probably the largest-leaved of all the hostas, sometimes reaching up to 30 cm (12 in) wide. It is entirely grown for its great leaves as the flowers are of no consequence in this species. It is sometimes still referred to as *H. fortunei robusta* or *H. glauca*. *H. × tardiana* is a group of blue hybrids of which my favourite is undoubtedly 'Halcyon', although 'Blue Moon' comes close behind. *H. tokudama* is a much smaller hosta, indeed it resembles a small version of *H. sieboldiana*. The last of the glaucous-foliaged hostas are some of the forms of *H. fortunei*.

Next, a quick look at some of the many hostas with variegated leaves. Of the white variegations *H. crispula* is one of the best, with wide white margins to the broad, wavy, dark green leaves. It is one of the earliest to flower, bearing pale lilac flowers. *H. decorata* has rounded dark green leaves and again a white margin. The flowers are a dark lilac in colour. *H. albomarginata*, as its name suggests, also has white margins, this time quite narrow, although it is also available as plain green. Very similar is *H.* 'Thomas Hogg'. *H. fortunei* 'Marginata

Alba' has sage-green leaves with a wide white edge. *H. undulata* 'Variegata' has quite small wavy leaves with the central area splashed and streaked with white and green margins.

Subtly different are those with cream or yellow variegations. Mention has already been made of *H. ventricosa* 'Variegata' as probably the best with this characteristic. This has dark green leaves margined with creamy-yellow. Its companion *H.v.* 'Aureo-maculata' has the same colour markings splashed over the centre of the leaf. *H. sieboldiana* 'Frances Williams' has a characteristic *sieboldiana* leaf, irregularly but broadly edged with yellow. There are so many, many more of these, all variations on the same theme, but all worth a look.

Not all the leaves are green or glaucous blue, some are yellow all over. *H.* 'Sun Power' has beautiful gold leaves with just a touch of very pale green. 'Midas Touch' has rounder cupped leaves of gold, wheres 'Piedmont Gold' is greener. 'Light Up' has small, narrow, wavy leaves of a gold yellow. *H.* 'Zounds' is a very good gold, with puckered leaves. *H. sieboldii* 'Kabitan' has rich yellow leaves with a narrow band of green on the margins. The form of the leaves is quite wavy. *H.* 'Vanilla Cream' has small, broad leaves of a pale green tending to gold. *H.* 'Excitation' has similarly coloured but narrower leaves.

I have tried to give not only some of my favourites, but an indication of some of the various variations and permutations that exist in the hostas. It is now up to the reader to go out, more aware of the great variations that exist, and look at them with new eyes and perhaps make up your own mind as to what plants you like or which would suit your garden.

Hostas grow best in rich soil in partial shade but they will tolerate quite a range of soils as long as they do not dry out too much. In spite of preference to partial shade, they will grow in full sun if they are kept moist and, certainly, they flower better in this position than they do in shade. They also make tighter, neater clumps.

Unless you are trying your hand at breeding, the only way to propagate hostas is by division. This can be achieved by lifting the plant and splitting it with a spade, although dividing by hand will not only provide more plants and less wastage, but also less chance of disease entering the wounds. Hostas in fact do not need disturbing and will grow and improve in the same place for years with no more than a dressing of compost. In order not to disturb the plant it is possible to remove part of a plant with a spade as it lays in the ground, just cutting off a small section or two.

The taste of hostas seem to be one of the greatest of delicacies as far as slugs and snails are concerned. (The taste is also appreciated by the Japanese who stir-fry the leaf stalks). Unfortunately one bite (by the slugs – not by the Japanese) into the emerging spike of foliage will result in the leaves looking like paper doilies, so anti-slug measures should be taken before and after the foliage has emerged. The other predator that may have to be kept at bay is the flower arranger, as hosta leaves are excellent for decorations indoors.

**INULA** (Compositae) – Inula, elecampane
After a considerable break we are back with the daisy family; they are never far away. This is quite a large genus with 200 members, but many are far too coarse for the garden. Indeed, those that are used in the garden are considered coarse by some people, but they do add stature and texture to a border. I think they are of more interest in a border than, say, the *Helianthus* (see page 180), whose overall appearance can be somewhat boring.

Of the various species in general cultivation I prefer the two extremes, the shortest and the tallest. The shortest is *Inula ensifolia* which only grows to about 30 cm (12 in) in height. It provides a dense clump of narrow-leaved stems producing golden yellow flowers, with a darker centre, in the late summer. It is very good for a position in the front of the border.

At the other end of the scale is *I. magnifica*, sometimes still known as *I. afghanica*. This is a tall plant reaching up to

Inula

*I. royleana* also has the same finely cut petals but in this case they are a darker orange-yellow. It is also shorter than *hookeri*, being only 60 cm (2 ft) tall.

They will all grow in any moisture-retentive soil as long as they have a sunny situation, although a certain degree of shade is tolerated.

Propagation is from either seed or division, the latter being especially easy with the more invasive members of the genus.

**IRIS** (Iridaceae) – Flags

This is one group of plants that is very easy for everybody to identify. They have characteristic flowers with three 'falls', which hang down as if weary of life, and three 'standards', which proudly stand upright. These make the plant really distinct whether it is only a few inches high or several feet. These characteristics apply to all the irises whatever type they are, and in gardening terms we can divide them first into bulbous and non-bulbous, of which the latter is of most interest to us. This can then be further split into several groups, of which two are of primary interest to us: bearded and beardless.

The bearded irises are those with a 'beard' of hairs at the root of the tongue-like fall. This group of irises tend to have big blousy flowers with an incredible range of shades and hues of colours. I can think of no other genus that has such a vast number of differently coloured flowers, all subtly different. Bearded irises are considered an essential ingredient of an herbaceous border, but they do have their problems. Colourful as they are in flower, out of flower, with one or two exceptions, they are deadly dull. The other problem is that the rhizomes must have as much sun as possible, which makes it difficult to grow other plants, which might cause shade, in close association with them. The answer that is usually resorted to, is to have beds devoted to nothing but irises. These are visited during the flowering season, but ignored for the rest of the year. Fine, if you have a big enough garden; if not, then another solution must be sought. The way round it is to plant them at

2.1 m (7 ft) or more. It needs a lot of space and is not a plant for the small garden, but where it can be used it lives up to its name and is magnificent. It is large in all its parts, with huge rough leaves and wide yellow flowers up to 15 cm (6 in) or more across in late summer.

For the smaller garden *Inula hookeri* is a better size as this only grows up to 75 cm (30 in), but it can be a rapid spreader so an eye should be kept on it. Its yellow flowers have very distinct narrow petals. In many plants this would be a sign of a miffy form, but in this case it makes an attractive feature, almost filigree in nature. It is hardy, but new growth can suffer from late frosts.

the front of the border where they are not crowded by other plants, and where the sun can penetrate to the rhizomes. Some of the bearded irises may be too tall for this position but, fortunately, they come in all sizes, including miniature ones only 20 cm (8 in) tall. They will still be tatty out of flower, but that is something you will have to put up with if you want their brief moment of glory.

The most commonly grown are the hybrids bred under the name of *Iris germanica*. There are literally thousands of these and in no way could I do justice to the vast range of colours that are available. Look at them in flower wherever you can and decide the ones you like, then search them out. Two others are worthy of mention, both possibly involved somewhere in the development of *I. germanica*. *I. florentina* is an iris that has been grown in gardens since earliest times, as much for its root as its very pale blue flower. It is orris root, used in the preparation of perfumes and potpourri. *I. pallida dalmatica* is the other I wish to mention. This is another ancient plant with lavender flowers and grey leaves. The leaves of this plant are almost as important as the flower as it is the only one of the bearded irises to have presentable leaves for most of the season. The form 'Variegata' has either yellow or white stripes and is doubly valuable.

Lovely as the bearded irises are, it is the beardless irises which give us more variation in flowering and in planting positions. Beardless irises prefer moist or damp soil: many are best seen to advantage by ponds or streams. Water is not essential as long as the soil can be kept moist or at least moisture retentive by the addition of plenty of humus. *Iris sibirica* is the most popular of this group. The flowers, as with all the group, are more refined than the bearded irises, smaller and with a crisper outline. In *sibirica* the falls are quite rounded and usually a variation on blue or purple, with white markings at the throat. There are a large number of cultivars available based on the colour variations, including white. They clump up quickly.

*Iris ensata*, still sometimes called *I. kaempferi*, has small standards and large falls. Again there is a tremendous colour range varying from white to purple. This is one of the few irises that dislikes lime. It will grow in water as will *I. laevigata*, a close relative, but with larger standards.

One of the gems of the genus is *I. chrysographes* which is a dark velvety violet-purple – sometimes so dark as to appear black. The *chrysographes* of its name refers to the gold pencilling at the top of the fall. Again it prefers a moist soil and will tolerate partial shade. Make certain you buy the darkest form you can find; 'Black Knight' is one of the best.

*Iris foetidissima*, the British native gladwin, is not a moisture lover in the sense that it grows by water, but it does appreciate the dampness of leafmould. Having said that it will tolerate any soil including chalk. It flowers in the shade and is particularly good for planting amongst shrubs or trees. Attractive as the bluish-yellow flowers might be, it is the bright red seeds that are exposed when the pods burst, that make this plant desirable. They not only look good in the garden but also as cut material. There is a more robust form with yellow flowers, 'Citrina', and a form 'Variegata' with variegated leaves.

For the front of the border, where you can get your nose down amongst its leaves, try *I. graminea*, the plum tart iris. This forms dense clumps of leaves, which unfortunately overtop the brilliant violet-blue flowers. The plum tart comes from the rich smell that the flower emits. In spite of the problem with the leaves, it is well-worth growing. Another front-of-border plant is *I. unguicularis* (*I. stylosa*), which again is overtopped by leaves and has a delicious scent, but the amazing thing about this plant is that it flowers in the middle of winter. Slugs can be a nuisance and reduce it to tatters so precautions should be taken. They should be picked in bud and brought indoors to open. There are several named forms. Both these two need a warm sunny position with well-drained soil.

With a different colour range is *I. innomi-*

*nata*. This comes from the warmer parts of the United States and the colours, particularly in the Pacific hybrids, reflect this, being hotter oranges and yellowy-browns, both with purple markings. A well-drained, sunny position at the front of the border is required for this short iris.

There are many, many more irises to explore, including the bulbous species which are strictly outside our remit, but it is worth giving them just a quick glance. The dwarf bulbous irises flower in the early spring – some when it is still winter – and brighten the dead borders. There are a lot of varieties based on *Iris reticulata* and *I. histrioides*, giving a mixture of blues and purples. Then there are *I. danfordiae* and *I. winogradowii* which offer yellow, and yellow-and-blue hybrids. They only grow to 7.5–10 cm (3–4 in), but are a good choice. The other group are the Spanish and Dutch irises, raised from *I. xiphium*, and English irises from *I. latifolia*, beloved by florists. These flower in a range of blues and yellows in the late spring and early summer. All the bulbous irises like a free-draining soil in full sun.

Propagation of irises is mainly by splitting the rhizomes or bulbs after they have finished flowering or in the spring. It might take them a year to settle down again.

In spite of their relatively short individual flowering periods, irises are one of those groups of flowers that can get into the bloodstream, converting their growers into fanatics. Fortunately there are societies for such fanatics and if you feel that you are getting hooked then you can always join one of them.

## KIRENGESHOMA (Hydrangeaceae)

Here is another genus that produces plants that instantly produce a response from the gardener and yet are not that frequently seen. It is a small genus with only one or two species (depending on which botanist you follow). They are woodlanders and are magnificent plants for a cool, moist shady border.

The species that is normally seen is *K. palmatum*. This has, as its name suggests,

**Kirengeshoma**

palmate (maple-shaped) leaves held on erect black stems. Both of these help to offset the yellow bell-shaped flowers that appear in the autumn. The whole plant reaches about 1.2 m (4 ft) in height. *K.p. koreana* or *K. koreana*, depending on your inclination, is a very similar plant except that it is slightly taller and the flowers open wider and are held slightly more erect. In the garden there is not a great deal of difference between the two species except that *K. palmata* is the more readily available.

The kirengeshoma like a moist leafy soil and light shade, making them ideal plants for the woodland garden, especially as they flower in the autumn when there are not many other plants in bloom. They can be increased by division or from seed.

## KNAUTIA (Dipsacaeae)

Although there are 50 members in this genus only one, *Knautia macedonica* from the Balkans, is normally seen in gardens. Even this would probably not be seen if it were not for the colour of the flower, as its size and shape are nothing at all special. However the colour is – a rich crimson.

It is very closely related to the scabious, with a similar pincushion-shaped flower held way above the basal leaves on 60 cm (2 ft) swaying stems. There are very few plants with this intensity of crimson, which makes it quite difficult to place in the border. The easiest association is with other red and purple plants or to give it an isolated position, backed by green or grey foliage. It combines well with taller campanulas.

With the interest in wild and meadow gardening, and the introduction of many wild flowers back into the garden, our native field scabious, *Knautia arvensis*, has been attracting more, well-deserved attention. This has pinkish-lavender flowers about the same size as *K. macedonica*. Both flower in the summer. This is an attractive plant and more easy to place in a border.

They are happy with any fertile soil but prefer full sun. Propagation is from seed, preferably sown fresh, or by division.

## KNIPHOFIA (Asphodelaceae/Liliaceae) – Red-hot poker, torch lily

Red-hot pokers have gained a lot in popularity, although it is not the red-hot, but the softer colours that seem to be getting the attention. They come from southern Africa which tends to throw some doubt onto their hardiness, but there are sufficient hardy varieties to satisfy most gardeners.

These are plants for vertical emphasis. The flowering stems vary in height from below 60 cm (2 ft) up to 1.8 m (6 ft), rising straight up out of clumps of untidy, grass-like leaves. The flower heads look like clubs on the end of their stems, each made up of large numbers of small tubular flowers,

generally sloping downwards. As these come into flower, the band of colour, usually, red, orange or yellow, spreads upwards leaving the dying tubes behind. These plants always look magnificent from a distance, but on closer examination it is very difficult to find a perfect head; there always seems to be too many buds yet to open at the top of the head, or dead material below it. Some of the creamier cultivars have the advantage that the dead material is the same as the main colour and so is not so noticeable, except by the closest examination.

In larger borders the tall varieties add an exotic, tropical look, quite different to most other hardy perennials. *Kniphofia caulescens* is unusual in that it is grown for its foliage as well as its flowers. This is a grey or blue-green and grows from a thick trunk-like stem which eventually flops over. It flowers late in the season, in autumn, when it produces soft coral-red spikes that turn greenish-yellow with age. Another tall member of the genus is *Kniphofia uvaria* with its large fat heads of red and yellow reaching 1.5 m (5 ft). It has a form, 'Nobilis', which is even taller (1.8 m/6 ft) high and has bigger and longer heads. *K. rooperi* (once called *K. uvaria* 'C.M. Prichard') is a late flowerer with a red and yellow flower. Another bicolour, 'Royal Standard', is an old favourite with red buds that open yellow. 'Wrexham Buttercup' is a good pure yellow, while 'Green Jade' is a cool pale green. 'Atlanta' is one of the earliest to flower and is useful if one wants to have a continuation of kniphofias throughout the summer. It is an orange-red.

*I. snowdenii* is a curiosity with well-spaced coral, orangy-red flowers that have a downward curve. It flowers later in the season and is reputedly tender, but I have seen it flowering happily right through winter, and it was certainly not killed during two winters of −14°C (7°F), but it was in well-drained soil.

While the original tall varieties are still popular, it is with the medium and short forms that interest is spreading. There seems to be a better range of colours and certainly there are some very fine soft and subtle tones. Being shorter they are more suitable for the smaller garden. Going straight to my favourite, 'Little Maid', this has an ivory flower and a good stiff green foliage touched with a reddish bronze. A marvellous plant that flowers in the late summer and into autumn. It is a miniature version of 'Maid of Orleans' (hence its name), one of the taller knophofias with ivory-cream flowers.

A contrasting colour is *K. galpinii* with its wonderful orange flowers and the similar *K. triangularis*, having brilliant orange-red spikes. Both of these only grow to 75 cm (30 in) and form nice clumps with grass-like leaves.

New varieties are continually being sought and once found introduced into general cultivation, so the number is constantly on the increase.

A moisture-retentive soil in a sunny position is needed for best performance. If there is any likelihood of losing plants over winter, give them a good covering with bracken or straw to keep some of the frost at bay. Slugs like kniphofias at all times of the year and have sometimes felled the tall stems like trees in my garden, so always take precautions, particularly in the winter if they are covered up.

Propagation is normally from division in the autumn or spring. Seed is produced, but it is unlikely that cultivars will come true and even the species vary in quality.

## LATHYRUS (Leguminosae) – Peas

One of the evocative plants of the cottage garden is the sweet pea. This and the everlasting pea are seen clambering over pea sticks or bushes in great profusion. *Lathyrus odoratus* is the sweet pea, but since it is only an annual it is, unfortunately excluded from this book. (I must say that I had the species self sowing itself in the garden for a number years so I suppose it qualifies for that group that I often call annual perennials.) The everlasting pea, *L. latifolius* (sometimes wrongly called perennial pea), is truly perennial like so many of the other species, and will tolerate a fair degree of frost, at least −14°C (7°F) and probably much more.

It has a strong growth of winged stems that rise to 1.8 m (6 ft) or more, producing frothy groups of pink or white flowers for quite a long time in summer and early autumn. The one drawback to this plant is that the flowers have no scent. If you have a hedge that does not need trimming too often, *L. latifolius* can look marvellous sprawling over it. It can be used to clothe a bush that flowers earlier in the season, or even be used to flop over an herbaceous plant that has finished flowering.

*Lathyrus rotundifolius*, the Persian ever-lasting pea, is a more delicate plant, with rounded, fresh green leaflets and rose-pink flowers that also look rounder than the previous species. It is not so free-flowering as *L. latifolius* and it has a tendency to be a bit invasive, but the fresh colour of the flowers make it an attractive plant to have if it can be placed where it will not become a nuisance.

Not all lathyrus are climbers. *L. vernus* grows to only about 30 cm (12 in) or so and has small reddish-purple and blue flowers. This plant would have little importance if it flowered in the height of summer, but it does so, in fact, in the early spring, one of the first of the truly herbaceous plants to flower, making it invaluable. I prefer the type, but there are also various named coloured forms, pink, and pink and white for example. Do grow it; you will enjoy its early flowers, and it is very little trouble.

Lathyrus do not seem to be too worried about soil conditions. In theory they should be in well-drained soil, but I have successfully grown them for years on quite heavy soil. They will do best if planted in the sun.

The easiest way to grow all of these is from seed, although it is also possible to divide them, particularly the last two species.

## LAVATERA (Malvaceae) – Tree mallow

This is mainly grown in gardens in one of its annual forms but increasingly one or other of the hardier forms are being seen. It is characterized by the typical funnel-shaped flowers of the mallow family (the hollyhock probably being the best known), usually in shades of pink.

191

The species most commonly seen is *L. olbia*. Strictly speaking this is a shrub, but it has for a long time been considered an honorary herbaceous plant. It is a tall plant growing 1.8–2.1 m (6–7 ft) or more in height, and almost as much in width. It is airy with slightly furry, grey-green leaves. The type is not often seen, as it is the form 'Rosea' which is generally available from nurseries. This has pink flowers with rose veining and eye. In recent years another form, 'Barnsley' has entered the arena and has been a runaway success. This has the same habit as 'Rosea' but the flowers are a much lighter pink with a dark eye. As its name might suggest, it originated from Rosemary Verey's garden at Barnsley House.

As *L. olbia* is not herbaceous, it should be pruned hard each spring. In windy areas it might be advisable to take off some of the top growth after flowering.

Another lavatera that should be grown more frequently is *L. cachemiriana*. This is about the same height as *L. olbia* but is a more upright plant with less spread. The flowers, which appear from summer into autumn, are a clear pink. The petals are narrower than in other species and the sepals can be clearly seen between them. This plant is more difficult to find, but can easily be grown from seed.

Unfortunately the tree mallows are not completely hardy. Their chances of survival are increased by being planted in a free-draining soil in a sheltered position in full sun.

Propagation is very easy from cuttings for *L. olbia* and from seed with *L. cachemiriana*. Both are not very long-lived plants and should be replaced every few years; they grow very fast and a cutting of *L. olbia* will be full height in a couple of seasons.

## LEUCANTHEMELLA (Compositae)

The only species here is *L. serotina* which has also been grown under the names of *Chrysanthemum uliginosum* (under which it is best known) and *Tanecetum serotinum*. This is a very tall plant, growing to 2.1 m (7 ft) or more in good soil. On top of these stems are typical white daisy flowers that always seem to be at an angle, rather than horizontal, as they follow the sun crossing in the late autumn sky. This latter ability means that it should not be planted on the southern boundary of your garden, otherwise your neighbour will benefit rather than you. It spreads reasonably rapidly, forming large clumps. It is not overly attractive, but the fact that it flowers in later autumn makes it useful if you have the space to accommodate it.

This plant does not seem too fussy about soil, but it does prefer a sunny position. Propagation can be easily achieved by division. It will also grow from seed and will self sow if seed has time to ripen before winter sets in.

## LEUCANTHEMUM (Compositae)

This is another refuge for plants made homeless from the demise of *Chrysanthemum*. The main plant of concern to us here is the shasta daisy which is covered by both *L. maximum* and *L. × superba*. This is rather a coarse plant, with large white flowers and a typical daisy yellow centre. They make an excellent display when they have made a clump, which they do quite quickly, and are excellent as cut flowers. Typically they are about 90 cm (3 ft) tall and although generally quite sturdy they may need support in exposed gardens. There are an increasing number of forms of this: some double, others with narrow petals and some pale yellow. Another species that is of interest, especially to wildflower gardeners is *L. vulgare* (originally *Chrysanthemum leucanthemum*), the oxeye daisy. This is a smaller and more refined plant, appearing with its main burst of flowers in early summer. It is mainly a plant of the fields and road verges, thus making it an ideal plant for a meadow garden. It has thinner stems than the shasta daisy and this gives it a wiriness that does not require staking.

Neither plant seems at all fussy about soils, although they prefer to grow in sun. Propagation can be by division, but they will also come from seed. *L. × superbum*, in particular, seeds itself around.

**LIATRIS** (Compositae) – Liatris, blazing star, gay feather

*Liatris* is a genus of some 40 species from North America, some of which have been used in gardens for two centuries or more. They are characterized by their parallel-sided spikes of purple flowers. One of the unusual things about these spikes is that, unlike most other similarly structured plants, the flowers at the top open first, progressing downwards as summer passes. Another surprising thing about them, until one looks closely, is that they are a member of the Compositae, the daisy family.

All the species in the garden are similar in appearance, varying mainly in height. The flowering stems all rise from a grassy foliage. *Liatris spicata* is the most commonly grown. This is about 60 cm (2 ft) in height. The dense flower head can be described as a bright rose-purple, perhaps not the easiest of colours to place in a garden, but it does well in a border with other purple plants. There are several good forms of *L. spicata* including 'Alba' and 'Floristan White', both white, and 'Kobold' (also known as 'Gnome').

The other commonly grown species has the strange-looking name of *L. pycnostachya* (literally 'dense spiked'). This is a much taller plant, reaching 1.2 m (4 ft) or so, with large mauve-pink spikes that flower over a long period. It is known in its homeland as the Kansas gay feather.

The gay feathers like a well-drained, but moisture-retentive, soil in a sunny position. Increase can be achieved by division in the spring or from seed.

**LIGULARIA** (Compositae) – Ligularia

We now move to another of the Compositae, but how different from the last. For a start this one looks like a daisy and secondly it revels in wet, almost boggy conditions. They resemble large forms of the senecios, to which genus they used to belong, with their narrow, golden orange petals. They originated in the Far East, mainly China and Japan.

Undoubtedly the most commonly seen is *Ligularia dentata* (formerly *L. clivorum*). This has large kidney-shaped leaves and daisies with orange-yellow petals and brown centres. There are several forms in general cultivation, of which 'Othello' and 'Desdemona' are two that are similar to each other. They are shorter and more compact than the type and have maroon-purple stems. Unlike so many cultivars these two come reasonably true from seed; so near that it is possible that many of the named plants on offer are in fact seedlings and not the true vegetative offspring from the original plants. Other forms that are sometimes seen are 'Orange Queen', 'Orange Princess' and 'Golden Queen'. Another golden-orange is the hybrid *L.* 'Gregynog Gold'. This is a taller plant than *L. dentata*, with conical heads of flowers.

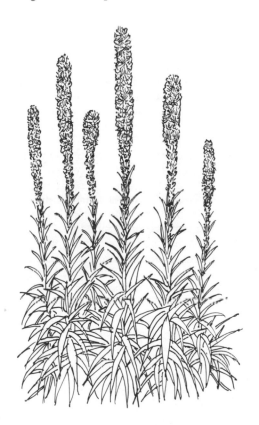

**Liatris**

**Ligularia**

There are quite a few other species represented in gardens, but I am only going to write of one more, *L. hodgsonii*. This is a smaller plant than the other species, being only about 90 cm (3 ft) high. This makes it preferable for a small garden. The flowers are not held in spires like the previous species, but in broad flattish heads. They are orange in colour, which contrasts well with the green, kidney-shaped leaves. In essence it looks like a smaller version of *L. dentata*.

All the ligularias like a moist soil and hate being dried out. They prefer a sunny position but they are often seen planted amongst trees where they only get an occasional shaft of sunlight. Protect from slugs and snails, who find them much to their taste.

## LILIUM (Liliaceae) – Lily

This is another of those genera that really is outside the scope of this book as they are bulbs, but who would want an herbaceous border or a mixed border without lilies? They have been grown in gardens since gardens began, and have been used as cut flowers, gathered from the wild, since before that. There is something about their shapes, colouring and fragrance that makes them very appealing and, consequently, popular. They are not particularly difficult to grow and many are perfectly hardy, which adds to their attraction. The genus is a very versatile one as species can be found that will grow in most places: in shade, sun, dry and even moist soil. They look perfectly at home planted amongst shrubs or herbaceous plants.

Lilies are a big genus and naturally they have been split up into various classes and subclasses, but it is beyond the scope of this book to go into that kind of detail. All that I can say is that it is a wonderful genus to explore and just list a few, taken at random, of my favourites which I think you will enjoy and start you off on what could become an exciting adventure. The first two are amongst the most popular, but are none the worst for that. *Lilium regale* has trumpet flowers of pure white, with a yellow throat.

*L. przewalskii*, is a popular species – surprisingly so, because I cannot imagine anyone actually asking for it at a garden centre or nursery with a name like that. In spite of its name it comes from China. It is the dark green, deeply-cut foliage that contributes towards its popularity. The stems are very dark, almost black, and the flowers yellow. There is a very good form that probably belongs to this species called 'The Rocket'. This is similar except the leaves are not so deeply cut.

In bud and on the reverse of the petals when they open, they are suffused with a wine red. The plant has a superb perfume, particularly in the evening. It is easy to grow, happy on a variety of soils and positions. Surprisingly, it is a relatively recent addition to our gardens, only being discovered at the beginning of this century. The other is the madonna lily, *L. candidum*. Unlike the previous, this has been known around the Mediterranean for thousands of years and is typically grown in this country in old cottage gardens. It is a wonderful white flower with a strong fragrance; again it has a trumpet shape, although this time more flared. Unfortunately the majority of the stock is produced vegetatively and has become heavily virused so it is not as common as it was formerly.

Moving now to the Turk's-caps, I must say I am particularly fond of the common *Lilium martagon*. This, as its vernacular name suggests, resembles a Turk's-cap hanging from a slender stem. The colour varies but is basically a spotted pink or purple. There are many different colour forms and many hybrids have been derived from it. Its natural habitat is amongst trees and so it is quite at home in shade. There are many other pendulous lilies, many deriving from the martagon lily, but also from other species. Although not difficult, *L. chalcedonicum* is not frequently seen in cultivation. This again is a Turk's-cap, with a brilliant pure red colour, and comes from Greece. Another bright red, this time from Korea, is *L. amabile*. Unfortunately there are some less interesting colour forms around. *L. henryi* is a late-flowering lily with a lovely deep yellow-orange colour. One of the most famous of this type of lily is undoubtedly the tiger lily, *L. lancifolium* (previously *L. tigrinum*) with its strong orange flowers spotted with dark purple.

A pendulous lily but with a shallow trumpet, or bell shape, is *L. szovitsianum*. This is a fabulous lily to grow amongst shrubs where it will grow up to 1.8 m (6 ft) with its yellow flowers showing up against dark green foliage.

For mixing with herbaceous plants where they can get some sun, are the Oriental Hybrids, many of them based on *L. auratum*. These are the big blousy lilies with open flowers, often of strong colours and with heavy spotting. These often have very strong fragrance.

This has been a very, very brief survey of what is a most beautiful genus. Look at as many as you can, get hold of specialists catalogues and then choose for yourself, but do not blame me if you get hooked.

Most are very accommodating with regard to soil types and can be grown on either under acid or limy conditions. On the whole they prefer a well-drained soil, but again there can be quite a range of tolerance. Lilies need not only be grown in the border; they are perfect candidates for growing in containers on a terrace or elsewhere.

With patience they can be increased from seed, but a more speedy method is by scaling bulbs. This involves removing the outer scales of the bulb and planting them into a moist compost. A third method is to plant the bulbils formed in the axils of some species, notably *L. lancifolium*.

**LINARIA** (Scrophulariaceae) – Toadflax
The linaria have 'snapdragon' flowers very similar to the antirrhinum, but they differ in that they all have a spur that sticks out of the back of the flower. It is quite a large genus, but includes many weeds, some invasive, such as the yellow British native *L. vulgaris*. This is very rampant and difficult to eradicate once it has been introduced to a garden.

Similar in appearance, but bigger in all its parts is *L. dalmatica*. The stems and leaves are a glaucous blue and the flowers a good yellow. It has an upright branching habit and grows to about 90 cm (3 ft) in height. This can also run and be a bit invasive, so be careful where you plant it. *L. purpurea* is an old cottage garden plant. This is a much more refined plant, with thin blue-grey stems forming an airy erect clump. The leaves are small, as are the flowers. The latter are normally purple but there is a good pink form known as 'Canon Went' and also a rare white form. It can grow to 90 cm

195

(3 ft), but is often somewhat less. This plant does not run; however, it does self sow, although it never becomes a nuisance. The self sowing can be useful as this is not a long-lived plant.

From time to time other linarias are seen in gardens and there are probably quite a number of garden-worthy species yet to be introduced.

The toadflaxes like a well-drained soil in a sunny position. They can be increased by division or from seed.

## LINUM (Linaceae) – Flax

No summer border would be complete without one of the two blue members of this genus. *L. narbonense* and *L. perenne* both produce a constant stream of daily flowers on long slender stems. These flowers are very dainty and tend to drop by late afternoon, making these unsuitable plants

**Linum**

for the evening gardener. They are both very similar in appearance, although it is often claimed that *L. perenne* is shorter-lived and so it is usually *L. narbonense* that is recommended. There are other members in the genus, of which *L.* 'Gemmell's Hybrid', closely linked to *L. flavum*, is the best. This is a wonderful golden yellow, but it is short and needs to be grown at the front of a border, although it would be better in a rock garden.

Linum prefer a light, well-drained soil in full sun. Seed provides the best method of increase.

## LIRIOPE (Convallariaceae/Liliaceae) – Liriope

This is a small genus from the Far East of only six plants, only one of which to my knowledge is in general cultivation. *Liriope muscari*, the plant in question, has not got a great deal to offer, but is at its best in late autumn, when not much else is around and in a position, shade, that most other plants shun at this time of year.

It is not a very big plant, only growing up to 30 cm (12 in). The foliage is very grass-like, in dense, arching clumps, from which rise spikes of mauve flowers which look more like round fruit than flowers. Indeed, they look like the flowers of the bulb *Muscari*, after which it is named. As I have already said, not a spectacular plant, but one worth growing for the added colour it can provide when little else is in flower. If you are lucky it will, in fact, continue to flower through early winter.

There are several forms around, but they are not very easy to find and one wonders whether they do their job any better than the type.

Liriope is not too fussy about the soil it will grow in, accepting quite dry conditions under trees and bushes. With its dense foliage, it is sometimes used as ground cover.

## LOBELIA (Campanulaceae)

Most people tend to think of lobelias as being low-growing trailing annual plants with small blue or purple flowers. It may come as a surprise to know that there are some perennials in the genus. I was careful to say 'perennials' rather than hardy perennials because they are not totally hardy, many coming from the warmer parts of the globe. The genus is surprisingly large with over 300 species, of which just a handful make it into our gardens. They belong to the Campanulaceae, the bellflower family, but apart from a few blue, it is the red-flowered species that have attracted the gardener's eye over the centuries.

One of the oldest in cultivation is *Lobelia cardinalis*, the cardinal flower, which was introduced as long ago as 1626. This comes from eastern North America and has 90 cm (3 ft) spikes of brilliant scarlet flowers. This is probably the most hardy of the reds. Similar, but with reddish stems and leaves instead of green, is *L. fulgens* (*L. splendens*). This, and its hybrids, are the gems of the genus but, alas, it is not very hardy and reserve plants should be overwintered indoors. The most spectacular are 'Bees' Flame' and 'Queen Victoria', with dark purple stems and the most brilliant red flowers. Another red lobelia on the tender side is *L. tupa* from Chile, which is worth attempting as it is a striking plant. It can grow up to 1.8 m (6 ft) when happy. The pointed leaves are a pale green and downy. The flowers are brick-red and of a curious shape. It should be grown in a sheltered position and protected over winter.

Moving to what is thought of as the more conventional colour of lobelias, we have *L. syphilitica* with its blue flowers. This comes from the eastern United States and is hardy in most areas. It grows to 90 cm (3 ft), with light green leaves and tall spikes of good blue flowers. There is a 'Blue Peter', said to be superior to the type. Unlike many of its brethren, this is a plant that will tolerate quite wet soils, including heavy ones.

Another plant that likes moist soil and that tolerate some shade is the hybrid, *L. vedrariensis*. The colour of the spikes of starry flowers vary from violet to a deep purple. There is a named cultivar, sometimes attributed to this hybrid, called 'Russian Princess' which is a clear pink.

The lobelias like to have a rich soil that does not dry out too much. They prefer a sunny position and it is a wise precaution to give them a sheltered site.

Propagation is from either division or seed. Many of the lobelias are short lived and this, combined with possible winter losses, make it a sensible precaution to propagate new material at frequent intervals.

**LUPINUS** (Leguminosae) – Lupin
Who could deny lupins a place in the herbaceous border? Perhaps some people might on the grounds that once they have finished flowering, they leave a hole for the rest of the season, but this applies to so many plants and, besides, when they are in flower they have a stateliness and form for which there is no substitute. Their shape, colour and peppery scent add a quality to the border in early summer that I would hate to be without.

There are over 200 species from the Mediterranean and North America, but it is from the latter that most of those grown in our gardens come. They all have spikes of the characteristic pea-like flower followed by pods, again pea-like in appearance.

The most commonly seen are the hybrids derived from *L. polyphyllus* plus some blood from *L. arboreus* and some of the annuals, which contributes to the shortness of their life. Although a plant commonly associated with the traditional cottage garden, it was only in the twentieth century that the vast, sophisticated range of colours has been developed, particularly by George Russell with his Russell strains. These are sturdy plants, growing up to 90 cm (3 ft) in height. Sometimes they are selfs, i.e. the flower is all of one colour; sometimes they are bicoloured, with the second colour being a contrasting one or just a subtle shift. Breeding is still going on and new strains are being introduced all the time. For the smaller or exposed gardens, dwarfer varieties are available.

Border lupins are short-lived, or rather they get past their best if left in the border for too long. Some gardeners treat them as biennials and replant every year with new stock grown from seed. While this may be time consuming, it does ensure a good display. However, it is possible to leave them *in situ* for a couple of years or so before replanting. It helps to prolong their life if the flowering stems are removed before the seed is formed. When planting, it should be remembered that it is always best to position the new plants or replacements in the autumn; the tap-rooted plants will not establish themselves quickly enough to produce a good show if transplanting is left until the spring.

There are several other lupins occasionally seen in cultivation, but I only want to mention one more because it is a favourite of mine. It has already been mentioned as one of the many parents present in the above hybrids, *L. arborescens*. Strictly speaking this is a shrub rather than an herbaceous plant but it is often seen in herbaceous or mixed borders. It can also be seen growing in the wild in Britain, naturalized on sandy soils, especially near the sea. The flowers are much smaller than the hybrids and a delightful pale yellow.

These plants do not like to be wet but, on the other hand, they appreciate moisture-retentive soil. An acid soil is best; they are not too happy on chalk. They are tap rooted and resent disturbance. A sunny site is the best position for them.

If you are not too worried about the colours, then lupins are very easily raised from seed; if colour strains, or named forms are required to be kept pure, then cuttings can be taken in the early spring. If allowed to self sow, the colours will eventually revert to a muddy purple.

## LYCHNIS (Caryophyllaceae) – Lychnis
One member of this genus is very well known as a garden plant, while others ought to be better known. They are bright, attractive plants that flower throughout the summer in a sunny position. There are not a great number of species in this genus which belongs to the *Caryophyllaceae* family. This means that they are related to the campions, which they resemble, and the dianthus.

Their flowers are in the form of flat discs, usually facing the sky, and often brightly coloured.

The most brightly coloured of them all, and the most popular is, *Lychnis coronaria*. This has brilliant magenta flowers, so dazzling that it is sometimes difficult to look them in the eye. These are held on branching silver-felted stems above similarly clad leaves. The silver sets off the magenta well, but can look a sorry sight in a wet season. Wonderful as these plants are, they are difficult to site and much thought is needed. The other problem is that they do tend to self sow, often in awkward places such as in the middle of choice plants. There are pure white forms, which I like very much, one of which has a pink centre, particularly when it ages. 'Alba' is the pure white and 'Oculata' the eyed form.

Another plant with a bright flower, although otherwise different in appearance, is *L. chalcedonica*. This is an upright plant with a flat head of brilliant vermilion flowers, each with deeply notched petals which give it its name of Maltese or Jerusalem cross. It is a plant that makes an impact when planted in groups particularly with a yellow achillea as a background. There is a white variety, but it is rarely seen; seeds and plants purporting to be this form invariably turn out to be a light salmony-cream form, pleasant but not outstanding.

*L. flos-jovis* has the same grey felted leaves and stems as *L. coronaria*, but it is a much smaller plant (only 45 cm/18 in) with more upright stems. The flowers are held in small clusters and are variations on a pink to red-purple theme. There is a dwarf, compact form, 'Nana', that is only a few inches high.

There is a short-lived hybrid, *L.* × *haageana* which is occasionally seen. This again is about 45 cm (18 in) high with dark green, unfelted leaves and red, white or orange flowers. This in turn has produced another hybrid *L.* × *arkwrightii*, which has startling orange-red flowers.

Lychnis seem happy in any fertile soil as long as they have sun. Increase is easily achieved from seed.

**LYSICHITON** (Araceae) – Skunk cabbage
The two species of this genus are found on either side of the northern Pacific, with *L. americanum* coming from North America and *L. camtschatcense* coming from Kamchatka in Asia. They are both plants of boggy or wet ground. In spring their flower spike is surrounded by a spathe or hood, in the case of the former plant it is yellow and the latter white. The flowers have a somewhat foetid smell, hence the vernacular name. Once the flowers are over the large, upright leaves grow to 1.2 m (4 ft) or even 1.5 m (5 ft) tall, slightly less in the case of *L. camtschatcense*. These plants are curious rather than beautiful, but form ground cover as they are likely to spread.

Lysichiton must have a wet soil, as already mentioned, and do well next to ponds and streams, as well as in bog gardens. Division can easily be carried out in spring.

**LYSIMACHIA** (Primulaceae) – Yellow loosestrife
This is a large genus of which an increasing number are coming into cultivation. One of the oldest to be introduced to our gardens is that of *L. punctata*. As the name implies it has yellow flowers, and it grows to about 90 cm (3 ft) high. It has a preference for moist soils, where it will run madly about, making it a plant for the wild garden, rather than the border. In drier soils it is shorter and not quite so fast in its travels. It is a somewhat better form of the British native, *L. vulgaris*, which it closely resembles.

*L. ciliata* is another yellow-flowered species but this is a plant with much thinner stems and in consequence flops. Attempts can be made to stake it or it can be grown as a tangled mass between other plants. This also prefers a moist soil. *L. clethroides* has spikes of white flowers that curve over at the top. Like so many others in this genus, it can be invasive. A more upright plant with greyish glaucous leaves, giving it an almost refined look, is *L. ephemera*. This also has spikes of white flowers, but the spikes are more upright.

All of these, besides being invasive, are

**Lysimachia**

reasonably tall, reaching about 90 cm (3 ft) or so. There is one, however, that concentrates its efforts at ground level. This is *L. nummularia* (creeping Jenny). This has creeping stems that quickly carpet the ground. The usual form seen in gardens is the golden one 'Aurea'. Again this prefers a damp soil and will grow in light shade and is a good woodland plant.

Propagation of all of these is by division.

**LYTHRUM** (Lythraceae) – Purple loosestrife
In spite of its name this genus is not related to the previous one. Although quite a large genus, it is only represented in gardens by a

199

couple of species, of which *L. salicaria* is the most common. This produces dense flower spikes of a deep purple colour that makes an attractive addition to the border. They reach up to about 1.2 m (4 ft) or so and appear in summer. There are quite a number of cultivars available, of which 'Robert' is the most popular. There is a slightly smaller, more slender species, *L. virgatum*, which is otherwise quite similar in appearance.

They prefer a moist soil and do particularly well beside a pond or stream, or in a bog garden, but they can also be grown in ordinary soil as long as moisture-retentive material has been added to it. They are not invasive like the previous genus, but are clump forming. These clumps can be easily divided in spring to provide new plants.

## MACLEAYA (Papaveraceae) – Plume poppy

It takes a bit of imagination to realize that the plants in this genus are related to the poppies. To the gardener's eye nothing about them resembles the flashy red plants that we all love so much. They are tall, up to 2.1 m (7 ft) or more, with feathery plumes of flowers that are too small to see individually unless you happen to be 2.1 m (7 ft) tall as well. They are a whitish brown in colour. The leaves are part of the joy of this plant: they are lobed in shape, and have a wonderful glaucous grey, infused with a coral colour, as are the stems.

The big disadvantage of this genus is that they are rampant and will travel through the soil at an astonishing rate. This means that they are really only for a garden or a large border. The species most commonly found is *M. microcarpa*, usually in the cultivar 'Coral Plume', which has plumes of flowers that glow with the named colour.

The only other species that is seen is *M. cordata* which is not such a large plant, although the individual flowers are much larger and usually white. It is supposed to be less invasive; try it if you dare. In spite of their invasiveness, both species are very handsome plants and deserve the space if it is available. They look particularly good

**Macleaya**

when the evening light shines through the leaves and plumes of flowers. Incidentally, the genus has previously been known as *Bocconia*.

Both species seem happy in moist soils and although they prefer sun, they will take a little shade. They can easily be propagated by digging up one or more of the suckers. Alternatively, root cuttings can be taken in winter.

## MALVA (Malvaceae) – Mallow

*Malva moschata*, the musk mallow, is a constituent part of any cottage garden. It is a British native and none the poorer for it. The flowers are typical of this genus as well as the closely related *Lavatera*. The main species has sugary pink flowers that have a wonderful clarity about them. If these take a lot of beating, then you should try the white form, *L.m. alba*, which has the purest of pure white flowers. These come very easily from seed and will usually self sow, so there is little excuse for not growing them. Although they will tolerate most soils, the plants are decidedly smaller in dry, under-nourished ones. They normally grow to about 90 cm (3 ft) in height. They are short-lived and should be replaced regularly.

*M. sylvestris* is a trailing species that spreads along the ground, although some-times getting up to 1.5 m (5 ft) in height. This has purple flowers. The form that is generally grown is 'Primley Blue', which, as its name implies, is blue. The only other species normally cultivated is *M. alcea*, of which the old cultivar 'Fastigiata' is the one that most people grow. This is a plant with pink flowers that continue throughout the summer and autumn.

Most will do well in almost any soil. They prefer a sunny position. They can be easily grown from seed, with the cultivars coming readily from cuttings.

## MECONOPSIS (Papaveraceae) – Blue poppy

Most gardeners dream of growing various members of this genus. There seems to be something very desirous about a blue poppy; I must admit they are very beautiful. However, they are not the easiest of plants to grow unless you have the right condi-tions. The easiest to grow, by far, is not blue at all, but yellow or orange. This is the Welsh poppy, *Meconopsis cambrica*. Some-times it can be surprisingly difficult to establish for some unknown reason, but once you have one plant you will have hundreds before you can blink. It is beauti-ful, but it can become a pest; self sowing into precious plants. This would not matter except that it has a deep tap root, which makes it difficult to extract. Regular dead-heading is the only way to keep it under control. It will tolerate a surprising degree of shade and looks especially good lighting up a dark corner, perhaps amongst ferns and hostas.

Now to the true blues. These need a moist situation where they can have a cool buoyant atmosphere similar to their native Himalayas. In Britain the best place to grow them is Scotland, and growers in that part of the country have some magnificent stands. Elsewhere they must be well fed with organic material to provide moisture and nourishment at their roots. If plants are in a light shade and in ground that is moist (but not sopping wet) – such as a woodland-type soil with plenty of leafmould – then the atmosphere around the plants will also be perfect. With this counsel of perfection there should be no problems; however they still can be temperamental so be prepared for failures.

One of the easiest to grow is *M. betonicifo-lia* (previously *M. baileyi*). This reaches up to 1.2 m (4 ft) and has good pale blue flowers, although they can be paler and more washed out on drier soils. As long as the plants are kept well fed with organic material, the plants are fully perennial. They can be increased by division in early spring or from seed. The latter should not be sown too thickly as the seedlings damp off very easily. Use fresh seed if you are not able to store it properly or able to get properly stored seed.

Arguably the best of the blue poppies is *M. grandis*, which in its best forms has dark blue flowers flushed with purple. Some forms have flowers that are purple or white. Unfortunately much of the seed and many of the plants sold under this name are in fact *M. betonicifolia*, so be careful when buying. This is also a true perennial and can be increased by division as well as by seed.

*M. × sheldonii* is a cross between the last two and has a greenish-blue flower. This must be increased vegetatively.

Unfortunately not all meconopsis are perennial; some are monocarpic, that is to say, once they have flowered and set seed they die. This may be in the same year as germination or it may be several years later. Some meconopsis seem to be either peren-nial or monocarpic depending on circum-stances. One of the most magnificent of the monocarpic species and one that will take the most degree of dryness is *M. horridula*, a short species with prickly stems and leaves. Justice cannot be done in words to the beauty of the flowers. Being monocarpic it can only be increased by seed. It is one worth trying.

There are so many meconopsis that are worth growing and I can only urge the reader that has the right conditions to pursue these further. Those who have to make the conditions should concentrate on the ones already mentioned and once they have conquered those successfully, should try others.

### MELISSA (Labiatae) – Lemon balm

*Melissa officinalis* is a herb that offers little to the open border, but may well earn its place in the herb garden. When it is young in the spring it has a fresh look about it, but as the year progresses and it comes into flower, it becomes rather straggly and unattractive. At this stage it is best to cut it down and let it regenerate with fresh growth. Another reason for cutting it down as soon as or immediately after it flowers, is that it has a tendency to self sow a bit too freely. There is a golden variegated form if you like that kind of thing.

Lemon balm is accommodating in that it will grow in most soils. Although it probably prefers sun it can be grown in light shade, but it gets even more straggly under these conditions.

### MENTHA (Labiatae) – Mint

Another plant that really belongs to the herb garden. Some forms are attractive enough for the border, but they have the unfortunate habit of being very rampant, requiring the gardener to chase the questing shoots to keep them out of the neighbouring plants. One form that I grow in the border is *M. longifolia* 'Buddleia' which is a tall form, 1.2–1.5 m (4–5 ft), with soft silver-grey leaves that can be very effective in association with other plants. Alas, like its relations, it runs and I have to dig around it each year to keep it confined. It also self sows, so it is essential to cut it down before it seeds everywhere.

Two plants that are occasionally risked in the border are the variegated apple mint,

*Mentha spicata* 'Variegata', which has creamy variegations against a soft green, and the ginger mint *M.* × *gentilis* 'Variegata', which has golden variegations set off against a bright green. The foliage of both make a colourful contribution to the border.

Mints will grow in most soils although they prefer a moist one. They can be easily propagated by division and they will self sow unless they are cut down before seedling.

### MERTENSIA (Boraginaceae) – Virginian cowslip

An increasing number of these plants are being grown in gardens. The main one, however, is still *M. virginica*. This is a

**Mertensia**

delightful plant for spring. It is grown for its violet-blue tubular flowers which are set off by its glaucous, grey blue-green leaves. The plant reaches about 45 cm (18 in) in height. It is not around for long and has disappeared below ground by midsummer, leaving the soil bare for something else. It likes a cool root-run in a woodland soil with plenty of leafmould in it. It prefers a lightly shaded position.

Two other species that are currently in favour are *M. asiatica* and *M. maritima*. These both have pale blue flowers and glaucous blue-grey leaves. They both prefer a much more free-draining soil than the previous species, and like a sunny position.

They can all be increased either from seed or by division.

## MIMULUS (Scrophulariaceae) – Monkey flower

This is a very large genus of plants, of which the majority are tender. However there are a few perennials that will stand a reasonably cold winter.

One of the most recent introductions has been that of *M.* 'Andean Nymph', collected by John Watson in Chile. This is a low-growing plant with lovely pink flowers suffused with yellow, and with deep pink spots in the throat and on the lower lip. Unfortunately it is promiscuous and therefore difficult to keep it pure, and there are now many different coloured offspring from it.

A more brashly coloured plant is *M. luteus*, which is yellow with large brown spots. This likes a moist soil. *M. guttatus* is very similar although it is taller. The best border mimulus is *M. lewisii*, especially in its white form. The usual colour of the tubular flowers is pink. This is quite a tall plant, growing up to 60 cm (2 ft) or more. Unlike the other plants this does not require a moist soil.

## MISCANTHUS (Gramineae)

*Miscanthus* is a genus of about 20 grasses, several of which are grown in the garden. They are clump formers which often grow up to 2.1 m (7 ft) or even 3 m (10 ft) high.

They are elegant and grown for both their leaves and feathery flower heads.

*M. sinensis* and its mass of cultivars are some of the best for garden purposes. Amongst the cultivars 'Silberfeder' ('Silver Feather') is one of the choicest. 'Gracillimus' is another good, graceful form with very narrow leaves. For those that want it there is a good variegated form, 'Variegatus', with a white stripe down each leaf. A more interesting variegated form is 'Zebrinus' which has broad bands of yellow *across* the leaves. It is known as the tiger grass for obvious reasons.

The other species that is commonly in cultivation is *M. sacchariflorus* which is one of the taller species forming statuesque clumps. It rarely flowers in Britain except after long hot summers.

All will grow in any reasonable garden soil as long as it does not dry out too much. They prefer a sunny position.

Propagation is by division in spring.

## MONARDA (Labiatae) – Bee balm, bergamot

For colour and evocative smells in the summer border there is nothing quite like the monardas. Even in winter when there is hardly any of the plant showing above the ground, the distinctive fragrance will immediately be released as you weed or otherwise tidy the plant. It is a garden smell I would not like to be without. The flowers are equally distinctive as they are carried on in tight whorls, one or two to each square stem.

The commonest in cultivation are some of the *M. didyma* cultivars and hybrids of which 'Cambridge Scarlet' is the brightest. 'Croftway Pink' is a good rose pink, while 'Beauty of Cobham' is a pale pink. There is a white form 'Snow Queen', but I have never found this a very robust or long-lived plant. These all require a degree of moisture in the soil and need to be regularly divided and replanted, else they become congested and languish.

There are a series of purple cultivars based on hybrids of *M. fistulosa*, of which 'Prairie Night' is one of the best. These are able to grow in a drier soil, but still do not like to be too dry. Both species will suffer from mildew if they become too dry.

All species and cultivars are easy to propagate by division of the creeping rootstock.

## MORINA (Dipsacaceae)

Although there are about 17 species in this genus it is only one, *M. longifolia*, that we have to consider in a garden context. This is a strange plant. The dark green leaves are very much like a thistle (to which it is related). These form a clump that enlarges for several years before putting up a flower spike 90 cm (3 ft) or so high. The flowers appear in whorls about this stem. They are narrowly tubular, white when they first appear, turning to pink and eventually to red. The flowering stems can be used in dried-flower arrangements.

In spite of its curiosity value, it is still an attractive plant. It looks best when planted in groups of three or more, rather than just as single plants.

It likes any ordinary garden soil, but it should be reasonably well drained. They seem to prefer a sunny position, but they will take a little light shade.

Propagation is from seed.

## NECTAROSCORDUM (Alliaceae/ Liliaceae)

I should make a brief mention of the two species that make up this genus. They are, in fact, refugees from *Allium*, the onions, and their affinity with that genus can be immediately appreciated by their smell. *N. siculum* and *N. bulgaricum* (or *N.s. bulgaricum* as it is usually considered a subspecies of the first) are tall plants reaching 90 cm (3 ft) or more. At the top of the straight stem is a cascade of bell-shaped flowers of pink, green and white. Once the flowers are over, the short flower stems become erect, carrying seed pods that give the impression of the towers of a fairy castle. Unfortunately, like most onions, they are very adept at self sowing and can become a nuisance. Both species are so close to each other in appearance that they are difficult to tell apart.

These are attractive plants and do well when placed amongst other plants about midway back in the border. Their smell and habit of rapid increase can be a bit trying.

They are not particularly fussy as to soil and prefer a sunny position. They can be increased either from seed or by division of the clump of bulbs that form around the parent.

## NEPETA (Labiatae) – Catmint

These plants are a welcome addition to the garden as long as you have not got a cat. This proviso is because cats tend to love the smell and taste of these plants (hence the

**Morina**

**Nepeta**

vernacular name) and can spend a lot of time chewing and rolling in them, much to the plants' disadvantage.

It is a very large genus of about 250 species, of which only a handful are in general cultivation. Most of the cultivated ones tend to be romantic plants with a mass of thin stems wreathed in a haze of pale blue flowers. One of the most commonly seen nepeta is *N.* × *faassenii*. This grows to about 45 cm (18 in) high and is a mass of arching and floppy sprays of mauve-blue flowers throughout the summer. It makes a good plant for the front of the border. There is a form *N.* 'Six Hills Giant' (sometimes referred to as *N. gigantea*) which is twice the size of *N.* × *faassenii*. This is a much

stronger plant than the latter and is a bit hardier. One of the parents of *N.* × *faassenii* is *N. mussinii* which, while similar to its offspring in appearance, is an inferior plant. *N. sibirica* has flowers of nearly the same colour, but is a more erect plant. 'Souvenir d'André Chaudron' is probably a form of the previous species. It is about half its height (45 cm/18 in) but otherwise similar. It also has a long season.

Of a different persuasion is *N. govaniana*. In cultivation this carries yellow flowers on its 90 cm (3 ft) airy stems, but in the wild it has also the more typical nepeta blue. It is not a densely floriferous plant, yet it is good for lighting up a shady corner. Much shorter, but very much worthy of the front of the border is *N. nervosa*. This has short, upright stems, densely clothed with bright blue flowers. Of a similar height, but a greyer leaf and lighter blue flower is *N. cataria* 'Citriodora', whose leaves smell of lemon when crushed.

Nepetas are not long-lived plants, especially in a damp position. They last and perform best in a well-drained soil in a sunny situation. Propagation can be easily achieved by division or by sowing seed.

**OENOTHERA** (Onagraceae) – Evening primrose
This is a large genus of mainly yellow-flowered plants, although there are also white and pink species. The naming is not always accurate and although botanists may have the names under control, gardeners certainly haven't and there is some confusion as to which plant is which. However, this is relatively unimportant as there are some very good garden plants in the genus. One of their characteristics, and hence its name, is that they tend to flower towards the latter end of the afternoon and evening. Most of the large dish-shaped flowers have a characteristic fragrance.

One of my favourites is the tall (1.2 m/ 4 ft) *O. stricta*. This is a short-lived perennial that happily sows itself around. The flowers are either a pale or deeper yellow, changing to an orangey red as they go over. It has a long flowering season as bud after bud opens up its stem. They can be floppy, but do not need staking. Another good species is *O. tetragona*, a shorter plant at about 45 cm (18 in) high. This has deep yellow flowers, usually red in bud. There are several forms to choose between, although 'Feuerverkeri' ('Fireworks') is currently the favourite. The flowers on this species and its cultivars are quite large, up to 5 cm (2 in) across, but it also has a subspecies *O.t riparia*, which is a much smaller plant altogether.

*O. speciosa* is a plant of increasing popularity. This again has 5 cm (2 in) flowers, although this time they are white and pink. The plants grow to about 60 cm (2 ft) high and are good for rambling through other plants. This one is a bit of a runner and some forms can be quite invasive. One of the most beautiful evening primroses is another pink form *O. caespitosa*. This has very large flowers, 7.5 m (3 in) or more across. Unfortunately this is short-lived and it never seems to set seed in Britain, which means that it has to be regularly re-introduced. This is a low-growing creeping plant. There is a similar large-flowered plant with yellow flowers, *O. missouriensis*. Both of the last two are suitable for the front of border.

There is another plant for the front of the border that looks like a small epilobium at a quick glance. This is *O. rosea*, which is different from the rest of the cultivated plants in that it is a very dark rose pink, almost carmine. Plants of this are offered under a variety of wrong names.

While at ground level it is worth looking at one final oenothera. This is *O. acaulis* that has large white flowers (or yellow in the form *O.a. aurea*). These are stemless. The resulting conglomeration of seed capsules looks like a hedgehog. It is as hard as iron and difficulty might be experienced in getting the seed out. Soak it in water before prying the pods open.

There are many more garden-worthy oenothera and it is difficult to know when to stop. Perhaps I should just mention one more. Strictly speaking this is biennial, but since it self sows freely it is an honorary perennial. This is *O. biennis*, with large green leaves and masses of yellow flowers in summer and into autumn.

Oenothera like a well-drained soil in a warm sunny position. They are all easily grown from seed and can also be increased by division.

## OMPHALODES (Boraginaceae)

There are two plants in this genus that are well worth growing in the shade garden. The first *O. verna* is about 30 cm (12 in) tall and scrambles about the woodland floor making a carpet, from which the blue, forget-me-not flowers appear in spring. *O. cappadocica* is a much smaller plant, only about 7.5–10 cm (3–4 in) high. This forms clumps in the leafmould of the woodland floor, with similarly shaped flowers which are a deeper blue.

Both plants like a moisture-retentive soil, preferably a typical woodland soil of leafmould, and a shady position. They can be easily increased by division or from seed.

Before I leave this genus, mention must be made of an annual that self sows regularly enough to be considered a perennial as it is always around. *O. linifolia*, again, has forget-me-not flowers, but these are pure white, beautifully set off against the glaucous grey leaves of the plant. It grows to 30 cm (12 in) or more, depending on the quality of the soil and how close the plants are together. This loves a sunny position and looks tremendous at the front of a border. Once it has established, it needs little attention other than to thin out when too many have germinated.

## OPHIOPOGON (Convallariaceae/Liliaceae)

This obscure genus has suddenly been projected into popularity as many gardeners discovered the black-leaved form called *O. planiscapus* 'Nigrescens'. It is the true blackness of the narrow leaves that hold the key to this plant's success. Omitting berries, there are very few true blacks in plantlife and so this has become an essential part of most gardeners' palettes. It is a low plant, growing no more than 15 cm (6 in) high. It is an ideal plant for the front of a border and will grow in full sun or light shade. There is

**Ophiopogon**

a similar green plant *O. japonicus* which will grow in the same conditions.

Ophiopogon do not seem to have any particular soil requirements. The plants are best increased by division.

## ORIGANUM (Labiatae) – Marjoram
The origanums are essentially herbs, but there are several that earn their place in the flower border in their own right. There are three major ones in this context. The first is *O. laevigatum* which I find very attractive both as a species and in one of its several forms currently being offered. It grows to about 45 cm (18 in) and flowers from late summer well through into autumn. The flowers are small and purplish pink, set off well against purple stems and calyces. The two forms that are current favourites are 'Hopley's' and 'Herrenhausen' both of which have larger, richer-coloured flowers.

One of the most attractive front-of-border plants must be the form of *Origanum × hybridum* 'Kent Beauty' which occurred at Washfield Nursery in that county. The flower heads consist of hop-like bracts in pink and green, from which the tubular pink flowers protrude. The species itself is also worth growing, but it has not the size or colour of its seedling.

The final origanum for the border is the golden form of the native herb, *O. vulgare* 'Aureum'. This forms a neat clump of up to about 30 cm (12 in) high of brilliant gold, which changes to green as the summer wears on and the flowers begin to appear.

For the herb garden the species required is *O. onites*.

Origanums like a well-drained soil in a warm sunny position. They can be increased by division or by taking basal cuttings in spring. Most will also come from seed, but the vegetative methods are best for cultivars.

## PAEONIA (Paeoniaceae) – Peony
This is a wonderful genus about which I have mixed feelings. At the risk of offending some of my readers, I must admit that I am not so keen on some of the big blousy double cultivars that, pretty as they may be, are unable to hold up their heads under their own weight, especially when full of rain. However there are many superb plants and one would definitely not like to be without them.

One of the earliest to flower has the terrible name of *P. mlokosewitschii* (usually known for simplicity as 'Molly the Witch'). This is a superb plant with soft yellow, single flowers held above glaucous, greyish foliage that has a reddish-purple tinge to it when it is young. Once it has finished flowering, it produces red-lined seed pots with plump black seeds, as well as some red undeveloped ones. Altogether a plant that no garden should be without.

Well where does one go from here as there are so many more good plants. Certainly the various species have returned to popularity in recent years. Their simplicity and purity often contrasts with the fussiness of so many of the cultivars. *P. cambedeseesii* (another mouthful) is another gem. This has deep rose flowers that appear in late spring. These are set off by dark green foliage that is an incredible purply-red on the reverse. This is about 45 cm (18 in) high.

*Paeonia officinalis* is an old-fashioned plant with crimson-red flowers. It is most commonly seen in double forms, but singles also occur. Another red is *P. tenuifolia*. This is only about 45 cm (18 in) tall but it has very finely cut leaves giving a very effective feathery background to the flower. *P. wittmanniana* is somewhat similar in appearance to *P. mlokosewitschii* except that it is taller and has paler yellow flowers. *P. emodii* is quite commonly available, and none the worst for that. It has pure white flowers enhanced by a wonderful golden boss of stamens in the middle. This is one of the peonies that like a light shade. It is also one of the tallest of the species, reaching up to 90 cm (3 ft). Another choice white is *P. clusii*, but unlike the last, this is one of the shortest at about 25 cm (10 in) high. Another very good white is *P. obovata alba*. This, like so many peonies, has a very good foliage that stands it in good stead when it is out of flower. This species has blue seeds, another bonus.

There are still more species and far too many cultivars to mention all of them here. The best suggestion I can make is to visit one of the nurseries that specialize in peonies while they are in flower, and make your choice from what you see.

Peonies are easy to grow. Once they have been planted out they will continue without the need to dig them up for many years. In fact they resent disturbance. Because of this the soil should be well and deeply prepared, with added organic material to help keep the soil moisture retentive. At the same time the soil should be well drained. Peonies are gross feeders and they should be top-dressed each year with further organic material.

Most peonies like a sunny position, although a few prefer light shade as mentioned above. Most species will stand without support, but the heavy-headed cultivars are likely to need some form of staking, especially if it is a wet spring.

The species can be increased from seed or by division in the autumn. Cultivars should be propagated by division only.

## PAPAVER (Papaveraceae) – Poppies

These are plants that have graced our gardens for centuries and have been much loved as cottage-garden flowers. The typical colour is red, but they also include whites and various shades of pink and orange.

The mainstay of the border is the oriental poppy, *P. orientale*. This is available in all the colours mentioned above, but it is especially impressive in the scarlets and oranges. One of its best offspring is the form 'Goliath', which has enormous flowers, almost dinner-plate size. It is an intense red, so intense that it is difficult to look it in the eye. The centre of the flower is jet black, including an enormous boss of funerial stamens. Another very fine, although quite

**Papaver**

different form, is 'Cedric Morris'. This is a pearly pink with very dark crimson blotches at the bases of the petals. 'Mrs Perry' is a clear pink, whereas 'Perry's White' is just that, white, but again with very dark patches at the base of the petals. 'Black and White' is similar, although larger. All these come into flower in the early summer on stems that need support. Once they are over they can become a bit of an eyesore and should be cut to the ground, preferably with later-flowering plants to spread over the spot where they were. Propagation is by taking root cuttings during winter.

A poppy that I would not like to be without is *P. atlanticum*. It is quite a modest poppy, only reaching about 30 cm (12 in) in height. The flowers are a soft orange and when it is in flower it is not easy to distinguish it at a quick glance from a *Meconopsis cambrica* of the same colour. It sows itself around but is never a nuisance. There is also a double form.

Some of the annual poppies make good border plants, becoming perennial by virtue of the fact that they regularly self sow. *Papaver somniferum* is the classic example of this. There are now many colour forms, varying from purplish-red to pale pink and mauve. There are also varying degrees of doubleness, with some having deeply cut petals. My favourite is a purple one with the flower shaped like a tulip. *P. nudicaule*, the Iceland poppy, is a short-lived perennial, but is usually treated as an annual. There are several colour strains and again there are doubles and singles. The flowers are usually large and look like crumpled tissue paper, the hallmark of so many poppies.

If you are looking for the blue poppy, you must be referred to the genus *Meconopsis* (see page 201).

Poppies tend not be too fussy about soil as long as it is reasonably well drained, but all require a sunny position. Cultivars generally need to be reproduced vegetatively, but otherwise they come readily from seed.

## PENNISETUM (Gramineae)
Grasses make a good contrast in the perennial border. This is a large genus but only a few are in cultivation. One of the most popular is *P. villosum*, a plant whose interest is not in its size (only 45 cm/18 in or so), but in the flower heads. These are bottle-brushes of light fawn that appear from the late summer, until the late autumn weather disperses them. *P. alopecuroides* is a plant of about twice the last's size. The flower heads are also large and are of a violet-purple colour. A further species, *P. orientale*, is intermediate between the two both in height and colour. The last two are valuable for the interest they give to the garden in the winter. They are all clump-formers and are not invasive.

Pennisetum like a well-drained soil in the sun. They can be increased by division or seed.

## PENSTEMON (Scrophulariaceae)
This is a large genus of which an increasing number are coming into cultivation. Of these the majority are smaller species that are finding their way into the rock gardens, but there are still a large number, especially of cultivars, for borders. Penstemons are not always hardy and it is advisable to take cuttings every autumn and overwinter them to ensure that you have plants for the following season. Having said that, many will stand most winters of down to $-15°C$ (5°F) or even less. There is a saying about the cultivars that the larger the flowers the less hardy they are, and there does seem some truth in this.

*P. campanulatus* is the species that has given rise to many of our cultivars. Amongst some of the best are 'Garnet', bright red; 'Evelyn', pink; 'Hidcote Pink', a salmony-pink; 'Stapleford Gem' (most plants labelled 'Sour Grapes' is in fact this plant) mauvy-blue; 'Alice Hindley', purply-lilac, and many more. These all have quite large tubular flowers. All of these flower in the summer and through well into the autumn, sometimes even into the winter.

A spring-flowering species that seems to be very hardy is *P. serrulatus*. In flower this plant is only about 30 cm (12 in) high and quite bushy; however, it does become rather leggy and floppy after it has flowered and should be cut back. It also seeds rather prodigiously, which is another reason for cutting back, although this habit does give a constant supply of new plants with which to replace the old ones. Its flowers are purple.

Most other species flower later in the season though. There are plenty of them to be had from nurseries and with the increasing tendency for many of them to stock the more tender plants, the number of them gets bigger each year. *P. barbatus* has narrow bright orange or red flowers. This is a truly hardy species, but it has got the annoying habit of being floppy, so requires support to raise it to its true 90 cm (3 ft). *P. hartwegii* also has red flowers, but these are much longer and the plant shorter. Another red, *P. isophyllus*, is even taller, reaching 2.1 m (7 ft) in good conditions. This has a pale throat. *P. confertus* has creamy-yellow or yellow flowers. A good blue can be found in *P. ovata*. The tall plant (1.2 m/4 ft) of *P. gentianoides* produces flowers of a purply-blue, while the confusingly similarly named 'Gentianoides' is more lilac blue.

There are many for the enthusiast to explore and enjoy.

Penstemons require a well-drained soil in a sunny position, although quite a number of the species grow in scrubland. The warmer the position, the more certain they are to come through the winter.

All cultivars should be grown from cuttings; similarly the species, but these can also be grown from seed.

## PENTAGLOSSIS (Boraginaceae)

*Pentaglossis sempervirens* may be an unfamiliar name to many gardeners, but the plant probably is not. This is what used to be known as *Anchusa sempervirens*. This is a coarse, bristly plant with forget-me-not-type flowers of blue that appear in spring. It is a useful plant for naturalizing in shady places, especially in the wild garden or large wooded areas. It grows to about 60 cm (2 ft) in height.

It prefers a moist soil and a shady position. It can be increased quite easily by seed, particularly as it self sows.

## PEROVSKIA (Labiatae)

This is one of those genera that is borderline to this book. Technically the species are shrubs, but they are usually treated as herbaceous perennials and cut to the ground in spring.

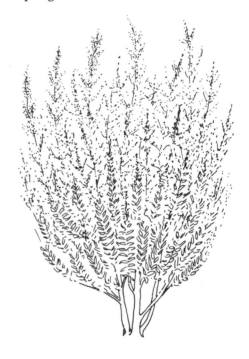

**Perovskia**

There are about seven different species but only one, *P. atriplicifolia*, is in general cultivation. It is a plant that is not seen that often, which is a pity as it is a fine, blue-flowered plant for late summer and early autumn. It grows to about 1.2 m (4 ft) tall with white furry stems and grey foliage. Sympathetically set against these are the small powder blue flowers that seem to create a haze around the plant. 'Blue Spire' is the form that is mainly seen. This seems to be a hybrid with another species *P. abrotanoides*, which is rarely seen in cultivation.

Perovskias seem to be fully hardy. They like a well-drained soil in full sun. Propagation is from basal cuttings in the spring although it is possible to divide them. They will also come from seed and occasionally self sow.

**PERSICARIA** (Polygonaceae) – Knotweeds
This is the refuge of many of the plants that have been thrown out of *Polygonum*. Most are a bit on the rampant side and should only be planted with this in mind.

*P. affinis* is a low-growing, carpeting plant that only reaches 23–25 cm (9–10 in) in height. In summer and autumn it throws up spikes of pale pink flowers that gradually turn red. Once they go over they turn a

**Persicaria**

lovely rusty brown, as do the leaves which provide colour in the border during the winter. There are several cultivars, such as 'Superba' and 'Donald Llowndes', but they are not the easiest of plants to distinguish between.

A much larger and vigorous plant (reaching 1.2 m/4 ft when happy) is *P. amplexicaulis*. This has leaves that can be confused with a dock at a casual glance. It is quite a coarse plant but it has good narrow spikes of flowers that go on for a long time throughout the summer and autumn. These are generally pink or red. Again there are different cultivars, usually dependent on the shape and colour of the flower head. 'Atrosanguineum', with crimson flowers, is the most frequently met.

In spite of this being a bit of a weedy and rampant genus, there are some good plants and besides giving house room to the above (in several forms) I also grow *P. bistorta*, another rampant species, especially when it has its toes in a moist soil. This has fresh green leaves which admirably set off the lovely pink cylindrical flower spikes. The form 'Superba' is the one that is usually grown.

*P. campanulata* is a spreading plant that reaches up to 1.2 m (4 ft) in height and is covered over a long period with little knots of pink flowers. It is really only a plant for the wilder areas of a garden. It likes a damp soil and light shade.

There are several more species, but they get progressively more invasive.

All can easily be increased by division.

**PHALARIS** (Gramineae) – Gardener's garters
*Phalaris arundinacea* 'Picta' is the only member that is in general cultivation. It is a very popular plant, although many gardeners have had cause to curse it, as it runs like mad and if let loose in a border it can cause chaos. However, it is a very attractive plant and if a wild corner or a place where it can be contained can be found, then it is well worth growing. The leaves are very fresh looking and are striped with white. It grows to about 60 cm (2 ft) in height.

It will grow in virtually any soil and likes a sunny position. Propagation is very easy as it just involves digging up a part of the clump and transplanting it.

## PHLOMIS (Labiatae)

This is another genus of mainly shrubby plants, but there are a few that are grown in the perennial border. Probably the best known is *P. russeliana*. This is a plant with a large basal clump of rough floppy leaves overtopped by stiff stems bearing whorls of soft yellow flowers in the summer. The whole plant reaches about 90 cm (3 ft) in height. Over the past few years *P. italica* has sudden risen in popularity. This has typical phlomis hairy leaves and whorls of pinkish-purple flowers. *P. tuberosa* is a taller plant (1.2 m/4 ft), with purple flowers and dark stems.

Phlomis require a well-drained soil in full sun. They can be increased by either division or from seed.

## PHLOX (Polemoniaceae)

Phloxes form an important part of the flora of our gardens. They can possibly be drawn up into three groups for our purposes. There are the dwarf ones that form mats and grow on rock gardens, the intermediate ones that are woodlanders and like a cool soil in light shade, and then there are the tall phloxes that grace our borders from the summer into autumn.

The first category really fall outside the remit of this book, but many people grow them as edging to borders, particularly when they can spill out over paths and patios. These are based on *P. douglasii* or *P. subulata* and flower in the spring. There are many cultivars to choose from, all with subtle differences in colour. They vary from strident magenta and purple through to white. The flowers are rarely more than about 1 cm (½ in) across and appear on mats of stems and foliage that rarely gets about 5–7.5 cm (2–3 in) high. They like a well-drained soil in sun.

The second group are very valuable for the shade garden. This is typified by *P. divaricata* and *P. stolonifera*. These are also spreading plants, although do not form the tight mats of the previous group; they are more open with flowering stems scrambling up to 30 cm (12 in). The flowers are also much larger, up to 4 cm (1½ in) across. The colours are more subdued and include, blues, lavenders, mauves, bluish-pinks and whites. These require a moist soil and do well in a peat garden or in any soil with plenty of leafmould added to it. They like cool, shady conditions.

The third group include much taller plants, some up to 1.5 m (5 ft) or more, but others are much lower at 60 cm (2 ft), while the average are about 90 cm (3 ft). These are based on *P. paniculata* and *P. maculata*. The flowers appear in late summer and autumn and are represented by a wide colour range from red to white, through purple and blue. Some are bicolours. There are many cultivars from which to choose. For those that like them, there are some forms with variegated leaves, of which 'Norah Leigh' is one of the best. The border phlox have a characteristic fragrance that adds to their charm. What detracts from them, however, is their proneness to eelworm, which stunts and distorts their growth. The only way to deal with this is to take root cuttings (which are immune to the eelworms) to start a new colony, and burn the old. Do not replant on the same ground.

This type of phlox likes a moisture-retentive soil with plenty of organic material added to it. They do best in the sun, although they will take a little shade. They lose vitality and vigour if they are not divided every three years or so.

Propagation is also by division.

## PHORMIUM (Agavaceae) – New Zealand flax

The New Zealand flax are much loved by garden designers because of their impressive shape that allows them to play a unique part in the appearance of a border. It is the long strap-like leaves that spray outwards from the plant, like a firework that impresses, rather than the flowers. The flowers are carried on wrought-iron prongs or candelabras that stick up well clear of the plant.

These are followed by impressive seed pods.

For all their popularity, there are only two species, although they have produced a large number of cultivars and hybrids

**Phormium**

between them. *P. cookianum*, the mountain flax, is the shorter of the two, getting to only about 1.2 m (4 ft), although the leaves are much longer. In this species they are inclined to be drooping rather than erect. The flowers are a yellowish-green. The seed pods hang down. *P. tenax* is altogether a much bolder plant: taller and more upright, reaching up to 3 m (10 ft) with the red flowers held even way above this height as are, of course, the erect seed pods. The grey-green leaves are edged with a narrow band of orange.

There are a wide variety of cultivars and hybrids which vary in their hardiness, and most are more tender than either of their parents. The distinguishing factor is nearly always the colour of their leaves which are usually variegated in combinations of green, brown, yellow, cream, orange, red, pink and purple. There are a few with single colours such as the smoky purple of 'Purpureum'.

Phormiums like a moisture-retentive soil with plenty of organic material. They prefer a sunny position but will grow in a light shade. They can be increased by division. Protect the cultivars and hybrids during the winter as these might not be hardy.

**PHUOPSIS** (Rubiaceae)

*Phuopsis stylosa* (previously known as *Crucianella stylosa*) is the only member of this genus. It is related to the bedstraws and like them produces a trailing mat of stems with leaves in whorls. It can be quite pungent especially after rain, when it smells, according to some, like the scent of foxes. Some find this repulsive; others like it. The flowers are quite stunning. Their heads consist of spheres of individual pink flowers about the size of a golf ball. It starts flowering in early summer and continues uninterrupted until the autumn.

The plant tends to root where it touches the ground so it can become a bit rampant, but it is not too difficult to control.

It seems happiest on well-drained soils. Although it prefers a sunny situation, it will grow in light shade. Propagation is by division of the rooted stems.

**PHYGELIUS** (Scrophulariaceae) – Cape figwort

This small genus of two plants from South Africa has become increasingly popular of late, as have so many plants that are marginally tender. A cold winter will cut them to the ground, but the roots will generally survive to rise again. They flower from late summer through to the end of autumn.

*P. aequalis* is the shorter of the two, typically reaching 1.2 m (4 ft) when happy. The curved tubular flowers are a dusky pink. There is a form 'Yellow Trumpet' which has, as its name implies, yellow flowers.

The other species is *P. capensis*, which is taller-growing with orange or red tubular flowers that curve in the opposite way to those of *P. aequalis*, namely upwards. *P. capensis* is hardier than its fellow species. There are a collection of hybrids between the two which have been collected under the general name of *P. × rectus*. The most popular of these have been 'African Queen', a dusky red; 'Moonraker', pale yellow; 'Salmon Leap', orange; 'Winchester Fanfare', red.

They are quite happy in any fertile garden soil and prefer a sunny position. They can be increased by careful division or from cuttings.

## PHYSOSTEGIA (Scrophulariaceae) – Obedient plant

The main plant in cultivation from this genus is *P. virginiana*. It is about 90 cm (3 ft) tall and carries spires of tubular flowers that

**Physostegia**

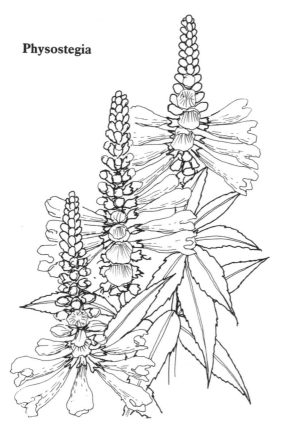

have the curious property of staying in whichever direction you point them – hence their vernacular name of obedient plant. The flowers are either pink as in the true species, or white as in the forms 'Alba' and 'Summer Snow'. There is also a variegated form. It isn't a spectacular plant, but it is pleasant enough and fills a spot in the border in the late summer.

They will grow in any good garden soil and prefer a sunny position. Propagation is from seed which is generally copiously set.

## PLATYCODON (Campanulaceae) – Balloon flower

The only member of this genus is *P. grandiflorum*. It has rich blue flowers, typical of the bellflower family. Before it opens to a shallow bell or dish, the flower, still in bud, swells up like a balloon. The plant is clump-forming and reaches about 60 cm (2 ft) in height. Needless to say there are several cultivars, of which 'Mariesii' is one of the oldest. This is shorter 45 cm (18 in) in stature and comes into flower earlier than the species. Shorter still is 'Apoyama'. There are also forms that are pink or white and semi-double forms.

Platycodon will grow in any reasonable soil. They prefer a sunny position. They can be increased by careful division, seed or by basal cuttings.

## POLEMONIUM (Polemoniaceae) – Jacob's ladder

This is a spring-flowering genus that always seems to have the freshness of spring about it. There are quite a number of species in cultivation and a corresponding number of cultivars. The general flower colour of the genus is blue, although there are variations on this. The vernacular name is due to the parallel leaflets on either side of the leaves which somewhat resemble a pole ladder.

The most common species is *P. caeruleum* which grows to a height of about 60 cm (2 ft). This is an old cottage-garden plant that has been in cultivation for generations. One reason for this is that it self sows, so that once it has been introduced into a garden it continues happily on its own. The flowers are blue, but there are also white forms.

*P. carneum* is a very pretty plant and typifies the spring freshness I wrote about earlier. This only grows to about 45 cm (18 in) and is a mound of fresh green leaves and covered with pinkish-lilac flowers. It is one of the parents of another pretty plant, 'Lambrook Mauve', whose flowers are slightly more blue in colour. I cannot imagine a spring garden without one of these two plants.

Most of the polemoniums have shallow funnel-shaped flowers, but in *P. pauciflorum* this is produced on the end of a long tube, more in the style of a trumpet. The colour is yellow suffused with pink.

There are quite a number of other plants in this genus to explore but the general gardener should find his or herself happy with any of the above.

Polemoniums enjoy any fertile soil as long as it is not too wet and will grow in either full sun or light shade. They can be increased by seed or division.

## POLYGONATUM (Convallariaceae/ Liliaceae) – Solomons's seal

This is another splendid genus that contributes much to spring. The species typically have tall arching stems with their leaves held stiffly out like wings and their delicate little bell-like flowers dangling beneath. The latter are white, usually suffused with green. Unless you are a connoisseur, there is not much to choose between the different species.

The general purpose one is *P.* × *hybridum*. This grows to about 90 cm (3 ft). The flowers are usually in groups of four. There is a variegated form of this species. *P. odoratum* has stems that are distinctly angular and flowers that are scented. This species has a double form, 'Flore Pleno', but you have to be quite close to appreciate this fact. *P. biflorum* has flowers that are in pairs as its name suggests. *P. latifolium* has much wider leaves than other species. And so on, all with just minor differences.

Solomon's seals love a cool root-run in a leafmould soil and when happy will run about forming large colonies. They like a light-shaded position and are ideal for planting in a woodland garden. They can easily be propagated by division in early autumn.

## POLYGONUM (Polygonaceae) – Knotweed

This is another of those genera where the species have been scattered to the winds. There has been two revisions in recent times, but it seems that it has at last settled down, with most of the perennials that we are interested in being moved into *Persicaria*.

## POTENTILLA (Rosaceae)

To the less experienced gardeners, potentillas nearly always mean shrubs; they are unaware that there is also a large number of herbaceous plants within the genus. Several of these are very garden-worthy plants and almost indispensable in the border.

*P. atrosanguineum* itself is not often grown, but it is one of the parents of a race of hybrids that are very popular. One of the most important is 'Gibson's Scarlet' whose 2.5 cm (1 in) flowers are a dazzling scarlet that quivers before the eyes. 'Flamenco' is another of the same colour; 'Yellow Queen' has yellow flowers; 'Monsieur Rouillard' a brownish-red; and 'William Rollison' an orange-red. All are scrambling plants, 45–60 cm (18–24 in) high. Their trailing stems will often poke up through other plants, but not in any way that is a nuisance. Indeed they are useful plants for binding the border together.

A similar group have been formed from *P. nepalensis*, of which 'Miss Willmott' is the star. The flowers of the latter are a pinkish-red. 'Roxana' is another favourite, with flowers of pinkish-orange and a diffused red eye.

The yellow-flowered *P. recta*, particularly in its cool form *P.r. pallida* (also known as 'Citrina' and 'Sulphurea') is a current favourite. This also grows to about 60 cm (2 ft) and loves to scramble up through other plants. A larger-flowered form is 'Warrennii', again with yellow flowers.

All the potentillas will grow in any good garden soil. They like a sunny position but are prepared to be shaded by other plants as long as they can get their head up into the sun.

Propagation is by division.

## PRIMULA (Primulaceae)

*Primula* is such a large genus that it is difficult to know where to begin. They have probably been used in gardens since gardens began. One of the earliest must have been the old cottage favourite: the common primrose, *P. vulgaris.* This is still much loved and can seen growing in many gardens. Its near disappearance from the countryside emphasizes that it should not be dug up from the wild, but bought or grown from seed. The cowslip, *P. veris,* is another popular country plant. Unfortunately if grown in a garden with other primulas about, neither of these two stay true and coloured forms start to appear. Much of this colour comes from another typical cottage-garden plant, the polyanthus. These are brightly coloured with almost the whole range of flower colour represented. Another variant of this group of primulas, besides the wide range of colours, is the Hose-in-Hose forms where there are two flowers, one growing from the centre of the other, looking like two layers of socks, hence the name. Another version is Jack in the Green, where the flower is surrounded by green leafy bracts that look like a ruff. A final old-fashioned variety that has become increasingly popular is the auricula. These have mealy leaves and bright flowers that usually have bands of different colours. There are countless cultivars currently available, but many of them are too delicate for growth in the open. There are however several, such as 'Dusty Miller', that have definite garden origins and can be grown at the front of the border.

Another distinct primula for the front of the border is the drumstick primula *P. denticulata.* The common form has a ball of lavender flowers, but there are now also many other colour forms, mainly various shades of purple. There are also white forms. These are usually named forms, but these primulas seed around producing their own colours, so there are many more shades than names.

As distinct as the round ball of flowers in the previous species is the spike on *P. vialii.* At a quick glance these spikes of pink flowers tipped with the red of the buds are just like orchids. In good conditions it will reach 60 cm (2 ft) in height. It is not a long-lived variety and needs to be constantly renewed from seed.

So far we have only looked at the shorter primulas that are good either for the front of the border or for tucking away in odd corners where they can be seen in spring before the main plantings obscure them. But there are much taller ones to consider, the candelabra primulas in particular. These can grow as much as 60–90 cm (2–3 ft) in good conditions and have whorls of flowers up the stem. One of the easiest to grow is *P. japonica.* This has a rosette of almost cabbagy leaves, then a stem carrying whorls of quite heavy flowers of white, pink or red, usually with a red or brown eye. There are a number of named forms such as 'Postford White' and 'Miller's Crimson'. *P. japonica* seeds itself around and once established will continue to flourish, especially if the soil is moist. *P. pulverentula* is a similar species but has a white, mealy stem. This floury deposit, called forina, is a feature of several forms. This has been crossed with several of the other candelabras to form new strains.

Much more delicate flowers are found on *P. bulleyana,* which has a yellowy-orange colour. *P. beesiana* is similar, but has deep pink flowers with a yellow centre.

Another race of tall primulas are those that have tassels of flowers hanging from the top of tall stems. Typical of this group are *P. florindae* and *P. sikkimensis,* both of which have yellow nodding flowers. These are the most commonly seen and easiest to grow, but there are many other species in the group to explore.

Primulas generally like a cool, moist shady position. The candelabra and *sikkimensis* types in particular like to have a dampish condition. The soil should be rich in organic material to offer nourishment as well as moisture retention.

*Stokesia laevis*
'Blue Star'. A good
purplish-blue
flower for the front
of border,
flowering during
the summer.

*Stachys macrantha*.
A good basic
border plant that
forms a large mat
covered with large,
mauve flower-
heads throughout
the summer.

217

*Ligularia przewalskii* 'The Rocket'. A dramatic plant for the border. It must have a damp soil, otherwise its leaves droop.

*Iris*. Few gardens can be without at least one of the many irises. Unfortunately they can be dull when they are not in flower.

*Lobelia* 'Cherry Ripe'. One of the few perennials to have flowers of such intense red. It needs a moist soil.

*Above: Lysimachia clethroides*. A spreading plant with flowers that appear like white fireworks going off in all directions.

*Hosta* 'Golden Tiara'. Hostas present some of the best foliage plants, especially as they are suitable for both sun and shade.

*Bergenia* 'Sunningdale'. The attractive green leaves are retained throughout the year and make an effective ground cover.

*Monarda*
'Cambridge Scarlet'. The bergamots are very aromatic plants as well as having curiously shaped, but effective, flowers.

*Platycodon grandiflorus*. The balloon flower, so-called because of its large inflated buds. A very good blue flower.

*Below: Phlomis russeliana* is a very good border plant with large floppy leaves that make excellent ground cover.

They can all be grown from seed, preferably sown when fresh. The seed pans should never be allowed to dry out. They can also be divided and this is important for individual cultivars.

This has been a quick run through of a very large subject; only a fraction of the species has been mentioned. Many books have been written on them and anyone who gets hooked by this fascinating genus should avail themselves of them.

**PULMONARIA** (Borginaceae) – Lungwort
The medicinal connection between this plant and lungs is that the spotted leaves look like a diseased lung, and hence in the eyes of the ancients it must have curative properties for that organ. If only medicine were that simple.

Herbalism apart, this is a wonderful genus of plants for the garden. The tubular flowers appear very early in the year, often starting in mid-winter and coming to their best in spring. However, once the flowers are done with, the leaves, especially those splashed with silver, continue to give interest and ground cover until the autumn.

The naming is getting a bit confused as the plants are promiscuous and frequently cross, producing many self-sown seedlings. *P. longifolia* is the British native mentioned above in connection with the vernacular name. This has long leaves with silver spots on them. The flowers are a bright blue, and in the case of the cultivar 'Bertram Anderson' intense blue. Another deep blue form is *P. angustifolia*. This has plain green leaves with a thin brown margin and is one of the dwarfest, reaching only about 23 cm (9 in) high. 'Mawson's Blue' is an old favourite cultivar of this species.

Once we move on to *P. officinalis* and *P. saccharata* the distinction between the plants gets less easy. The latter usually has narrower and more attractive leaves and is a slightly taller plant, reaching about 30 cm (12 in). In both, the colour of the flowers of the various cultivars varies from pale blue to pink and purple. The flowers on one plant often changes through all three of these colours as they age. There are also white

forms such as *P. o.* 'Sissinghurst White'. One of the best forms is now allocated to *P. vallarsae* and that is 'Margery Fish'.

Pale blue flowers are represented by *P.o.* 'Cambridge' and *P.* 'Frühlingshimmel'. The reds, without any blue present, are achieved in *P. rubra*, which has plain, light-green leaves. Needless to say, it too has several cultivars.

Pulmonarias will grow in any good soil, but they do not like to get too dry, otherwise the leaves go very limp. They prefer a light shady position, although can be grown in sun as long as the soil is kept moist.

Propagation is usually by division. They can also be grown from seed if you are prepared to take a gamble as to what you will get.

**PULSATILLA** (Ranunculaceae) – Pasque flower
I must confess this is one of my favourite genera. The sight of an opening dish of dark purple, centred with a golden boss of stamens, on a sunny day is enough to take anyone's breath away.

Pulsatillas are closely related to *Anemone*, to which genus they once belonged. There are quite a number of species, but they are so similar that it is very difficult to tell them apart unless you are a botanist. The plants in cultivation are so interbred that it is almost impossible to say which of the species is the parent of most of them. However it is probably true to say that *P. vulgaris* is the commonest and has had most to do with those in our gardens. This is typically a pale mauve in colour but there are colour forms that vary from white to such a deep purple that it is almost black. This latter looks particularly stunning when it first opens, as the contrast with the golden boss of stamens is indescribable. There are also red forms, one actually named 'Rubra', although it should not be confused with the species *P. rubra*, however similar the two may appear. In recent times there has been discovered in Czechoslovakia cut-petalled forms that could be considered semi-double. These are very attractive indeed and are just entering the market. There is a rare form called 'Budapest' that has pale flowers and golden hairs.

*P. halleri* is very similar to *P. vulgaris. P. slavica* is likewise, except that it has got distinctly broad leaflets. There are also some forms that have very wide flowers, up to 10 cm (4 in) across when open fully.

A much taller plant is *P. alpina*. This has glistening white flowers in the type plant and yellow ones in the form *P.a. apiifolia*. There is a smaller plant in *P. vernalis*, which is not very long-lived. This has white flowers, flushed with blue on the reverse. This is the only pulsatilla that is evergreen.

There are several other species that could be described, but the above provides a good introduction to the genus.

Pulsatillas like any well-drained soil. A sunny position serves them best. The easiest method of propagation is by seed, although cherished forms can be increased by root cuttings.

## RANUNCULUS (Ranunculaceae) –
Buttercups

Most gardeners spend a lot of time trying to keep buttercups out of the garden, so it may seem a bit bizarre to suggest that some should be introduced. Needless to say not all of them are a nuisance. I would certainly be wary of introducing any of the field varieties into the garden. Even the double form of *R. repens*, 'Pleniflorus' should be treated with healthy respect as it can get as invasive as its single parent. *R. acris* 'Flore Pleno' is a clump-former and is much better behaved. Another native double yellow buttercup that is better behaved and which is worth acquiring is *R. bulbosus* 'Pleniflorus' (now refererred to as *R. constantinopolitanus* 'Plenus' and in the past as *R. speciosus plenus*). This is an old cottage-garden plant that can grow up to 45 cm (18 in) if well suited.

Another invasive plant, but one that might be considered for larger gardens is the lesser celandine *R. ficaria*. This forms extensive colonies as its small tubers get moved around the garden by digging and weeding. Fortunately it dies down below ground by the end of spring so if you can

put up with it in the meantime it is worth it. Not perhaps for the species, although this can be attractive, but for its various forms. One of the best is 'Brazen Hussy' which has deep bronze leaves that set off the golden flowers so well. Another interesting form is 'Cupreus' which has deep orange flowers. There are also several doubles.

Of all border buttercups one of the best is *R. aconitifolius* (the fair maids of Kent). It is a clump-forming plant with airy branches, reaching up to about 90 cm (3 ft) in height and carrying pure white flowers. However it is the double-flowered form that is the plant to get, as the flowers make delightful pompoms of white, often referred to as bachelor's buttons.

If you want a yellow buttercup for the border then *R. gramineus* should fit the bill. This has narrow grass-like leaves as its name suggests. The rich yellow flowers are larger than the British buttercups and are carried over a long period in the spring and early summer. It is not invasive, although it does occasionally self sow. The plant grows to about 45 cm (18 in).

There are many, many more species in this genus that are worth considering for the garden, many of them being superlative, but they really belong to the rock garden rather than the open border where they would get swamped.

Buttercups will grow in most soils, but they do prefer them to be moisture-retentive. They grow best in full sun although some will take a degree or so of shade. Propagation is by division or from seed. Seed should be sown as soon as it is gathered.

## RHAZYA (Apocynaceae)

This is a small genus of only two species, of which *R. orientalis* is the only one in general cultivation. It is a clump-forming plant with a woody rootstock. It has heads of pleasant blue flowers, a bit like miniature periwinkles, that flower in the early summer. This fresh-looking plant is about 60 cm (2 ft) tall. It will grow in any fertile garden soil in a sunny position. It can be increased by division or from seed.

**RHEUM** (Polygonaceae) – Rhubarb

There are quite a number of different rhubarbs, of which several are grown in gardens, but the only one of any real value is *R. palmatum*. This reaches about 2 m (7 ft) tall and has large jagged-edged leaves and gigantic plumes of white, pink or red flowers and red seeds, much in the style of an oversized dock. The cultivar 'Atrosanguineum' has red or purple foliage when it is young, a colour that is retained on the undersurface even when they age. This form has pink flowers. There are several other cultivars, but you will need a large garden to grow more than one variety and still have room for other plants.

*Rheum × hybridum* belongs in the kitchen garden as it is the culinary rhubarb. *R. alexandrae* is a spectacular plant if you can grow it, but it really needs a cool damp atmosphere, such as can be found in Scotland. It is a plant of the monsoons and has developed impressive bracts that hang like tiles over the flowers to protect them, which gives the plant its distinctive appearance. When well suited it will grow up to 1.2 m (4 ft).

Rhubarbs need a rich, well-fed soil with plenty of humus and moisture. They will grow in either sun or light shade.

**RODGERSIA** (Saxifragaceae)

This is a small genus of only six species and all are in cultivation. They are mainly grown for their impressive foliage, but their plumes of flowers are also not without merit.

*R. podophylla* has the advantage of being impressive throughout the time it is above ground. The young digitate foliage (radiating like fingers on a hand) is suffused with a bronzy-purple which slowly changes to green as the season progresses. During the summer plumes of creamy-white flowers are produced and then, in the autumn, the leaves take on the reddish coloration typical of that time of year. The leaves are almost triangular, with the edge away from the centre jagged. A plant with similar leaves, except that they have a rounded, smoother outer edge and are deeply veined – the whole looking like the leaf of a horse chestnut – is *R. aesculifolia*. These can be suffused with bronze. The flowers are white.

*R. pinnata* has leaves that are pinnate, i.e. the leaflets are arranged opposite each other in the manner of an ash tree (*Fraxinus*). The flowers of this species can vary from white to deep pink. Like the preceding two plants this can be up to 1.2 m (4 ft) in height. It has a form 'Superba' that has bronze-tinged leaves, especially when they are young. Sometimes the pinnate leaves are nearly palmate as the leaflets contract towards each other.

Another pinnate-leaved species is *R. sambucifolia* (meaning elder-leafed). This has white flowers that tend to be held in sprays rather than plumes. The distinctive *R. tabularis*, with its rounded leaves and white flowers has been moved off to become *Astilboides tabularis*.

The rodgersias are moisture lovers and must not be given a dry situation. They do particularly well near a pond or stream, or in a bog garden. They should also be given a position in light shade, although if they have constant moisture a sunny position may be used. They can be increased by division.

**ROMNEYA** (Papaveraceae) – Californian tree poppy

The flowers of this small genus are very beautiful and will often create a talking point. Depending on your botanical outlook *Romneya* consists of either one or two members.

The species *R. coulteri* is the main one. This is a great colonizer and will soon run right through a border, so it needs placing well. The great joy of this plant is the pure white flowers that have the same tissue-paper quality of the poppy. These large flat discs are enhanced by the great boss of golden stamens in their centres. The plant itself grows up to 1.8 m (6 ft) although often less. The leaves are grey.

The other species or subspecies, depending on your view is *R.c trichocalyx* which only differs in small ways, such has having narrower leaves and more slender stems.

Romneya will grow in most good garden

**Romneya**

soils. It should have a sunny position,
sheltered from strong winds. Surprisingly
since it runs a great deal, it is not easy to
increase by division unless a great lump of
earth is taken as well. It is much more easily
propagated from root cuttings.

**ROSCOEA** (Zingiberaceae)
This is an intriguing genus of the ginger
family (the Zingiberaceae) that comprises
about 15 species, of which only a handful
are in cultivation. They have large hooded
flowers that can be said to resemble certain
orchids, although they are in no way
related. There are only really two or three
that are in general cultivation, although
these are not seen that often.

   *R. cauteloides* has pale yellow flowers,
which grow to about 30 cm (12 in). The

purple-flowered species that is also seen is
*P. humeana*. This is slightly shorter at up to
25 cm (10 in). Similar in colour but a bit
taller is *R. purpurea*.

   Roscoeas can be grown in the border, but
perhaps are best located in a peat bed or
rock garden where they will not be
swamped by plants. They like a moisture-
retentive soil in either sun or shade. They
do not appear above ground before early
summer so do not write them off too quickly
if they fail to appear in the spring. They
should be labelled to avoid accidentally
overplanting.

**RUDBECKIA** (Compositae) – Coneflowers
Of all the genera of golden daisies this must
be one of the best from the gardener's point
of view. It is characterized by the prominent
black centres of the flowers which give its
vernacular name, coneflower. They are

**Rudbeckia**

easy-to-grow plants that contribute a lot to the late summer and autumn scene in the border.

*R. fulgida* is one of the most useful. It is a spreading plant with stems up to a height of about 90 cm (3 ft). This is a typical rudbeckia with golden-yellow flowers and a dark centre. It has a cultivar, 'Goldsturm', which is slightly shorter, but none the worst for that. This continues flowering from late summer well into the autumn and is a plant that most gardeners would consider indispensable. Although best in the sun, this will also grow well in the shade. *RR. speciosa, deamii* and *newmanii* have all been taken into this species. *R. hirta* is a similar plant.

Most of the other species are taller plants that can be a bit floppy, requiring staking. The tallest is probably *R. laciniata* that grows up to 3 m (10 ft). The flowers, if you can see them, are the usual yellow, but have a very pronounced green cone. A much shorter version of this is the similar *R. nitida*. It is usually seen in the form 'Goldquelle', which is a double form.

One of the best of all of the rudbeckias, *R. echinacea purpurea*, has been hived off into its own genus *Echinacea*.

Rudbeckias will do well on most soils as long as they do not dry out. They like a sunny position. Propagation is by division.

## SALVIA (Labiatae) – Sage

Gardens would be all to the poorer if this genus did not exist. It is enormous, comprising over 700 species of which quite a number are in cultivation. However, if we exclude the annual, shrubby and tender ones we are down to not much more than a large handful, but a handful I would rather not be without.

The ones that create the biggest impact in the perennial border are those that form a mound of violet-purple flowers during the summer and into the autumn. Foremost amongst these is *S.* × *superba*. This plant reaches about 90 cm (3 ft). This is an old cultivar, but in recent times there have been many new cultivars that challenge its supremacy. Of these I think 'Blauhügel' is one of the best. It is shorter than *S.* × *superba* and

is of a wonderful colour, slightly bluer perhaps, and almost luminous. Other good forms include 'Mainacht' ('Maynight'), 'East Friesland' and 'Lubecca'. Most of these forms, as their names indicate, have come from the continent. Most of these are small and strong enough to not want support except in windy areas.

Another very recent introduction is *S. verticillata* 'Purple Rain'. This has individual whorls of soft purple flower along the stem, a bit in the style of the fur on a poodle's tail. Do not allow this one to self sow, otherwise it will introduce inferior forms. *Salvia farinacea* 'Victoria' is a more leafy plant with less flower spikes. It is on the tender side and usually used as a bedding plant.

A plant that has leapt into sudden popularity is *S. uluginosa*. This plant has very tall stems, reaching 1.8 m (6 ft), that are topped by small heads of bright sky-blue flowers. It flowers in the autumn when few blue flowers are around. Other variations on a blue flower is supplied by *S. patens*. These are perennials, but usually treated as annual bedding plants, either grown from seed each year or overwintered as cuttings. The flowers vary from light to dark blue.

There are several other plants that are liable to disappear during the winter, either because they are tender or short-lived. *S. sclarea* is just one such. This is a tall (up to 1.5 m/5 ft in good conditions) bushy plant with very large pinkish white bracts that are a distinctive feature. Another is its foxy smell. This is one of the worst plants to try and get seed from. It is very sticky, making it difficult to get the seed out, and before long your hands and clothes are covered with a sticky substance, reeking of fox. Fortunately it does self sow, but make certain that you have enough seedlings to replace those lost in the winter. There is a variety *turkestanica*, which is probably not in cultivation, those sold under that name differing little, if at all, from *S. sclarea*.

A plant similar to the previous one but on a smaller scale is *S. haematodes*. This is covered with blue flowers. Older plants of this sometimes disappear over winter and seedlings should be kept for replacement purposes. This is a very worthwhile plant.

Many of the sages are sticky. Probably the worst has already been mentioned but another that I grow is *S. nubigena*. This and its very close, and more common, relative *S. glutinosa*, have yellow flowers, lined and spotted with purply-brown. It is a tall plant (1.5 m/5 ft) and the flowers are sparsely distributed along its sticky stems, so it is really a curiosity rather than a decorative plant.

While yellow is not a very common colour in salvias, red is; although apart from the popular bedding plants it is a colour of which not much has been seen until recent times. However there has recently appeared a number of bright red-flowered species. The majority, if not all, are tender and the plants or cuttings from them must be overwintered to ensure their survival for another year.

Some of the shrubby plants are widely used in perennial borders. I am thinking here of forms of the culinary sage, *S. officinalis*. The purple form 'Purpurascens', the golden one 'Aurea', and the variegated 'Ictarina' are particularly useful.

All sages like a well-drained soil. Many of the winter losses are, I am sure, due more to the presence of moisture than to cold. They also like a warm sunny position. The species can be grown from seed and they will often obligingly self sow. Cultivars and hybrids need to be grown from cuttings or by division.

## SANGUISORBA (Rosaceae) – Burnet

This is a small, but intriguing genus of plants, all having cylindrical flower heads not unlike the bottle-brushes. *S. officinalis* is the great burnet which grows to about 2.1 m (7 ft), which I find a bit too tall for its short crimson flower heads to be enjoyed. It self sows. A more interesting plant, with darker green leaves and fluffier flower heads is *S. obtusa*. *S. canadense* has white flowers that look a bit like the sparkler firework as the flowers gradually open up the long flower spike.

**Sanguisorba**

The sanguisorba like a moist soil and will grow in either sun or shade. Some support is often needed, especially in windy positions. They can be increased either from seed or by division.

## SAPONARIA (Caryophyllaceae) – Bouncing bet, soapwort

This is an attractive plant that flowers late in the season, but it must be treated with caution as it runs like mad and can become a pest in a border. A place in the wild garden or even restricted in a herb garden might be a better position. Alternatively, a patch growing wild besides a cottage garden hedge would look good. It is usually seen in its double-flowered forms, with 'Roseo Plena' being pink, 'Alba Plena' white and 'Rubro Plena' a purplish-red. These are all forms of *S. officinalis*.

**SCABIOSA** (Dipsacaceae)

*Scabiosa caucasica* forms the backbone of this large genus as far as the gardener is concerned. These plants produce a constant supply of delightful flowers throughout the summer and autumn that are not only beautiful in the border, but also make good cut flowers for the house. There are quite a number of different cultivars, all in pastel blues and pinks, and creamy whites. 'Clive Greaves' is lavender blue, 'Moerheim Blue' a deeper lavender blue, 'Miss Willmott' and 'Bressingham White' and 'Loddon White' all white and so on. These plants all reach about 60 cm (2 ft) in height.

*S. ochroleuca* has only a small flower, but it is a lovely yellow, again flowering over a long season. The foliage is deeply cut and quite refined, making it a plant well worth acquiring.

A very recent introduction has been 'Butterfly Blue' which is a low-growing plant, only about 45 cm (18 in) high. It has the foliage of the previous plant and cool lavender blue flowers, again over a very long period.

Two garden plants with typical scabious flowers have been moved off into other genera. These are *Cephalaria gigantea* (previously *S. tartarica*) and *Knautia macedonica* (previously *S. rumelica*).

The scabious like a well-drained soil, preferably on the alkaline side of neutral, otherwise they tend to be short-lived. They like a warm, sunny position. They can be increased by basal cuttings taken in spring or, if you are not too fussy about what you get, from seed.

**SCHIZOSTYLIS** (Iridaceae) – Kaffir lily

The Latin name of this two-species genus is a bit of a mouthful; perhaps enough to frighten many people from asking for it at a nursery, but they should not be deterred as it is a very garden-worthy plant. *S. coccinea* is the species in cultivation and, along with its numerous cultivars, it provides us with a plant that flowers from early autumn into the winter. The flowers are crocus-shaped, but there the resemblance ends as they are carried as spikes on the end of 60 cm (2 ft)

**Schizostylis**

stems. Not all the flowers open at once and there is a continuing succession. The stems tend to be a bit floppy and because the plant has the general appearance of an iris with stiff, pointed leaves, it is difficult to support inconspicuously. However the flowers have a good satiny quality, varying in colour from light pink to a crimson.

Surprisingly schizostylis like a moisture-retentive soil and it should be rich in humus; they do well by water. They like a sunny position.

Increase by division.

**SEDUM** (Crassulaceae) – Stonecrops

This is an enormous genus on which some people get hooked, while others remain indifferent. The vast majority are too small for our purposes and we are restricted to a handful of species and their cultivars. The

231

border varieties flower mainly in the autumn and are much beloved by butterflies and bees. They would be worth growing for this alone, but they also provide a good splash of colour in the border just at a time that it is needed.

Starting off with one of the mainstays of the genus, *S. spectabile* is a tall plant of about 60 cm (2 ft) with glaucous bluey-green leaves and paler stems. It has large flat heads of pink to rose-pink flowers. Cultivar names to watch out for are 'Carmen,' a lavender-pink; 'Iceberg', a white; 'Brilliant', a deep pink; and 'September Ruby', a dark pink. This species can become floppy and benefits from some form of support.

Slightly taller, but in other ways quite smaller is *S.* 'Autumn Joy' or *S.* 'Herbstfreude' as it should strictly be known. This is one of the most popular of all sedums. The flat heads of flowers are a dark pink in colour, changing to crimson and eventually a rich rust colour. This is purportedly a hybrid between the previous species and *S. telephium*. The latter is a British native and often known as orpine. It has grey-green leaves and stems, whose typical waxy texture christens these species 'ice plants'. The flower heads are smaller than the preceding two plants and the colour is a purple-red that can be quite dark.

*Sedum maximum*, which should now strictly be called *S. telephium maximum*, is a more robust plant, but is spoilt by having undistinguished yellow and pink flowers. However, it has a form named 'Atropurpureum' which has good purple leaves, for which it is widely grown. A plant found by Joe Eilliott in a cottage garden and named after the owner, Vera Jameson, is possibly a hybrid of the latter. It is a shorter plant with very good purple foliage and heads of white starry flowers with rose centres. A similar plant *S.* 'Sunset Cloud'.

One parent of the latter is *S.* 'Ruby Glow', which has grey-green leaves and heads of a wonderful rich purple.

One could go on for ever about these plants. In some respects there is not a great deal to choose between them unless you want to make a collection. The selection of one or two at random may well suffice most gardeners' needs.

They all like a well-drained position in full sun.

Propagation is by division or by cuttings, with no particular problems with either.

## SENECIO (Compositae) – Ragwort

From a very large genus to a gigantic one with around 3000 species. *Senecio* is a very varied genus and includes trees 9 m (30 ft) tall as well as annuals such as the pestilent groundsel (*S. vulgaris*) from which most gardeners suffer. However, there are some rather respectable perennials that we must consider. Before we mention these it must be pointed out that quite a number of the garden species have been moved out to *Ligularia*; similarly, although it does not really concern us here, many of the shrubby ones have become *Brachyglottis*.

There are three perennials that one must look at. *S. tanguticus* is a tall plant, reaching 1.8 m (6 ft) or more. The yellow flowers are held in large conical heads that are both feathery and airy. It is a wonderful plant for the early autumn, but it does have the drawback that it runs around quite a bit and needs to be checked every year. Once the flowering is over it produces attractive fluffy seed heads, which last into winter.

A plant with more conventional daisies is *S. smithii* from South America and the Falkland Islands. This is rather a coarse plant with large fleshy leaves and heads of large white flowers with yellow centres. It is a good plant for growing in damp places, especially besides ponds or streams.

Another plant that gets away from the senecio's yellow image is *S. pulcher*. This has dark green leaves and, surprisingly, flower heads of reddish purple or magenta. This is a fresh-looking plant that is late in coming through the soil and flowers in the autumn.

As stated, *S. smithii* needs a wet soil, but the other two will grow in any fertile garden soil. They prefer a sunny position.

Propagation can be by division or by sowing seed, preferably fresh.

**SIDALCEA** (Malvaceae)

Although there are quite a number of species in this genus, it is only *S. malviflora* and *S. candida* that need detain us; but detained we must be as these are rather attractive border plants. They have flat funnel-shaped flowers (looking a bit like satellite dishes) in the style of the mallows and hollyhocks. The plants grow to 1.2 m (4 ft) with spikes of pink flowers that open over quite a long period in summer. There are quite a number of cultivars, some of which are much shorter and, in sheltered positions at least, do not require staking. These cultivars vary in colour from pale pink through to quite a deep pink, almost red.

*S. candida* is a shorter plant which has smaller white flowers.

Sidalcea

They both like a moisture-retentive soil in full sun. Increase can be by division or from seed if you are just growing the species.

**SILENE** (Caryophyllaceae) – Campion

These are not among the best plants for the border, but they are good to use in the wildflower garden, or simply to plant alongside a hedgerow.

*S. dioica* is the red campion of the countryside. The flowers are in fact pink and appear in quite some profusion in the late spring on 60 cm (2 ft) plants. The white equivalent is *S. alba*. Occasionally crosses appear between the two, producing pale pink flowers. There is one species that is sometimes seen in the border that is similar to *S. alba*, but it has deeply cut petals. This is *S. fimbriata*.

The sea campion, *S. maritima* (or *S. uniflora* as it must now be called) makes a good carpeting plant for the edge of a border. The glaucous, almost waxy leaves are covered with a mass of white flowers emerging from bloated calyces. There is now a rather good variegated form of this.

**SISYRINCHIUM** (Iridaceae)

This is quite a large genus, of which a number of the smaller species are grown in the rock garden. However there is one that frequently features in the open border. This is *S. striatum* (or rather was, as it has now been moved to the equally tongue-twisting *Phaiophleps nigricans*). The plant has fans of iris-like leaves from which emerge a flowering stem carrying small creamy-yellow flowers pressed against it. There is a fine variegated form, 'Aunt May', which has leaves striped with cream, which contrasts well with the grey-green.

They like a well-drained soil in full sun. Propagation can be by division, which is easy as the plants fall apart in the hand, or from seed, which is also easy as they have a tendency to self sow everywhere.

**SMILACINA** (Convallariaceae)

The genus is represented in the garden mainly by *S. racemosa*. It is closely related to the Solomon's seals and as such likes to have a similar cool position, such as light shade in a woodland setting. Indeed, such a position is also ideal from a visual point of view as these are plants to light up a dark corner.

**Smilacina**

Instead of the hanging bells of the polygonatum, the smilacina has frothy plumes of creamy white flowers that appear at the end of the arching leafy shoots. It flowers in the late spring and is good for cuttings for the house. The leaves are held on either side of the stem much in the manner of the polgonatum. The plant runs a bit, making dense clumps when it is happy with its conditions. When the smilacina fruits the flowers are replaced by bright red berries.

There are a couple of other species in cultivation but these are really collector's items as they make little impact on the garden.

Smilacina generally like a lime-free leafy soil, but I have seen them growing, and growing well, in an alkaline soil. Perhaps the secret is to keep them moist. They prefer a lightly shaded position such as under trees or against a north wall. Propagation is by dividing the rhizomatous rootstock. It can also be raised from seed if it is available.

**SOLIDAGO** (Compositae) – Golden rod
Although solidago is a large genus, only a few are in cultivation as the majority are a bit weedy. Some gardeners may think they are all a bit weedy, but they have their place in the midsummer and beyond. It is a very old plant of gardens and here perhaps lies the problem, as the old cultivars of *S. canadensis* were tall, rather invasive, hungry and prone to mildew. What you got for this was a swaying mass of yellow flower heads, each made up of small individual florets. Modern cultivars are better behaved and have dropped the height from 1.5–1.8 m (5–6 ft) to around 75 cm (30 in), producing a much better plant. Most of these hybrids are based on *S. cutleri* (previously *S. brachystachys*). There are now quite a number to choose from, varying in the deepness of their yellow colour and the shape of the plant, some being more bushy than others.

Golden rods are happy in most soils and will grow in light shade as well as a more open situation. They should be increased by vegetative means, such as by division or basal cuttings. The old-fashioned *S. candensis* tends to self sow.

× **SOLIDASTER** (Compositae)
× *Solidaster luteus* is a bi-generic hybrid, that is to say it is a result of the crossing of two genera rather than two species which is much more usual. In this case it is the interaction of *Solidago* and *Aster* that have brought this cross about. It looks very similar to some of the shorter solidagos with loose heads of tiny flowers that are lemon

yellow with darker centres. They have a very fresh look about them. One of the most popular forms is 'Lemore' although others have recently been introduced.

It is happy in most soils, but prefers a sunny position. Increase by division.

## STACHYS (Labitae) – Woundwort

Not all of this genus are friendly and I would have serious reservations about introducing the native hedge woundwort *S. sylvatica* even to a wildflower garden, as it can become very invasive. However, that aside, there are also some good plants.

Perhaps one of the first of this genus that most gardeners are aware of is the lamb's ears, *S. byzantina* (previously *S. lanata*). This is valued for the very silvery leaves that are covered in a woolly felt. This is a carpeting plant, making a dense ground cover. The upright flowering stems are also very hairy with very small pink flowers just managing to emerge at the top. Many gardeners dislike these stems and their flowers and remove them. There is a cultivar, 'Silver Carpet' that is a non-flowering clone. This is a very valuable border plant as it will mix well with so many other plants. It is essential that it has a free-draining soil and is in full sun. It looks ghastly in a wet summer when it is likely to be reduced to a mush.

Another valuable border plant is *S. macrantha* (previously *S. grandiflora*), which, unlike the preceding, is grown for its flowers. These are again produced as upright spikes appearing from a mat of foliage, growing to about 60 cm (2 ft) in height. They are much more prominent in this case and are mauvish-purple. This plant will tolerate some shade.

*S. officinalis* could be included in the British wildflower garden as it is the native betony. It is not so impressive as the previous plant, but can still hold its place in a border. It has reddish-purple flowers but there are also forms with pink and white flowers.

These are plants of reasonably well-drained soil and full sun. They can readily be increased by division.

## STIPA (Gramineae) – Feather grass

To most gardeners this genus is mainly known through the species *S. gigantea*, which grows in great elegance to a height of about 2.1 m (7 ft), each graceful stem topped with a large flower head that moves beautifully in the wind. This plume is purple when it first opens but eventually turns a light golden yellow. Sparrows love to destroy the heads and often break down the stems in the process with their weight. *S. pennata* is a much smaller plant of the same ilk, but with a white head. *S. calamagrostis* is between the two in height, reaching about 1.2 m (4 ft). This has violet flowers that also turn yellow as they age.

These are all clump-forming plants giving no cause for concern over rampancy. They all like any fertile soil that is not too wet, and a sunny position. They can be increased by division in spring.

## STOKESIA (Compositae)

This is represented solely by *S. laevis*, although this has got a couple of cultivars. It is a relatively sprawling plant growing not more than about 45 cm (18 in) high. The flowers are a mauvy-purple. They are quite wide, up to 10 cm (4 in) across, and appear around midsummer. There are a few cultivars that vary the colour a bit, but often not noticeably. There are, however, distinct white forms and pink forms.

Stokesia will do well in most fertile garden soils and should be given a sunny position. They can easily be increased by division.

## STYLOPHORUM (Papaveraceae) –
Celandine poppy

Only one of this small genus is in general cultivation, namely *S. diphyllum*. It is a useful yellow-flowered plant for the shade garden. The flowers are typical of the poppy family and are a golden yellow, set off well against the green leaves. They are very useful for lighting up a shady area. The plant is not very big, reaching only 45 cm (18 in) in height.

The not too dissimilar *S. lasiocarpum* has recently begun to appear in cultivation.

These are plants of the woodland and enjoy a leafy soil or any other soil that has had organic material added to it. It is a good plant for either under trees or shrubs or against a north wall. It can be best increased from seed, although division is possible.

**SYMPHYTUM** (Boraginaceae) – Comfrey
These are plants that all gardeners should think at least twice about before planting as they are terribly invasive. Any small piece of root left in the ground will immediately start off a new colony. You have been warned. However, having said that, it must be admitted that they have got a place in our gardens as the spiral of buds that unwinds as each comes into flower has a curious beauty that makes one forgive its rampant nature and the coarseness of the rest of the plant.

**Symphytum**

Really they are plants for the wilder part of the garden, where they can be left to run as they wish. They make excellent ground cover, and the foliage makes very nutritious compost.

*Symphytum ibericum* (also known as *S. grandiflorum*) is a species commonly seen. This produces flowers in the spring that are basically white, but flushed with blue and red, giving them a tricolour appearance. This is a relatively short member of the genus and only grows to about 45 cm (18 in). There is also a variegated form which has cream and green leaves. It is prone to revert to plain green. *S. caucasicum* is a much taller species reaching up to 90 cm (3 ft). This has pure blue flowers that are tinged with purple when they first open. *S.* × *uplandicum* is a similar plant with the flowers being pinker when they first open. It has a very good variegated form, 'Variegatum'.

As a contrast, another hybrid, *S.* 'Rubrum' has very good, deep red flowers, attractively set off against the dark green leaves. This is one of the best forms and I have seen it in borders, but it has to be kept under control. This is another tall form but one of the shortest is *S. tuberosum* which is about 38 cm (15 in).

All the comfreys like a rich, moist soil, but will do well in virtually any garden soil. They will grow in full sun or light shade. Propagation is usually by division of the rampant rootstock. They will also come from seed if needs be. Their speed of progress can be reduced and the appearance of the plant improved by shearing it over after flowering.

**TANECETUM** (Compositae)
The genus *Tanecetum* has really come into its own lately. A few years ago the only plant that one would have thought garden-worthy was the native tansy *T. vulgare*, a rather coarse plant with feathery leaves and flat heads of golden yellow flowers, shaped like buttons. It might appear in the border, but it was more likely to show up in the herb garden or wildflower patch. However it has come into more prominence as plants have been moved in from the now almost defunct

genus of *Chrysanthemum*. One is an old-fashion garden plant that has suffered many changes of name in the past, although its vernacular name, feverfew, has remained fairly constant. The plant in question is *Tanecetum parthenium* (previously *Chrysanthemum parthenium*) amongst others). It is a pretty plant with airy sprays of white daisies with yellow centres, but it is usually grown in the garden in one of its two forms: the golden-leaved one, 'Aurea', which is supposed to be very good for headaches (hence its vernacular name), and the double-flowered form 'White Bonnet'. The golden-leaved form is often grown for this feature alone, and the flowers are either cut off, or the whole plant scrapped once it reaches flowering stage (the plant often turns greener at this point anyway). *T. parthenium* has a tendency to seed itself all over the garden, but it is easy enough to pull out and, besides, it is often useful for filling up the odd spot. It has the advantage of being able to provide flowers throughout most of the growing season.

Another group that has finally settled here having been through *Pyrethrum* and *Chrysanthemum* is *T. coccineum* and its cultivars. These are the border pyrethrums: first rate, fresh-looking daisies for the summer border. They are not very tall plants, being only up to 60cm (2 ft), but they are a bit floppy and really need some form of support. The leaves are finely cut and feathery, much in the manner of the tansy mentioned earlier. The flowers cover a range of pinks through to reds and includes white. Some are doubles. Some of these coloured forms are good enough to have been given cultivar names, eight of which are currently available.

*Tanacetum* will grow in any good garden soil and generally prefer a sunny position. They can be grown from seed, but cultivars should be raised from basal cuttings taken in the spring or by division.

### TELEKIA (Compositae)

*Telekia speciosa* is the only garden representative of this genus. It was previously known as *Buphthalmum speciosum*. This is a tall 1.5–1.8 m (5–6 ft) plant with golden-yellow daisy flowers that have thin petals, looking a bit like a ligularia with its large fragrant leaves and untidy flowers. It certainly is a bold plant, forming large clumps. It spreads both by rhizomes and by self sowing.

It likes a moist soil and looks well when planted beside water. Full sun or light shade will suit it. Propagation can be by division or from seed.

### TELLIMA (Saxifragaceae)

The solitary member of this genus is *T. grandiflora*. This is not in the first rank of border plants, but it nonetheless has a contribution to make, especially in the shady garden. It is closely related to the

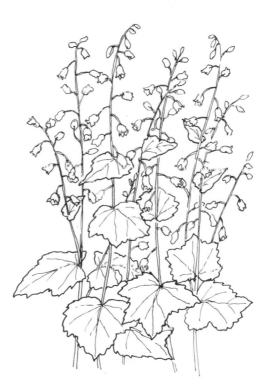

**Tellima**

heucheras and tiarellas and this shows in both the shape of the leaves and in the flower spike. The leaves are a dark green, often having a tinge of dark purple along the veins during the winter (it is evergreen). The flowers and the flowering stem are a light green. They appear in late spring and early summer.

This makes a very good ground-cover plant as long as the soil is moist enough. It prefers to grow in the shade and makes an ideal plant for carpeting under shrubs or trees. It can be increased by division or from seed.

## THALICTRUM (Ranunculaceae) – Meadow rues

Few gardens can be without at least one of this very attractive genus. Surprisingly perhaps, it belongs to the Ranunculaceae, the buttercup family to which it seems to bear little obvious resemblance. The majority have very delicate fern-like leaves overtopped by airy foaming flowers.

The first to flower is *T. aquilegiifolium*, so called because of the resemblance of its leaves to those of aquilegia, indeed, it is often mistaken for that plant when it is out of flower. The flowers, however, are quite different. They are small with prominent stamens which give them a light fluffy appearance, especially when they are collectively seen in the large heads that they form. Their colour is either lilac or creamy white and they appear in late spring and early summer. They are followed by large flattish seeds which hang like great clumps of earrings and are very sensitive in their own right. However if they are left they do self sow copiously.

This is followed by a welter of different species. *T. flavum glaucum* is a much heavier-looking plant with thick glaucous bluish-green stems and similarly-coloured leaves. The flowers are light yellow and do not appear so light and airy as other species. In spite of making it sound not very garden-worthy, this plant is still very useful and has much to offer.

*Thalictrum minus* varies in height, usually being either a little above or below 45 cm

(18 in). It is a bit rampant and quickly forms dense clumps of tangled roots. The very small flowers above the delicate foliage are yellowish in colour. It can be a bit floppy in a windy position and may need support.

One of the gems of the border is undoubtedly *T. delavayi* (previously known as *T. dipterocarpum*). It is a very refined plant with dainty foliage and large airy sprays of light flowers. These flowers are mauve with a mass of creamy stamens. The whole plant is about 2.1 m (7 ft) tall and may need supporting to prevent it falling over. The cultivar that most people grow is 'Hewitt's Double'. This is a much shorter plant and the double flowers do without the colour of the stamens. It has a long flowering season, but does not appear above the ground until late in the spring, so do not accidentally dig it up or overplant it.

The final one that I wish to mention is *T. diffusiflorum*. This species reaches a moderate 90 cm (3 ft). The foliage is again very attractive, with delicate blue-green leaflets. The flower heads are much looser than in other species and consist of large bell-like flowers that are lilac in colour with the typical cluster of yellow stamens. It makes a very attractive plant.

The choice between these various plants is not easy and it is said if you are restricted to one, particularly as there is more to explore than I have mentioned here.

They all like a moisture-retentive soil that is rich in humus. They will grow in sun or light shade. Propagation can be from seed or divisions.

## TIARELLA (Saxifragaceae) – Foam flower

Once these plants have been seen it is easy to appreciate why they are called foam flowers. The flowers are very small, but are carried in such numbers on the 30 cm (12 in) tall flowering stem that they appear like a cloud, or the foam of their name.

*Tiarella cordifolia* is the species normally grown from this small genus. This has maple-like leaves, which like several members of the saxifrage family, are often tinged with purple or bronze during winter. The white flowers appear in late spring. It spreads rapidly to form a large colony and can be used as ground cover.

Another species, which has been gaining in popularity lately, is *T. wherryi*. This is a more sophisticated plant with more deeply cut leaves and more dainty flowering spikes. This carries pink-tinged white flowers which are pink in bud, often giving the appearance of a firework going off and lighting up the dimness under trees or shrubs. This is not a runner and only forms small clumps. A very desirable plant for a shady spot.

Both species will thrive in any moisture-retentive soil, but become unhappy if it dries out. They prefer light shade and are ideal either under trees and shrubs or under a north wall.

**TRADESCANTIA** (Commelinaceae) – Spider wort
This is quite a large genus, but the plants that are grown in gardens are generally hybrids of *T. virginiana* called *T.* × *andersoniana*. These are rather untidy plants with sprawling stems and narrow leaves that clasp the stem. Bright three-petalled flowers make an appearance at the tips of these stems. The colour can be any of a whole range of blue through purple to magenta. There are also white forms. The flowers are not very big, but the brightness of their colour means that they shine out from the scramble of stems and leaves. Some are double. Flowering is over a long period from late summer until the frosts. The whole plant is about 60 cm (2 ft) tall.

Tradescantia are not at all fussy as to their soil, but they prefer to have a sunny position. They can be increased by division, although if the colour is of little matter, they can be grown from seed. They self sow.

**TRICYRTIS** (Convallariaceae/Liliaceae) – Toad lilies
This is an intriguing group of plants, although it is difficult to see their resemblance to lilies-of-the-valley (*Convallaria*), to which they are related. The intrigue lies in the flowers, whose six narrow petals are funnel-shaped and surmounted by a fusion

**Tricyrtis**

of styles and stamens which are usually the same colour as the petals. The colouration adds to the effect, as in most species there is pale background colour overlaid with darker spots. The whole plant is somewhere in the region of 60–90 cm (2–3 ft) in height and forming large clumps or colonies. The leaves usually clasp the stem, although not always up the complete length of the stem.

*T. formosana* (also called *T. stolonifera*) is one of the most frequent found in cultivation. This has pale lilac petals heavily spotted with purple. As its synonym implies it is stoloniferous, forming large colonies. The lower leaves do not clasp the stem. *T. hirta* is another popular species. Its flowers also have a pale lilac colouration overspotted with purple, but it is not a stoloniferous plant. All leaves clasp the stem.

*T. latifolia* (also called *T. bakeri*) has wider leaves as its name implies. The flowers are yellow, spotted with a reddish-brown. *T. macrantha* is the odd one out as its yellow flowers not only have more substance, but they hang down, showing spurs at the base of the flower.

The toad lilies are plants of the woodland and therefore like to have a cool leafy soil, which never dries out, in light shade. Method of increase is usually by division.

## TRILLIUM (Trilliaceae/Liliaceae)

No garden that has any shade in it should be without at least one species of trillium. It is a truly beautiful group of plants. All the parts are in threes: three petals, three sepals, three leaves.

One of the most popular in gardening terms is the white wake robin (*T. grandiflorum*). This is only about 30 cm (12 in) or so high, but the three pure white petals shine out very clearly against its green leaves. Although slow, they eventually will form a large colony. The form 'Flore-Pleno' is a double of exquisite beauty. Another good form that is slowly spreading is a pink one, 'Roseum'.

The next in popularity is a plant whose name is currently much confused. It has been called *T. sessile* for many years, but the true plant of this name has rather miffy, short brown flowers whereas the garden plant is handsome with its three long petals upstanding and a very rich mahogany-red. Some are calling *T. chloropetalum*, which is very similar, but I believe the correct name is *T. kurabayashii*. The large leaves are a dark green with darker mottling. These plants look stunning when in dappled shade, with rays of sunlight passing through the petals.

Another species with outstanding, but much smaller petals is *T. luteum*. Here the petals are a lemon yellow and the flower has a very attractive fragrance. Another with small, but erect petals is *T. erectum*. Here there is quite a range of colours including white and a very good red.

There are several more to choose from and one can become a collector of these intriguing plants if the right site is available. The majority are woodlanders and like to have a cool root-run in a leafy soil. It goes without saying that they like a light shade.

Propagation is not easy. For the inexperienced, seed possibly presents the best bet, but it must be fresh and it can take several years before a flowering plant is reached. It is also possible to increase them by careful division.

## TROLLIUS (Ranunculaceae) – Globe flower

This genus gives us some very useful flowering plants for the early summer border. Most are yellow and in many respects they closely resemble their close cousins, the buttercups, except the petals are fuller, often almost making a complete sphere, hence their name.

**Trollius**

One of the most popular is *T. chinensis*, sometimes still labelled under the old garden name of *T. ledebourii*. This is a strong orange colour with the inner petals being narrow and held upright in a very distinctive manner. There is a whole group of truly cosmopolitan hybrids between this species, *T. asiaticus*, and *T. europeus* that go under the name of *T. × cultorum*. One of the best of these is the very pale yellow, 'Alabaster'. Another good one is 'Feuertroll' or 'Fireglobe' which is a rich orange.

The native European species, *T. europeus* is not quite so spectacular as some of these and can become overlooked, but it is a very attractive plant in its own right. This is not quite so tall as some of the others, but is still 75 cm (30 in) or so. At the other extreme is the delightful *T. pumilus* in which the flowers are held only about 20 cm (8 in) above the relatively low foliage. The flowers are golden yellow.

These are plants of boggy soil, but they will take most garden conditions as long a they are not too dry. Plenty of organic material added to the soil will please them. They are perhaps at their best if planted next to a water feature such as a pond or a stream. They appreciate a sunny position, although they will take a bit of light shade.

Propagation is by division, but the species can also be grown from seed, as long as it is sown while it is fresh.

## TROPAEOLUM (Tropaeolaceae)

The idea of nasturtiums in most gardeners' minds is restricted to the annual *T. majus*, but there are quite a lot more of these exotic-looking flowering plants that can be grown, although it must be admitted that not many are hardy.

*T. speciosum* is one of the most spectacular, with flame-red flowers, similar to those of the nasturtium. It is a climber and likes nothing better than to scramble up through some bushes or a hedge. It flowers throughout the summer and autumn and can well be grown through bushes such as small rhododendrons which have long finished their flowering. They look particularly attractive against the dark green of yew hedges. They prefer cool conditions and will grow best on the shady side of the hedge or shrub as long as the soil is moist.

*T. polyphyllum* as we know it in cultivation, has yellowy-orange flowers held in great profusion above the long, trailing stems of greyish foliage. This is a more tender species, but the roots seem to protect themselves by delving down very deeply, as anyone knows who has tried to dig them up – the shoots emerge sometimes 'miles' away, giving the impression that the plant has been moved. This looks best cascading down over a wall. Unlike the previous species this one likes the sun and must have a well-drained soil.

The final plant, *T. tuberosum*, is tender and has to be dug up each year unless it is in a very favoured position or covered with a very deep layer of mulch. As its name suggests, this is a tuberous species. This is another climbing form and can be planted under a shrub. The flowers are much smaller and less flared than the previous two species, but they are produced in profusion, making an attractive sight. They are coloured orange and red. They flower in the late autumn but there is a form called 'Ken Aslet' which fortunately flowers from summer through into autumn. This needs a well-drained soil and will flower in either sun or light shade.

All can be propagated from seed. They can also be increased by taking basal cuttings.

## UVULARIA (Convallariaceae/Liliaceae)

This is a curious genus of plants that is really for the collector rather than the gardener who is trying to provide a decorative border. They are related to the Solomon's seal but have yellow flowers rather than the latter's white ones. In appearance they have more in common with another of the same family, the disporum. It is only a small genus with up to five species and they can be quite difficult to tell apart.

They are generally upright plants that droop towards the top of the stem, from which hang small yellow flowers, whose petals dangle like limp bits of rag. They are

**Uvularia**

typically about 2.5 cm (1 in) long and are various shades of yellow.

The commonest in gardens is *U. grandiflorum*. This plant is up to 60 cm (2 ft) in height and carries large (5 cm/2 in) flowers of a citrus yellow colour. It has a form 'Pallida', which has much paler flowers.

Another plant that is seen relatively frequently is *T. perfoliata*. The name refers to the perfoliate leaves whose bases clasp and enclose the stem. Unfortunately this plant is not unique in this way as the previous also has this tendency. However it can be differentiated by its smaller stature and smaller flowers, which are also paler in colour.

The only other species that is grown to any extent is *T. sessilifolia*. Again this is a

property of the plant that is not very useful as the previous two are also sessile, that is without a leaf-stalk. However they are not perfoliate and its flower-shape is more bell-like. They are a pale greenish yellow.

Like the Solomon's seal these are plants of the woodland, so they enjoy a cool root-run in a leafy soil that does not dry out. They also like light shady conditions. They are quite large in appearing above ground so be careful not to disturb them or dig them up during a spring clean-up.

Propagation is by division or from seed if it is available.

**VALERIANA** (Valerianaceae) – Valerian
Considering that this is a very large genus, it is surprising that there are few garden-worthy plants.

*V. officinalis* is a British native and would do well as a summer-flowering plant for a wildflower garden or even as a group in a border. It is a tall plant, reaching 1.2 m (4 ft) high and carrying pale pink flowers. The leaves are decoratively pinnate.

A plant of quite different character is *V. phu*. This plant eventually reaches 90 cm (3 ft) with tall stems holding the white flowers well above the foliage. It is mainly in the form 'Aurea' that it is seen and this is grown for its golden, spring foliage. This is at its best when it is still in a low hummock, prior to sending up its flowering shoot. Many gardeners cut off the flowers as the two colours, dirty white and golden green are not very sympathetic and their main interest in the plant is in its foliage.

Both plants will grow in any good garden soil and will do well in either sun or light shade. They can be increased by division.

**VANCOUVERIA** (Berberidaceae)
With the upsurge of interest in epimediums, there has been more interest in this closely related genus. They are good ground-cover plants with at least one species retaining its leaves throughout the year. Both flowering stems and those of the leaves are very wiry. The plants quickly make large colonies and should not be planted near other choice plants.

Up to now the main species has been *V. hexandra* which has deciduous leaves, the leaflets of which are roughly hexagonal. The airy displays of small flowers are white.

The plant that is eventually going to overtake this in popularity is *V. chrysantha*. This is evergreen and makes very good ground cover. The leaves are smaller, but they are leathery, It is a good idea to shear them over towards the end of winter so that the new growth can be better appreciated. The flowers are about the same size and just as airy as the previous species, but they are yellow.

Like the epimediums, the vancouveria are woodlanders. They like a leafy soil in which they can quickly spread around. They also appreciate light shade. Both these plants are running ones and they are easy enough to propagate by simply dividing off a piece.

## VERATRUM (Melanthiaceae/Liliaceae) – False hellborine

These are plants of good garden value as they are attractive both when they are just in leaf and when they are in flower. The former is probably just as well as it can take up to seven years before the plant is ready to flower. They are very statuesque plants for a cool position, preferably without slugs which can reduce the beautiful leaves to tatters. The clumps of basal leaves are wide and deeply pleated and make very good foliage feature.

One of the most spectacular of the genus is *V. nigrum*. This has bold clumps of leaves from which eventually emerges a tall flowering stem that reaches 1.5 m (5 ft). It has side branches from which cluster hundreds of small, starry, dark red flowers, that look particularly effective with the evening sun shining through them. Once they are over, the branches are hung with seeds.

The white equivalent is *V. album*. This is a similar plant although it is often taller. Here the flowers are pale green or greenish white.

There are other species, although these are two of the best and most commonly available.

**Veratrum**

They must have a moisture-retentive soil but can be grown in either sun or light shade. Propagation can be from seed but this can be a lengthy process. Fortunately, however, they can also be divided, with care.

## VERBASCUM (Scrophulariaceae) – Mullein

Few gardens should be without these stately plants. Many are very tall, sometimes reaching 2.4 m (8 ft) but fortunately there are also many smaller species that are eminently suitable for the smaller garden. A large number are annual or biennials, but since they are likely to self sow they can be considered honorary perennials.

*V. bombyciferum* and *V. olympicum* are both statuesque biennials although the latter can also be a short-lived perennial. These are the giants that one often sees rising up to

The Complete Book of Hardy Perennials

2.1 m (7 ft). Moving down the scale to about 90 cm (3 ft) we come to *V. chaixii*. This is a more refined plant, but still with the same characteristics of its bigger brothers and still with yellow flowers. The centres are purple. There is a white form *V.c.* 'Album', which is rightly very popular. For different colours we must turn to *V. phoeniceum*, the purple mullein. As its vernacular name implies it has purple flowers, but it also has a range of cultivars with alternative colours from pink and lilac to terracotta. Whites and yellows are also present. They go under such names as 'Gainsborough', sulphur yellow; 'Bridal Bouquet', white; 'Pink Domino', mauvy-pink; and 'Cotswold Beauty', salmony-brown. These all have much thinner stems than other verbascums, and have the general feeling of being much lighter plants, more airy.

*V. nigrum* has more the feel of *V. chaixii* about it, more refined than the big species but still on the stiff side. This has small yellow flowers, although there is also a white form.

Verbascums like a well-drained soil and an open situation. The shorter forms do not usually need support; the taller ones may do, especially if they are in an exposed position. The caterpillar of the mullein moth can reduce the leaves to tatters. However, it can be easily controlled by being picked off. None of the verbascums are very long-lived and constantly need renewing. They come easily from the copious amount of seed they produce and can usually be depended on to provide enough seedlings from self sowing. The coloured cultivars need to be increased vegetatively and this can be done by taking root cuttings.

**VERBENA** (Verbenaceae)

This is a large genus with quite a number in cultivation, but unfortunately, for our purposes, many of these are tender. However there are still a number worth mentioning.

*Verbena bonariensis* (much confused lately with *V. patagonica*, a low alpine) is one of the tallest, often reaching 1.8 m (6 ft) or more. The stems, however, are very slender

and wiry and stand well against wind. On top of these tall stems is a small head of purple flowers. Individually they do not amount to much, but in a colony of several plants makes a pleasing sight, either at the back of a border, peering over other plants, or even at the front, where the stems are not thick enough to prevent the eye travelling through them to the rest of the border. They are not very long-lived plants but do self sow, providing a continuance.

*V. rigida* (previously called *V. venosa*) is very similar to the previous plant in terms of flowers and colour, but it is much shorter, only reaching about 60 cm (2 ft) tall. Another plant of this height that has flowers of a more luminous blue is *V. corymbosa*. This is a wonderful plant to have in the border, except that it has a nasty habit of running madly in all directions. It is one of those plants that you are never short of a bit to give to a visitor.

Some of the more tender ones such as *V.* 'Sissinghurst' can be brought through quite cold winters simply by mulching them on cold nights with conifer branches or even sheets of newspaper.

Most verbenas can be propagated vegetatively by division or from basal cuttings. They can also be increased by sowing seed. They need a well-drained soil in a sunny position.

**VERONICA** (Scrophulariaceae) – Speedwell

This is a wonderful race of plants for the border. They supply tall members for the back as well low carpeters and clump-formers to decorate the front. Most are in wonderful shades of blue, some brilliant blue, but there are also white and pink cultivars.

Starting with one of the tallest at up to 120 cm (4 ft) there is *V. longifolia*. This is a clump-forming plant that carries both narrow leaves and narrow spikes of blue flowers. *V. exaltata* is a very similar species, but a better garden plant. A shorter plant, and one more frequently seen in gardens, is *V. gentianoides*. This is a mat-forming plant with shiny green leaves from which arise

244

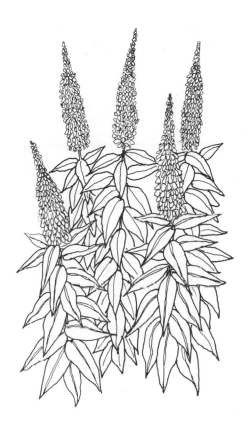

**Veronica**

45 cm (18 in) flowering stems, bearing pale blue flowers. This is a very attractive, spring-flowering veronica. There is a white form of this and a form with variegated leaves.

Lower still are a whole series of plants that do well towards the front of the border. *V. spicata* is the tallest of these, varying from 30–60 cm (12–24 in). This forms clumps with many flowering spikes, each covered with blue flowers of differing shades which give rise to quite a number of cultivars and hybrids. Some of these have produced white and pink flowers. *V. spicata incana* was considered a species in its own right until recently. This is a similar plant to the above except that it has a silvery-grey foliage. Several of the greyer-leaved *V. spicata* forms are a result of crossing with this subspecies.

Another species that has disappeared in its own right is *V. teucrium* which is now considered a subspecies of *V. austriaca*. Again there are several cultivars, some of them an intense blue. These are up to 45 cm (18 in) tall and make good fillers amongst the plants towards the front of the border.

Veronicas will grow in most garden soils and appreciate a sunny position. It is best to cut off the flowering stems once the flowers are over. Propagation is by division, or from seed for the species.

**VERONICASTRUM** (Scrophulariceae)
*V. virginica* is sometimes included in *Veronica* and sometimes here. It is a very good border plant. It grows to about 1.2 m (4 ft) and has spikes of blue flowers. There are also pink and white forms. It is a very elegant plant which, in spite of its height, rarely needs staking.

It will grow in any soil, but can languish if the soil becomes too impoverished. A sunny position is the most favoured. Increase can be by division or from seed. It will self sow.

**VIOLA** (Violaceae) – Pansies, viola, violets
This is a very large genus and one that needs a whole book to do it justice. Violets are a bit on the small side for growing in a border, but some of the early flowering ones can be over and finished well before the bigger plants get moving. Most like shade and therefore are good for planting under shrubs or trees. Violas and pansies are big enough to look after themselves in the border and make excellent edging plants.

Most of the violets are species. One of the most popular is the sweet violet, *V. odorata*. In its typical form this is a deep violet purple. There are also cultivars varying from white to red as well as differing blues. Several white violets are in cultivation of which one of the most popular is the fat-flowered *V. septentrionalis* 'Alba'. Another popular white form, this time speckled with blue is *V. sororia* 'Freckles'.

One colour for violets that is not often seen is yellow, although there are a surprising number of species of that colour. *V. glabella* and *V. pensylvanica* are two such that we have in our gardens. *V. labradorica* is valuable for its purple foliage as well as its purple flowers.

There are two violets that enjoy scrambling through other plants. *Viola elatior* is a surprisingly erect plant with pale blue and white flowers. The scrambler *par excellence* is *V. cornuta*, which can either be grown as a clump or allowed to climb up through bushes and other plants. This has either mauve or white flowers.

The flowers of the last species are bigger than most other species and similar in size to the many violas that now appear in our borders. Every year there seems to be more and it is impossible to keep track of them all. However there are a number of tried and tested plants of which just a few can be mentioned.

One of the cheekiest is 'Jackanapes' which is yellow with the upper petals a rich crimson. Unfortunately it is not a very strong plant and needs frequent replacing. 'Maggie Mott' is more sedate, with quite large, rounded flowers that are a light mauvish-purple with a pale yellow centre. 'Irish Molly' is a greenish bronze that has an oily appearance. Both 'Penny Black' and 'Molly Sanderson' have very good black flowers.

There are also many slightly smaller flowering forms of which 'Nellie Britton' (also called 'Haslemere'), pale purple, and 'Ardross Gem', yellow and blue, are amongst my favourites.

A final plant that should not be forgotten is *V. tricolor* that appears almost as a weed in many people's gardens. The flower colour is variable, but is mainly a rich purple and yellow. I let odd patches of it build up in places where it looks good and then scrap the lot and let it reappear somewhere else. There are always masses of seedling everywhere, yet they are not difficult to get rid of if they are not required. They flower throughout the year, but another self sower that appears all over the garden, although only in spring, is the delightful *V. rupestris rosea*. This has small, fresh-looking, pink flowers in abundance. Yet another plant not to be without.

**YUCCA** (Agavaceae/Liliaceae) – Adam's needle, palm needle

This is a genus of very distinctive plants, with strong, sword-like leaves and a huge, stiff-flowering spike that can rise up to 2.1 m (7 ft) or more, and carry large creamy-white bells, sometimes tinged with pink. Variegated-leaf forms are amongst the most popular.

At a casual glance many of the yuccas look the same and if only one is required it probably does not matter which is chosen. *Y. filamentosa* is one of the most frequently seen in cultivation. This has curled threads along the margins of the leaves. This has a short, floriferous cultivar form 'Ivory' which only grows to 1.2 m (4 ft) as well as a variegated form. *Y. flaccida* is a similar

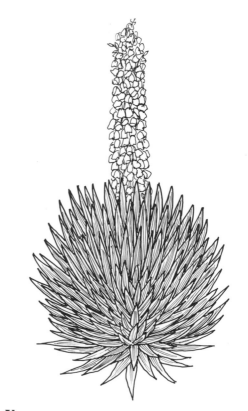

**Yucca**

plant, although somewhat shorter and the leaves not so rigid. *Y. recurva* is again not dissimilar but has recurved leaves.

There are several other species to look at if you get interested in them, but the average gardener is likely to be more than satisfied with one of the above. They like a well-drained soil in full sun.

Propagation can be achieved by breaking of the offsets that appear round the base of the plant. They can also be grown from seed, if it is available.

## ZANTEDESCHIA (Araceae) – Arum lily, lily-of-the-Nile.

Although there are several species in this genus only one, *Z. aethiopica*, is hardy and that is only marginally so. Everybody knows this serene white flower, but its association with funerals puts a lot of people off growing it. The pure white part of the flower is in fact the spathe, that wraps round the true flower, which shows as the yellow spike in the middle. The flowers are well set off by the shiny green leaves. There is a form called 'Crowborough' that is hardier than most, but even the species will come through some very cold winters if mulched or if grown in 30 cm (12 in) or more of water.

This plant likes a moist soil and is even prepared to grow in water. It prefers a sunny position. Propagation is generally by division or from root cuttings, but it can also be grown from seed.

## ZAUSCHNERIA (Onagraceae) – Californian fuchsia

This is another small genus of tender plants of which one, *Z. californica* is hardy enough to survive most winters. Strictly speaking this has been moved to the genus *Epilobium*, under the name *E. canum*, but there is still hope that this change may not be generally accepted.

This is a bushy plant growing no more than 30 cm (12 in) or so high. The leaves are grey and slightly furry which sets off well the orange or scarlet, tubular flowers. These are a bright addition from late summer and into autumn. There are an increasing number of cultivars and hybrids on offer.

Plant in a free-draining soil, possibly on a wall or bank where the plant can hang down slightly. It must have a warm, sunny position. Increase can be effected by cuttings taken in the late summer. These will also insure against winter loss.

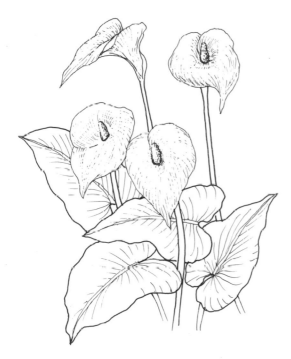

Zantedeschia

# APPENDICES

## Plants for Special Uses

Unless the number of plants involved in any of the categories below is only one or two, only the genus name is given. This does not mean that the whole genus is suitable for that particular purpose and the reader is referred to the text to see which of its plants fall into the group required.

### Plants for shady areas

Aconitum
Actaea
Ajuga
Alchemilla mollis
Anemone
Aquilegia
Arum
Aruncus
Astilbe
Astrantia
Bergenia
Brunnera
Bupthalmum
Caltha
Campanula latifolia, C. persicifolia, C. trachelium
Cardamine
Cardiocrinum
Cimifuga
Codonopsis
Convallaria
Corydalis
Dactylorhiza
Dicentra
Disporum
Digitalis
Dodecatheon
Doronicum
Eomecon
Epimedium
Eranthis
Euphorbia amygdaloides, E.a. robbiae
Filipendula
Gentiana asclepiadea

Geranium
Glaucidium
Helleborus
Heuchera
Hosta
Hyacinthoides
Hylomecon
Iris foetidissima
Kirengeshoma
Lamium
Lathyrus vernus
Leucojum
Lilium
Liriope
Lobelia cardinalis, L. syphilitica, L. vedrariensis
Lunaria
Lysimachia
Meconopsis
Mertensia
Myrrhis
Omphalodes
Paeonia
Paris
Persicaria
Phlox divaricata
Podophyllum
Polygonatum
Primula
Pulmonaria
Ranunculus
Rodgersia
Sanguinaria
Saxifraga fortunei

Smilacina
Smyrmium
Stylophorum
Symphytum
Telekia
Tellimia
Tiarella
Tolmiea
Trillum
Trollius
Tropaeolum speciosum
Uvularia
Vancouveria
Veratrum
Viola
Zantedeschia

### Plants for moist soil

including water gardens and bog gardens
    Those plants that will grow in wet soil or water are marked (W)
Acorus (W)
Ajuga
Astilbe (W)
Caltha (W)
Astrantia
Cardiocrinum
Cautleya
Cimifuga
Claytonia
Darmera (W)
Dodecatheon
Eomecon

Eupatorium
Euphorbia palustris
Filipendula (W)
Gentiana
Glaucidium
Gunnera (W)
Hosta
Houttuynia (W)
Inula
Iris
Kirengeshoma
Ligularia (W)
Lobelia (W)
Lysichiton (W)
Lysimachia
Lythrum (W)
Meconopsis
Mentha (W)
Mimulus (W)
Monarda didyma
Persicaria
Primula
Ranunculus
Rodgersia
Schizostylis
Senecio smithii
Symphytum
Trollius (W)
Veratrum
Zantedeschia (W)

## Plants for dry soils

Acanthus
Alstromeria
Alcea
Anaphalis
Anemone × hybrida
Armeria
Artemisia
Asarina
Asphodeline
Asphodelus
Aubrieta
Ballota
Brunnera
Campanula
Catananche
Cherianthus
Cortaderia
Corydalis
Crespis
Dianthus
Dictamnus
Echinops

Eremurus
Eryngium
Erysimum
Euphorbia
Filipendula vulgaris
Foeniculum
Gaillardia
Geranium
Gypsophila
Helleborus
Hieracium
Incarvillea
Iris
Kniphofia
Lamium
Lavatera
Limonium
Linaria
Linum
Lychnis
Macleaya
Malva
Nepeta
Origanum
Papaver
Perovskia
Phuopsis
Romneya
Sedum
Stachys byzantina
Yucca
Zauschneria

## Plants with ornamental foliage

As well as the plants listed below many species have variegated forms that are grown for their foliage. All silver-leaved plants also fall into this category.

Acanthus
Ajuga
Alchemilla
Aruncus
Astilbe
Bergenia
Bupthalmum
Cardiocrinum
Centauria dealbata
Cephalaria
Cortaderia
Crambe
Cynara
Darmera

Echinops
Epimedium
Eryngium
Euphorbia
Filipendula
Foeniculum
Geranium
Glaucidium
Gunnera
Helleborus
Heuchera
Hosta
Iris
Kirengeshoma
Kniphofia
Lamium
Ligularia
Liriope
Lobelia
Lysichiton
Macleaya
Meconopsis
Miscanthus
Morina
Myrrhis
Paeonia
Phlaris
Phormium
Polygonatum
Pulmonaria
Rheum
Rodgersia
Sanguisorba
Selinum
Sisyrinchium
Tellima
Tiarella
Valeriana
Vancouveria
Veratrum

## Ground-cover plants

Acaena
Acanthus
Ajuga
Alchemilla
Anthemis
Asarum
Bergenia
Brunnera
Calytonia
Convallaria
Crambe
Darmera
Doronicum

Epimedium
Euphorbia
Geranium
Gunnera
Heuchera
Hosta
Houttuynia
Lamium
Liriope
Ophiopogon
Persicaria
Petasites
Phlomis
Prunella
Pulmonaria
Rheum
Smilacina
Stachys
Symphytum
Tellima
Tiarella
Tolmiea
Vancouveria

## Silver and grey foliage plants

Achillea
Anaphalis
Anthemis
Artemisia
Centaurea
Convolvulus cneorum
Crambe
Cynara
Dianthus
Echinops
Eryngium
Hieracium
Hosta
Kniphofia caulescens
Lupinus

Lychnis
Lysimachia ephemerum
Mentha longifolia
Mertensia
Nepeta
Omphalodes linifolia
Perovskia
Potentilla
Romneya
Rudbeckia maxima
Salvia argentia
Sedum
Sisyrinchium striatum
Stachys byzantina
Thalictrum
Verbascum
Veronica
Yucca

## Perennials for cut flowers

Achillea
Alstroemeria
Anemone
Anthemis
Anthericum
Argyranthemum
Armeria
Asphodelus
Aster
Astilbe
Bupthalmum
Centaurea
Cimifuga
Cephalaria
Chrysanthemopsis
Convallaria
Coreopsis
Delphinium
Dendranthema
Dianthus

Dicentra
Doronicum
Echinops
Erigeron
Eryngium
Gaillardia
Galega
Gaura
Geum
Gypsophila
Helenium
Helianthus
Heliopsis
Helleborus niger
Hemerocallis
Hesperis
Heuchera
Hosta
Iris
Kniphofia
Lathyrus
Leucanthemella
Leucanthemum
Liatris
Limonium
Lupinus
Lysimachia
Lythrum
Monarda
Paeonia
Penstemon
Phlox
Physalis
Primula
Ranunculus
Rudbeckia
Scabiosa
Tanacetum
Thalictrum
Trollius
Veronica
Zantedeschia

# Societies

One way of extending a gardener's knowledge of his subject is to join a society. These provide information and help in a variety of ways including journals and other publications. They also provide an opportunity to meet and talk with other people of like mind, especially if the society has local groups that meet regularly. Beside publications, national societies usually provide a seed exchange which in some cases runs into thousand of varieties on offer each year, many not available elsewhere. At local level there are usually lectures and plant sales as well as garden visits. In Britain, the main society to join for those concerned with hardy perennials is undoubtedly the Hardy Plant Society, but there are also many other, often specialist societies that may well be of interest.

Most societies do not have full-time offices and the address of the secretary is likely to change. If there is any problem in locating the one you want, write to either the Royal Horticultural Society or the American Horticultural Society for the current address.

American Hemerocallis Society, 1454 Rebel Drive, Jackson, MS 39211, USA

American Herb Association, PO Box 353, Rescue, CA 95672

American Horticultural Society, 7931 East Boulevard Drive, Alexandria, Virginia 22308, USA

American Hosta Society, 5206 Hawksbury Lane, Raleigh, NC 27606, USA

American Iris Society, (Carol Ramsey), 6518 Beachy Avenue, Wichita KS 67206, USA

American Penstemon Society, 1569 S. Holland Court, Lakewood, CO 80226, USA

American Primrose Society (Brian Skidmore) 6750 W. Mercer Way, Mercer Island, WA 98040, USA

British Hosta and Hemerocallis Society (R. Bowden), Cleeve House, Sticklepath, Oakhampton, Devon EX20 2MN

British Iris Society (Mrs E.M. Wise), 197 The Parkway, Iver Heath, Iver, Buckinghamshire, SL0 0RQ

Cottage Garden Society (Mrs C. Tordoff), 5 Nixon Close, Thornhill, Dewsbury, W. Yorks. WF12 0JA

Cyclamen Society (Peter Moore), Tile Barn House, Standen Green, Iden Green, Beneden, Kent TN17 4LB

Hardy Plant Society (Pam Adams), Little Orchard, Great Comberton, Nr Pershore, Worcs, WR10 0DP

Hardy Plant Society of Oregon, 33530 SE Bluff Road, Boring, OR97009, USA

Perenial Plant Association, 3383 Schirtzinger Road, Columbus OH43026, USA

Royal Horticultural Society, Vincent Square, London SW1P 2PE

# Bibliography

Billington, Jill, *Architectural Foliage*. Ward Lock, 1991

Bird, Richard, *Propagation of Hardy Perennials*. Batsford, 1993

Bird, Richard, *Woodland Gardening*, Souvenir Press, 1992

Bird, Richard, *Lilies*. Apple Press, 1991

Clausen, Ruth Rogers, and Ekstron, Nicolas H., *Perennials for American Gardens*. Random House, 1989

Cobb, James L.S., *Meconopsis*. Helm, 1989

Cribb, Phillip and Bailes, Christopher, *Hardy Orchids*. Helm, 1989

Grenfell, Diana, *Hosta*, Batsford, 1990

Jellito, Leo and Schacht, Wilhelm, *Hardy Herbaceous Perennials*. 2 vols. Batsford, 1990

Lacey, Stephen, *Scent in Your Garden*. Frances Lincoln, 1991

Lacey, Stephen, *The Startling Jungle*. Viking, 1986

Lewis, Peter and Lynch, Margaret, *Campanulas*. Helm, 1989

Lloyd, Christopher, *The Well-tempered Garden*. Collins, 1970

Lloyd, Christopher and Bird, Richard, *Cottage Gardening*, Dorling Kindersley, 1991

Mathew, Brian, *Hellebores*. Alpine Garden Society, 1989

Mathew, Brian, *The Iris*. Batsford, 1981

Phillips, Roger and Rix, Martyn, *Perennials*. 2 vols. Pan, 1991

*The Plant Finder*. Headmain, annual

Swindells, Philip and Mason, David, *The Complete Book of The Water Garden*. Ward Lock, 1989

Thomas, Graham Stuart, *Perennial Garden Plants*. 3rd edn. Dent, 1990

Yeo, Peter, *Hardy Geraniums*. Helm, 1985

# Index